Covenant Theology is a way of  from Genesis to Revelation as es and anyone who writes on it must not only be familiar with biblical themes, but must also be able to integrate historical, systematic and practical theology in such a way that what results is comprehensive and comprehensible. McKay manages to all of this with breathtaking ease. I have been waiting for over twenty years for such a book. This is it.

Dr Derek W. H. Thomas
Reformed Theological Seminary,
Jackson, Mississippi

Covenant theology is the staple diet of all Reformed dogmatics, and this volume does justice to the task of presenting it in simple but comprehensive fashion for the 21st century. This robust restatement of covenant theology is not a backwards looking exercise, but drawing on a comprehensive knowledge of the past the author applies the doctrines and insights of covenant theology to the contemporary scene. He does so in a clear and engaging style, not shirking from dealing with difficulties and controversies, but always focusing matters on the life of the individual and the church. The passage of time does not invalidate the truth, and this book applies vital Scriptural insights that need to be learned and practised afresh.

Professor John L Mackay
Free Church College,
Edinburgh

David McKay has accomplished a remarkable goal in this book. He covers the full range of the topics of Christian doctrine from the standpoint of Covenant Theology, showing the relevance of the covenant in all aspects of faith and life. This is, in fact, a covenantal systematic theology. Particularly useful is McKay's treatment of contemporary issues from a covenant perspective: e.g., neo-orthodoxy, the New Age Movement, feminism, evolutionism, the 'open view of God,' etc. He interacts with an amazing range of Reformed authors, from Calvin to the Puritans to Murray, Van Til, and Reymond. I enthusiastically commend this work, and will use it in my Seminary courses.

Dr. Wayne R. Spear,
Reformed Presbyterian Theological Seminary,
Pittsburgh

In many Christian circles there is no awareness of the biblical concept of the covenantal aspect of redemption. Even when it is discussed in doctrinal works, it is often little more than a theological fragment, a segment of the whole which is dealt with on its own, but not related to other doctrines. My colleague, Dr McKay, views the entire field of Christian doctrine in a covenantal framework and does so successfully and convincingly. In these pages we are shown the relevance of the Covenant of Grace for the individual Christian, the Church and the nation. Exegetically sound and warmly devotional, this stimulating work is highly commended.

Principal Frederick S. Leahy,
Reformed Theological College,
Belfast

One of the most important, yet most neglected themes of Scripture is that of Covenant. The fact that the two parts into which the Bible is divided are called, literally, 'Old Covenant' and 'New Covenant' ought to be enough to tell us that the whole principle of covenant is a major key to understanding how its message holds together. Yet the average Christian is ignorant of these things. Here is a book that will go a long way to remedy this deficiency. It provides us, not merely with a theology of covenant, but a genuine covenantal theology. David McKay explores this central theme of Scripture in such a way as to show how it provides cohesion to the message of the Bible, gives us a reliable world and life view and ultimately leads us into a deeper knowledge of Jesus Christ, the Covenant King.

Mark G. Johnston
Grove Chapel, Camberwell

The Bond of Love

*Covenant Theology and
the Contemporary World*

David McKay

Mentor

© David McKay
ISBN 1 85792 641 2

Published in 2001
by Christian Focus Publications,
Geanies House, Fearn, Ross-shire,
IV20 1TW, Great Britain

Cover design by Owen Daily

Contents

Contents

Introduction

Most Christians, if they have heard of Covenant Theology at all, think of it as cold, obscure, speculative, old-fashioned, artificial, a straitjacket imposed on the Bible. It is tragic that that is the case. No doubt there have been proponents of Covenant Theology who at times have been obscure, speculative, and many other undesirable things. Covenant theologians are, after all, fallible human beings, and sinners too, (although, we trust, saved sinners). At its best, however, Covenant Theology is faithful to the Word of God and full of the warmth of the love of God. When God makes a covenant with his people, it really is 'a bond of love', that brings salvation and an eternal hope to people who were dead in sin, 'without hope and without God in the world' (Ephesians 2:12).

Covenant Theology does not in any way minimise or overlook the wrath of a holy God on sin, but its focus is on the loving relationship which God in his infinite love establishes with those he takes to be his people. 'I will walk among you and be your God, and you will be my people' (Leviticus 26:12) is a promise to fill the Christian's heart with joy, and one to make those who are not Christians reconsider what they are missing by living as they do. Could anything be more beautiful than the gracious covenant which the Lord makes with saved sinners?

The theme of God's covenant with his people runs all the way through the Bible, from Genesis to Revelation, and relates in one way or another to every area of theology. In the course of this study, therefore, we look at subjects ranging from the nature of God, through the provision of salvation in Christ, to the 'last things' in what is known as 'eschatology'. We will try throughout to listen to what Scripture says, without forcing it into a preconceived framework or attempting to make its teaching neater than it actually is. We believe, however, that the approach adopted by Covenant Theology serves to show the wonderful unity of God's revelation to us, without in any way hiding its rich diversity. To see the way in which the Lord deals with his people by means of a covenant stirs wonder and evokes worship.

The biblical truths that we will be considering have come under attack all through the history of the Church. We will face some of the most important and the most recent challenges to show how the Word of God provides solid answers. Covenant theologians from different periods are quoted frequently, not because they have an authority equal to the Bible, but in order to show some of the riches that their writings contain.

The material out of which this book grew first saw the light of day at the Free Church of Scotland Summer School in Theology in Larbert, and was later repeated at Korea Theological Seminary in Pusan. I am grateful to Malcolm Maclean of Christian Focus Publications for encouragement to write and for his acceptance of my proposal for this book. I greatly appreciate the stimulus of teaching at the Reformed Theological College, Belfast, with supportive colleagues and with students who refuse to be fobbed off with easy answers. In producing this book I wish to thank Diana Kirkpatrick, whose proof-reading was meticulous. My wife Valerie typed the entire manuscript and gave support for which no words of thanks begin to be adequate. 'She is worth far more than rubies' (Proverbs 31:10).

1

Setting the Scene

It is fashionable today, at least in Europe and North America, to rubbish any philosophy or system that claims to explain 'life, the universe and everything'. According to many of the most influential intellectual figures of the day, it is simply impossible to provide a single overarching explanation of everything that exists. They argue that no such explanation exists and that the search for it is utterly misguided. At best we may find what is 'true for us' – what enables us to cope with life – but that may be entirely different from what is true for anyone else. Any claim to have a 'world-and-life-view', for example by Bible-believing Christians, is dismissed as a delusion.

In their approach to the Bible Christians may, even unconsciously, be affected by this climate of suspicion. They may be very reluctant to accept any claim to explain the 'big picture' as far as the Bible is concerned, any claim to have a system that ties together the diverse parts that make up the Christian Scriptures. Should that system have been developed several centuries ago, it has even less chance of being taken seriously in a culture that puts the highest value on what is thought to be contemporary and original.

In such a climate it would seem to be a waste of time and energy to try to persuade Christians to take Covenant Theology seriously. Here, after all, is a theological system that claims to find a single thread running right through the Bible, tying all its parts together. 'Covenant', it is said, provides a vital key for understanding the Bible as a whole. If these claims are true, however, they cannot be ignored. To reject a fruitful approach to the study of God's word is ultimately to dishonour the divine author and impoverish our own spiritual life.

We should not allow ourselves to be put off by the fact that the main elements of Covenant Theology were identified and assembled several centuries ago. The Bible itself, after all, is many centuries old! Our culture may encourage us to follow the latest thinking and to despise what is regarded as old-fashioned. The Bible, however, teaches us to respect the wisdom of the old who have long experience of God's ways. Among covenant theologians there have been many godly men who served the Lord in some of the Church's best days. At the very least they deserve a respectful hearing.

The main purpose of this introductory chapter is to explain briefly what Covenant Theology is and to show that in its broad outlines it is an accurate expression of what the Bible teaches. There have been differences of opinion among covenant theologians on various issues in the course of history, but there is a substantial area of agreement which unites those who hold to Covenant Theology. These men are, of course, fallible and we cannot endorse everything that has been said or written in the name of Covenant Theology. Our only infallible rule of faith and practice is the Bible which stands in judgment over all our theological thinking.

Having laid the foundations in this introduction, we will devote the rest of our study to tracing how the theology of the covenants relates to a range of doctrinal issues. Not every subject can be considered, but our chosen topics should show something of the range and richness of Covenant Theology.

One particular aim will be to apply Covenant Theology to some of the important challenges which contemporary Christians have to face in the culture in which they live and witness. In so doing, we will see that, far from being an outdated relic of seventeenth century 'Reformed Scholasticism', Covenant Theology is of the utmost contemporary relevance.

What is a covenant?

It is clear from the evidence provided by Scripture that 'covenant' plays a very significant role in God's dealings with His people. A covenant is established, for example, with Noah (Gen. 6:18), with Abraham (Gen. 15:18), with the Israelites (Exod. 24:8) and with David (Ps. 89:3). In the New Testament we also find Jesus applying covenant terminology to the Last Supper: 'This cup is the new covenant in my blood' (Luke 22:20). But what is a 'covenant'?

A useful, concise definition is provided by one of the great Scottish covenant theologians, Robert Rollock, in his 1597 work *A Treatise of God's Effectual Calling*: 'The covenant of God is a promise under some certain condition.'[1] Although Rollock wrote four centuries ago, the work of biblical scholars in the intervening period has confirmed the accuracy of his words. Two aspects of 'covenant' can be identified.

(i) a promise

The essence of God's covenant is summed up in the promise repeated throughout Scripture, 'I will be your God and you will be my people'. This promise is found, for example, in Leviticus 26:12, but even when the precise form of words is not used, the promise is always the same. Look, for example, at the following verses:

Genesis 17:7: 'I will establish my covenant as an everlasting covenant between me and you and your descendants after you for the generations to come, to be your God and the God of your descendants after you.'

Exodus 6:7: 'I will take you as my own people, and I will be your God. Then you will know that I am the LORD your God, who brought you out from under the yoke of the Egyptians.'

Jeremiah 32:38: 'They will be my people, and I will be their God.'

Ezekiel 37:27: 'My dwelling-place will be with them; I will be their God, and they will be my people.'

2 Chronicles 6:16-18: 'Now LORD, God of Israel, keep for

your servant David my father the promises you made to him
when you said, "You shall never fail to have a man to sit before
me on the throne of Israel, if only your sons are careful in all
they do to walk before me according to my law, as you have
done." And now, O LORD, God of Israel, let your word that you
promised your servant David come true. But will God really
dwell on earth with men? The heavens, even the highest heavens,
cannot contain you. How much less this temple that I have built!'

It is striking that in the perfection of the final state, in the
new heaven and the new earth, God's promise is the same: 'Now
the dwelling of God is with men, and he will live with them.
They will be his people and God himself will be with them and
be their God' (Rev. 21:3). From Genesis to Revelation, the
covenant promise is unchanging, as the God who makes it is
unchanging.

It is important to stress that a covenant is first and foremost
a promise. When God makes a covenant, His is the initiative.
He is the almighty, sovereign God who freely decides to enter
into covenant. His covenant with His people is not in any sense
an agreement between equals. God and man do not sit down
together to hammer out the terms of their relationship, like
management and trade union negotiators. God decrees the terms:
it is for man to accept them humbly and willingly. This
asymmetry between the parties to the covenant must always be
kept in mind, especially in relation to salvation.

(ii) condition(s)
'While the covenant is unilateral in establishment, it is mutual
or two-sided in accomplishment.'[2] Without in any way
compromising the sovereignty of God, Scripture also stresses
the necessity of a response of faith and obedience on the part of
those who are to be His covenant partners.

Thus it was in the case of Abraham. In Genesis 17:2 God
confirms his covenant with Abraham and promises numerous
descendants, whilst in verse 1 He sets out the requirement, 'walk
before me and be blameless.' Such a life of obedience would

be the fruit of faith and, as Romans 4 shows, faith was an outstanding characteristic of Abraham.

This is how it must always be in the covenant. The divine initiative must be met by the response of faith, which inevitably issues in obedience if it is genuine. As Ephesians 2:8-9 demonstrates, even such faith is the gift of God. By the gracious working of the Holy Spirit, God enables His people to fulfil the conditions of the covenant. All the glory, therefore, belongs to God.

Some Reformed writers have baulked at the use of the term 'condition' in relation to the covenant, believing that it compromises the sovereignty of God and opens a door to unbiblical ideas of human merit as a contribution to salvation. Most covenant theologians, however, have recognized that it is proper to speak of a condition attached to the covenant if the term is carefully and biblically defined in the way that we have sought to do. To speak of a 'condition' in this sense does not compromise God's sovereignty or grace in any way.

We might note how often in Scripture God commands His people to keep the covenant that He has made with them, by their obedience to His commandments. Thus we read in Deuteronomy 29:9, when the covenant with Israel is renewed in Moab: 'So keep the words of this covenant to do them' (NASB). The essential place of obedience is made clear in, for example, Deuteronomy 7:9, with its reference to 'the faithful God, keeping his covenant of love to a thousand generations of those who love him and keep his commands'. The absolute sovereignty of God in no way destroys human responsibility. Obedience is the pathway to covenant blessings (Lev. 26:1-13), whilst disobedience brings down covenant curses (Lev. 26:14-39).

It is by means of a covenant, therefore, that God has freely chosen to relate to man and indeed, as we shall see, covenant also plays a part in relationships within the Trinity. A useful illustration of the nature of a covenant is the institution of marriage. Both parties enter freely (at least in normal

circumstances) into the marriage covenant which establishes
the relationship between them. A bond of *love* is forged, and it
is important to stress this, lest the concept of a covenant should
seem to be a cold, legalistic transaction. It is nevertheless a
bond: it binds the parties to fulfil certain obligations concerning
which they have made solemn promises. Thus in a marriage
the cry, 'We don't love each other any more' does not remove
the obligations or end the marriage. On the other hand, when
love is missing, the marriage covenant becomes a bondage. Love
and obligation should be held in balance, since both are integral
to the covenant relationship.

The covenant language of marriage is used by the Lord to
describe His relationship with His people in a number of
passages of Scripture, often in the context of their unfaithfulness
to the covenant. Jeremiah 3:1, 20 are such an example as is
Ezekiel 16:1ff. where the Lord says, 'I gave you my solemn
oath and entered into a covenant with you' (v. 8). The whole
book of Hosea describes the sin of Israel and Judah in terms of
the adulterous breaking of their marriage covenant with the Lord.

We may sum up the nature of God's covenant with His people
in the words of one of the most important seventeenth century
covenant theologians, Francis Turretin:

> 'covenant denotes the agreement of God with man by which God
> promises his goods (and especially eternal life to him), and by man,
> in turn, duty and worship are engaged... This is called two-sided
> and mutual because it consists of a mutual obligation of the
> contracting parties: a promise on the part of God and stipulation of
> the condition on the part of man.'[3]

The biblical covenants

To understand the structure of Covenant Theology we must
examine the covenants which are to be found in Scripture, the
covenants which chart the course of God's dealings with
mankind. If Covenant Theology is not rooted and grounded in
Scripture, it can make no claims on our belief or allegiance.
What, then, are the most significant biblical covenants?

(i) the covenant in Eden

At first sight there does not appear to be anything resembling a covenant in the arrangements put in place by the Lord for Adam and Eve in the Garden of Eden. (Note the apostle Paul's assumption that Adam was just as much a historical figure as Jesus was, Romans 5:12ff.) A closer examination of the biblical record, however, shows that the first human beings were indeed in a covenant relationship with God.

A very significant text in this regard is Hosea 6:7, which deals with Israel's sin of covenant breaking. According to the most satisfactory reading, the verse reads, 'Like Adam, they have broken the covenant' (NIV, NASB).[4] The implication of the verse is clearly that Adam was a party to a covenant in Eden, with the Lord obviously being the other party.

Other basic elements of a covenant may be discerned in the record of Genesis 1–2. Thus certain God-given provisions govern the life of Adam (and Eve) in Eden. In general, there are commands regarding procreation and dominion in Genesis 1:28-30. More specific direction is provided in Genesis 2:16-17, regarding the prohibition on eating from 'the tree of the knowledge of good and evil'. Although there is only one prohibition, the whole future of Adam (and of his descendants) hangs upon it.

Adam is left in no doubt regarding the covenant requirements that God has laid down for him, and the divine sanctions against the covenant breaker are made equally clear. In Genesis 2:17 the warning is given that 'in the day that you eat from it you shall surely die' (NASB). Subsequent events will show that what is in view is death in its fullest sense, primarily as loss of fellowship with God.

As Donald Macleod points out: 'This is a rather peculiar covenant because, in essence, it is not so much a conditional promise as a conditional threat.'[5] As he goes on to show, however, the grace of God is present in great measure in the covenant in Eden. We must remember that Adam was provided with an abundance of good gifts by his Creator, and that he had been created perfectly holy, in the image of God, and so was able to keep his covenant obligations. God was under no obligation to make such lavish provision for one of His creatures.

Furthermore, the threat of judgment on the covenant breaker implies a corresponding gracious promise on God's part. If death was to be the consequence of disobedience, then obedience would entail the continuance of 'life', not simply as biological existence but as life in its fullest sense, life in fellowship with God. What more could Adam desire? His relationship of love and trust with God would continue; God would be glorified and man would find the fulfilment for which he was created.

Many covenant theologians have argued that Adam in the Garden of Eden was placed 'on probation'. In other words, God was testing him for a limited period of time regarding his obedience to the divine command not to eat of the tree of the knowledge of good and evil. In the view of the majority, if Adam had passed the test, his state of holiness would have been confirmed permanently, he would have been put beyond the possibility of falling and would probably have been elevated to 'eternal life' in heavenly glory.

Much of this, however, is highly speculative and builds on a very small amount of evidence in the Genesis record. There is no indication that Adam was on probation for a set period of time and the record is silent regarding some 'higher' life which would be conferred after the test had been passed. It therefore seems best to say that as long as Adam continued in faith and obedience he would enjoy the bliss of fellowship with the Lord which had already been granted to him. Since God had decreed a different course of events, it seems fruitless to speculate about a hypothetical 'what if' situation. It may well be that at some point Adam would have experienced a transition to heavenly glory, but this cannot be proved. The reference in Genesis 3:22 to eating of the tree of life and living for ever may indicate the possibility of confirmation in a state of holiness or of sin, but little is said about the role of the tree of life and so too much should not be built on this verse.

What is clear from the rest of Scripture, however, is that Adam in Eden acted not only as an individual but as a representative of the whole human race that would derive its existence from him. Adam can thus be described as the 'federal (i.e. covenant) head' of the human race.

In support of this view, we may note that the consequences of Adam's disobedience, as detailed in Genesis 3, have as much reference to his descendants as to Adam himself. Thus death is the lot of every human being – not through personal repetition of the pattern of temptation and fall in Eden but as a result of spiritual solidarity with Adam. In 1 Corinthians 15:22 Paul expresses it in this way: 'in Adam all die'. The other consequences of Adam's sin, including the corruption of marital relationships and the struggle to secure food from a resistant earth, affect all his descendants even though they did not personally eat the forbidden fruit.

Further evidence is provided by New Testament passages which show that the solidarity between Adam and his descendants is parallel to the solidarity between Christ and His people. This is clear in a fuller quotation from 1 Corinthians 15:22: 'as in Adam all die, so in Christ all will be made alive.' Just as those who are united to Christ receive the benefits of His redemptive work, so those who are united to Adam (the whole human race) receive the poisoned fruit of his disobedience.

The parallels between Adam and Christ are explored most fully in Romans 5:12-19. The heart of Paul's argument is summed up in verse 19: 'For just as through the disobedience of the one man the many were made sinners, so also through the obedience of the one man the many will be made righteous.' In due course we will consider Christ's federal headship of His people in the Covenant of Grace, but for our present purpose, this passage shows that Adam held a position of federal headship in relation to the whole human race in the covenant in Eden.

If it should be thought unfair that other people should suffer because of the sin of Adam, an objection often raised against this doctrine, two considerations must be kept in mind. First, it is God who lays down the standard of what is fair and just, and human thinking must be submitted to Him. As Paul asks in Romans 9:20, 'who are you, O man, to talk back to God?' Secondly, if we reject the possibility of human sinfulness arising through union with Adam, we must also reject the possibility of human righteousness being granted through union with Christ. It is therefore the gospel that is at stake if the concept of federal headship is rejected.

Up until now we have not made use of the title most commonly applied to this covenant, namely, the Covenant of Works. Some theologians have preferred other designations, such as the Covenant of Nature, but most have opted for Covenant of Works. If this term is to be used, it must be defined carefully. Some have refused to speak of a Covenant of Works because of a fear that this suggests an ability on the part of man to accumulate merit with God and thus earn a right to blessing.[6]

It must be stressed that man can never, of himself, put God under obligation to bless. The principle stated by Jesus in Luke 17:10 is always true: 'when you have done everything you were told to do, [you] should say, "We are unworthy servants; we have only done our duty." ' Nevertheless God may choose to bestow blessing on the basis of His servants' obedience or lack of it. It is in this sense that the obedience of Adam in Eden was of such importance. To fail to render the obedience that God required would entail spiritual ruin for himself and for his descendants. The reason for Adam's expulsion from Eden, with all that this involved, is clearly disobedience.

We find nothing unworthy of God in His making blessing dependent on man's obedience. His doing so was a free, gracious act. He was not placed under any obligation by man; He placed Himself under obligation when He established a covenant. When He says to His people, 'I will be your God', He is taking wide-ranging obligations upon Himself, but He is never less than absolutely sovereign in doing so. The view of God that emerges from discussion of the Covenant of Works is entirely consistent with what He has revealed about Himself in the rest of Scripture.

It is also important to note that believers' salvation depends on the obedience of Christ, which is in fact compliance with the requirements of the Covenant of Works. Thus Romans 5:19 states, 'through the obedience of the one man the many will be made righteous.' The effects of the disobedience of Adam are reversed for believers by the obedience of Christ.

(ii) the Covenant of Redemption

The divine remedy for the sin of the human race is provided by means of covenant. Most covenant theologians have recognised that Scripture describes two sets of relationships that are involved in the divine plan of salvation. On the one hand there is a relationship between God the Father and God the Son (also involving the Holy Spirit) and on the other hand there is a relationship between the Triune God and the sinners that He chooses to save. Although these relationships are seen as being part of a single covenantal plan of God, for the sake of clarity covenant theologians have usually designated the first the 'Covenant of Redemption' and the second the 'Covenant of Grace'. Some eminent theologians, like the eighteenth century Scot, Thomas Boston, have rejected this division of God's covenant of salvation. We may use the terms, however, if we keep in mind the comment of W. G. T. Shedd: 'The covenant of grace and that of redemption are two modes or phases of the one evangelical covenant of mercy.'[7]

Whatever the theologians say, however, the concept of a Covenant of Redemption may be used only if its existence can be proved from Scripture. The word of God does indicate that there is such a covenant between Father and Son, but when speaking of something which takes place within the Trinity, great reverence and humility are required. We must be careful not to speculate beyond what God has revealed to us. Nevertheless, like the doctrine of the Trinity, the doctrine of the Covenant of Redemption may be assembled from the information which the Bible provides.

To begin with, it is significant that during His earthly ministry the Lord Jesus Christ showed a deep awareness of having been given a particular task to perform. This is especially clear in the Gospel of John, where Christ is shown to be sent with a mission to carry out. 'I seek not to please myself but him who sent me' (John 5:30). 'I have come down from heaven not to do my will but to do the will of him who sent me' (John 6:38). The following verses in John 6 specify that will: 'that I shall lose none of all that he has given me, but raise them up at the last day. For my Father's will is that everyone who looks to the Son and believes in him shall have eternal life...' (vv. 39-40). Clearly Christ has been sent to provide salvation for a people *given* to Him by His Father. (See also John 17:2, 6, 9, 24). The note of satisfaction is evident in John 17:4: 'I have brought you glory on earth by completing the work you gave me to do.' That the giving of a people to Christ took place before creation is expressed in Ephesians 1:4: 'He chose us in [Christ] before the creation of the world.'

Other texts demonstrate more explicitly that the arrangement made between Father and Son takes the form of a covenant. Thus in Psalm 89:3 God says, 'I have made a covenant with my chosen one; I have sworn to David.' The necessary background for understanding this statement is to be found in 2 Samuel 7:12-14, recording God's covenant promises to King David. As the quotation from this passage in Hebrews 1:5 shows, however, the ultimate reference is to David's greater descendant, the Lord Jesus Christ.

Further evidence is provided by Isaiah 42:6: '[I] will make you to be a covenant for the people and a light for the Gentiles.' The one addressed is the Servant of the Lord. Some take this as no more than a reference to Israel, but the language of Isaiah 42:1-7 strongly suggests that an individual is in view. In addition, the language of the passage is often used in the New Testament to describe the work of the Messiah, as for example in Luke 2:32 when Simeon speaks of 'a light for revelation to the Gentiles'. It would seem to be necessary to regard Christ as the one appointed 'as a covenant'.

Mention has already been made of the parallels between Adam and Christ in 1 Corinthians 15:22 and especially in Romans 5:12-19. The language of 'in Adam' and 'in Christ' is the language of covenantal representation. Adam and Christ represent two groups of people, they hold positions of headship. Adam was constituted head of the human race by the Covenant in Eden. Christ was constituted head of His elect people by the Covenant of Redemption.

What, then, was required of Christ in the Covenant of Redemption? In the most general way, we can say that His work was to undo the results of Adam's failure to keep the Covenant of Works. To be more specific – two elements were involved in His saving work. On the one hand, He was to make atonement for the sins of His people, thus dealing with their liability to eternal punishment. On the other hand, He was to keep the Law of God perfectly on behalf of His people, thus securing for them eternal life.

Both of these elements may be seen in Christ's designation as 'surety' (*engyos* in Greek, translated 'guarantee' in NIV and NASB). The term is used in Hebrews 7:22, 'Because of this oath, Jesus has become the guarantee of a better covenant.' A surety is one who undertakes to be responsible for the meeting of another party's legal obligations. It was therefore necessary for Christ to bear the punishment due to the sins of His people, and it is remarkable how often in the Gospel records He speaks of the necessity of His sufferings, as for example in Luke 24:26: 'Did not the Christ have to suffer these things and then enter his glory?' This element of His work is described in 1 Peter 2:24, 'He himself bore our sins in his body on the tree, so that we might die to sins and live for righteousness.'

The work of Christ also entails meeting His people's obligation to obey God's Law. It is not just that their past sins are wiped out, leaving them in a neutral position before God: they are constituted positively righteous in God's sight. The obedience of Christ, which was perfect in every detail, is counted as belonging to Him. Thus believers are said to 'become the righteousness of God' (2 Cor. 5:21) in Christ who is 'our righteousness' (1 Cor. 1:30).

All of these obligations Christ willingly took upon Himself in the Covenant of Redemption and so could say to His Father, 'I desire to do your will, O my God; your law is within my heart' (Ps. 40:8, as interpreted in Heb. 10:5ff.).

As far as the Father is concerned, then, what promises did He make to His Son in the Covenant of Redemption? In the most comprehensive sense, Christ was promised everything necessary for the accomplishment of a glorious redemption, including the resulting multitude of redeemed sinners 'that no-one could count' (Rev. 7:9). The nature of the promises may be derived in part from explicit biblical statements and in part by deduction from the provision and promises which Christ is said to enjoy.

One example of the Father's provision for the Son's atoning work relates to His incarnation. As Hebrews 2:17 says, 'he had to be made like his brothers in every way, in order that he might become a merciful and faithful high priest.' Verse 14 shows what this implied: 'Since the children have flesh and blood, he too shared in their humanity.' How this is linked to the Father's provision is made clear in Hebrews 10:5, where Psalm 40:6-8 (in the Greek translation) is attributed to Christ. In particular He says, 'a body you prepared for me', and the one to whom He speaks must be the Father.

It is impossible to consider the Father's promises to the Son of all necessary provision without making reference to the work of the Holy Spirit. This serves as a healthy reminder that the Spirit is vitally involved in the Covenant of Redemption: He does not stand aside as an idle spectator. Each Person of the Trinity plays a full part in all of God's works.

As far as the work of redemption is concerned, in Isaiah 42:1-2 the Father refers to the Son as 'my servant whom I uphold, my chosen one in whom I delight, ' and states, 'I will put my Spirit on him.' The Son is the Anointed One, the

Messiah, and says, 'The Spirit of the Sovereign Lord is on me, because the Lord has anointed me to preach good news to the poor' (Isa. 61:1; Luke 4:18). Not only is the Spirit given to equip Christ with everything necessary for His work, He also plays a part in the atonement that must be made. Thus Hebrews 9:14 speaks of 'Christ, who through the eternal Spirit offered himself unblemished to God'. It is that same Holy Spirit who applies the finished atonement of Christ to sinners for their salvation. Acts 2:33 can therefore speak of Christ in this way: 'Exalted to the right hand of God, he has received from the Father the promised Holy Spirit.' It is in the power of the Spirit that the Church is to fulfil its mission (Acts 1:8).

The promises of the Covenant of Redemption make doubly sure what was already sure – the success of Christ's redemptive work. Such double assurance is also seen in God's swearing an oath regarding Christ's priesthood (Heb. 7:17ff.). He is promised that His sacrifice will result in an innumerable spiritual seed (Isa. 53:10; Pss. 22:27; 72:17; Rev. 7:9). This should be linked with the promise of universal dominion indicated in, for example, Matthew 28:18 and Ephesians 1:20-22. In Philippians 2:9 it is significant that after describing Christ's atoning work Paul says '*therefore* God exalted him to the highest place'. Exaltation flows from his obedience unto death (v. 8).

The work of Christ must therefore be thought of in terms of obedience and consequent reward. As Donald Macleod says, 'The covenant-*breaking* of the First Man (and of all mankind) is covered by the covenant-*keeping* of the Last Man, the Lord Jesus Christ.'[8] He has secured a complete salvation for His people, including both their change of status (justification, adoption, etc.) and their change of condition (regeneration, faith and repentance, etc.). Everything required in the Covenant of Grace has been provided by a sovereign and loving God in the Covenant of Redemption.

(iii) the Covenant of Grace

Mention of the Covenant of Grace leads us to think of how sinful men and women actually benefit from the redemptive work of Christ. The Covenant of Grace is made by the Triune God of grace who shows Himself to be willing to pardon sin and restore sinners to Himself through the Saviour whom He provides. He is the one who sovereignly declares the terms on which sinners may become His people.

There has been some debate among covenant theologians as to the identity of the other party in the Covenant of Grace. The best view would seem to be that the covenant is made with those sinners who were chosen in Christ before the creation of the world (see Eph. 1:4). This view treats the covenant from the perspective of the results it achieves, namely the salvation of all those whom God 'foreknew' in eternity (Rom. 8:29-30).

A useful definition of the Covenant of Grace is given by Louis Berkhof, who describes it as, 'that gracious agreement between the offended God and the offending but elect sinner, in which God promises salvation through faith in Christ, and the sinner accepts this believingly, promising a life of faith and obedience.'[9]

As we will see at a later point in our study, Scripture also indicates that there is a sense in which the children of believers are to be considered as within the circle of the covenant. This will occupy our attention when we come to consider baptism, and so it will not be considered in detail here. It is in this sense that the Covenant of Grace can be said to be made with 'believers and their seed'.

As far as the promises made by God in the Covenant of Grace are concerned, they may be summed up in the words of Leviticus 26:12: 'I will walk among you and be your God, and you will be my people.' It is significant that God speaks these words in the context of deliverance from bondage (in Egypt, verse 13) and uses the special covenant name usually translated as 'the LORD'. It is clear that the God of the Covenant brings His people into a warm and loving fellowship with Himself. The language is the language of family.

This basic promise recurs constantly throughout Scripture, indicating that 'covenant' is a unifying theme in the unfolding of God's redemptive purpose. Thus when God establishes His covenant with Abraham in Genesis 17, He promises 'to be your God and the God of your descendants after you' (v. 7). When the Old Testament prophets look forward to the 'New Covenant', the promise it will embody is the same: 'I will be their God and they will be my people' (Jer. 31:33). Further examples are to be found in Jeremiah 32:38 and Ezekiel 36:28, 37:27. It therefore comes as no surprise that when the new heaven and the new earth are described in Revelation 21, the 'loud voice from the throne' declares, 'Now the dwelling of God is with men, and he will live with them. They will be his people, and God himself will be with them and be their God' (v. 3). From Genesis to Revelation the covenant promise is the same, a fact which has a very important bearing on many of the subjects that will be discussed in the rest of this book.

The central covenant promise sums up all that God undertakes to do for His people in the Covenant of Grace. It is of course a promise of salvation, since His people 'were by nature children of wrath, even as the rest' (Eph. 2:3, NASB). The relationship with God provided by the covenant requires that sin be dealt with. As Isaiah 59:2 puts it, 'your iniquities have separated you from your God; your sins have hidden his face from you, so that he will not hear.' Such a diagnosis underlines the necessity of the redemptive work of the incarnate Son of God.

Within the central promise that we have noted, a number of things are included, all provided by the grace and love of the Lord. That provision was made, as has already been indicated, in eternity according to the Covenant of Redemption, and is bestowed in the course of history as directed by the sovereign God. Thus God promised temporal blessings along with spiritual blessings in Old Testament days (see e.g. Deut. 11:13-15). These temporal blessings are often symbolic of spiritual blessings and provide some of the language that is used to describe spiritual blessings in the New Testament. God also promises to confer upon His people justification, adoption and eternal life (enjoyed already in the present world). He promises the Holy Spirit to apply the redemption purchased by Christ and to convey all the blessings of salvation, including sanctification. The Covenant of Grace cannot fail, as is shown by the promise of final glorification which will mark the entrance of resurrected believers into the fullness of eternal life in fellowship with God. Such passages as 1 Corinthians 15:12ff and Philippians 3:20-21 reveal a little of the wonders that God still has in store for His covenant people. Since many of these matters will be discussed more fully later, we will confine ourselves for the moment to this brief summary.

The Covenant of Grace of course requires a response from the side of man. That response is to be a humble acceptance of the terms of the covenant: God does not enter into negotiations with sinners to find a mutually agreeable set of terms. It is for the sovereign God to decree the terms upon which sinners may come to Him, and it is for them to accept (or reject) His terms. Acceptance is possible only by the grace of God, every element of salvation being by grace (Eph. 2:8-9), but it is genuinely *man's* response.

The acceptance required of the sinner embraces every aspect of his being: his thinking, his emotions and his will are all included. The self-giving of God in the Covenant of Grace ('I will be your God') must be met by man's total self-giving to God ('My Lord and my God', John 20:28). It must be a response of heartfelt, faithful devoted love, bearing out the truth of 1 John 4:19: 'We love because he first loved us.' The call of the gospel, summoning sinners into the covenant, must be answered with true repentance and saving faith in the Lord Jesus Christ. Such trust in Christ and commitment to Him will result in a life of joyful obedience to God's covenant law (John 14:15; 1 John 5:2-3). Nothing less is sufficient for a fallen son of Adam to have a share in the glorious blessings of the Covenant of Grace.

Where next?

The rest of this study will be devoted to a consideration of the relevance of the covenant theology that has just been outlined to various aspects of Christian doctrine and life. We will be concerned not least with the practical outworking of covenant theology, since all of God's revelation in Scripture should contribute to believers' growth in grace. Covenant Theology is not some obscure set of conundrums to tickle the intellectual palate of ivory tower theologians, although it has often been caricatured in that way. We will also be concerned to address the significant trends in modern thought which challenge the Christian faith and to which Covenant Theology provides so many biblical answers.

Notes

1. Robert Rollock, *A Treatise of God's Effectual Calling*, 1603 edition, translated by H. Holland in *Select Works of Robert Rollock* (Edinburgh, 1849), p. 34 (ch. 2).

2. P. A. Lillback, 'Covenant' in *New Dictionary of Theology*, edited by Sinclair B. Ferguson and David F. Wright (Leicester/ Downers Grove, 1988), p.173.

3. Francis Turretin, *Institutes of Elenctic Theology*, translated by G. M. Giger (Phillipsburg, 1992), Locus 8, Q3, para 3 (1.574).

4. The proposed alternatives are unconvincing. 'Like man/men, they have broken the covenant': how else could men break the covenant but 'like men'? On this translation the verse is stating the obvious. 'As at Adam, they have broken the covenant': no-one can suggest what (presumably well-known) episode is in view if this is the correct translation, not to mention how forced a translation of the Hebrew text it is.

5. Donald Macleod, *A Faith to Live By* (Fearn, 1998), p. 92.

6. See e.g. the views of Herman Hoeksema in *Reformed Dogmatics* (Grand Rapids, 1966), part 3, ch. 5. Hoeksema rejects any suggestion that the biblical covenants were agreements.

7. W. G. T. Shedd, *Dogmatic Theology* 1889-94 edition. (Nashville, 1980), 2.360.

8. Macleod, op. cit., p. 98.

9. Louis Berkhof, *Systematic Theology* (Edinburgh, 1958), p. 277.

2

A Personal God

By its very nature, a covenant must be established by personal agents, even when they are acting in a representative capacity. The covenants described in Scripture are made by personal agents and constitute personal relationships: between God and Adam (and his descendants) in the Covenant of Works; between Father and Son in the Covenant of Redemption; between God and His people in the Covenant of Grace. To say this is really to state the obvious, but sometimes the obvious needs to be stated if there are some who try to deny it.

The fundamental perfection (or attribute) of the God of the covenants is that He is personal. Among a multitude of personal activities ascribed to Him in Scripture are *speaking* (e.g. to Adam, in Genesis 2:16-17), *promising* (e.g. to Abraham, in Genesis 17:4ff.), *loving* (e.g. David, in Psalm 89:24, 28) and *choosing* (e.g. His people in Christ, Eph. 1:4). Also significant are the personal titles which God uses to describe Himself, such as *shepherd* (Ps. 23:1), *husband* (Jer. 31:32), *king* (Isa. 43:15) and *father* (constantly on the lips of Jesus).

Those who are brought into covenant with God relate to Him in a personal way. Thus He commands the Israelites, 'Love the LORD your God with all your heart and with all your soul and with all your strength' (Deut. 6:5). The same command is to be found in Jesus' summary of the Law in Matthew 22:37: 'Love the Lord your God with all your heart and with all your soul and with all your mind.' Clearly God is as personal as the neighbour who is also to be loved, according to verse 39. Covenant life is a personal relationship with God which expresses itself in prayer, obedience, repentance and other activities which require a personal object.

It is very significant, as Christopher Kaiser has pointed out,[1]

that in considering the ways in which God is described right at
the beginning of the Bible, in Genesis and Exodus, we do not
find abstract or technical terms such as 'omniscient' or 'infinite'.
Instead we find descriptions of God in terms of His relationship
with individuals, along with accounts of His mighty deeds on
their behalf.

This may be illustrated by God's dealings with the patriarch
Abraham. The blessing pronounced by Melchizedek in Genesis
14:19-20 is, as Kaiser demonstrates, full of significance:
'Blessed be Abram by God Most High, Creator of heaven and
earth. And blessed be God Most High, who delivered your
enemies into your hand.' God has entered into a personal
relationship with a particular man at a specific point in history.
The following chapters in Genesis recount the development of
that relationship as God elaborates His promises and as Abraham
grows in his understanding of and response to God. In this
context God makes a covenant with Abraham (Gen. 15) and
later reaffirms it (Gen. 17). A similar pattern can be traced in
the experience of Isaac and Jacob in subsequent chapters.

Reference has been made previously to the central covenant
promise 'I will be your God and you will be my people' (Lev.
26:12). God relates to His people person-to-person. To be a
child of God is not merely to hold certain intellectual convictions
and perform certain religious rituals: it is to know God and be
known by Him in a personal way. That is why Jesus, in the
following quotation from Isaiah, condemned the people of His
day who did not move beyond correct belief and ritual : 'These
people honour me with their lips, but their hearts are far from
me' (Mark 7:6, quoting Isa. 29:13). Covenant life entails
personal relationships.

The covenants, indeed, are full of the love of God. When the
Lord explains to the Israelites why they have been chosen as
His people, He makes it clear that it is not because of any
distinctions that they possess. Rather, the ultimate explanation,
beyond which it is impossible to go, is 'it was because the LORD
loved you' (Deut. 7:8). No more, no less. His love was such

that He fulfilled His covenant promise to their forefathers in every detail (v. 8).

The depth of God's love is illustrated in a rich variety of ways throughout Scripture. In Hosea He describes Himself as the husband of an unfaithful wife, yet His love is such that He says, 'How can I give you up, Ephraim? How can I hand you over, Israel?' (Hos. 11:8). It is of course at the cross of Calvary that the covenant love of the Lord is most beautifully demonstrated. Thus Paul can speak of 'the Son of God, who loved me and gave himself for me' (Gal. 2:20). It was out of an infinite love for specific persons that Christ shed His 'blood of the covenant' (Mark 14:24).

God the Absolute Personality

Great care must be taken when speaking about 'a personal relationship with God' that it is God who is kept at the centre of our thinking. In recent years there has been a tremendous upsurge of interest in 'spirituality', a very broad category embracing a bewildering range of religious options. Most, however, focus on the individual who is seeking some kind of spiritual satisfaction and whatever 'works' is acceptable. Such an approach leaves people open to all kinds of thoroughly unbiblical ideas and practices.[2] A healthy personal relationship with God in the covenant He establishes will focus on Him as He has revealed Himself to us.

Essential to God's self-revelation, as we have seen, is the fact that He is a personal God. But what kind of person is He? Some of the persons we encounter may be weak, indecisive, dependent – not characteristics to command respect or loyalty. What are we to say of the personal God of the covenants? We may rightly describe Him as 'absolute personality',[3] a phrase that sums up some important things that the Bible says about Him.

A vast range of intellectual and moral activities is attributed to God in Scripture, including willing, ruling, commanding, redeeming and judging. In none of His activities, however, does

God depend on anything outside Himself. He is entirely self-sufficient within His own being. It is in this sense that He can be described as 'absolute'. Every other being is dependent on someone or something else – God alone is self-contained and has within Himself an infinite richness of perfections. God is thus qualitatively different from everything else that exists and is not merely 'humanity writ large'.

Nothing stands above God as a standard to which He must conform Himself. As Cornelius Van Til puts it, 'There were no principles of truth, goodness or beauty that were next to or above God according to which he patterned the world.'[4] Indeed truth, goodness and beauty are attributes of God and He Himself is the standard for each of them. All creatures are finite and dependent, even when personal, whilst God is infinite and absolute.

The Source of all things
Covenant Theology proclaims that the ultimate source of all things, of the universe and of personal beings (angelic and human) is *personal*. All can be traced back to their origin in a personal Creator and all exist as a result of His purposeful action. The universe has a personal Source in the covenant God.

Such a view would be rejected out of hand by many of the most prominent popularizers of modern science. Stephen Hawking can theorize with dazzling erudition about the origins of the universe in his best-selling *A Brief History of Time*, yet feels under no compulsion to appeal to a personal source for anything, not even for human personality.[5] Astronomer Carl Sagan is even more blunt when he claims, 'The Cosmos is all that is or ever was or ever will be.'[6]

This materialistic view of the universe, propounded widely through the media, treats the universe as a closed system which requires no divine input at its beginning or at any other stage. It is a faithful reflection of the 'secular humanism' set out, for example, in the 1973 *Humanist Manifesto II*, which declares, 'We find insufficient evidence for belief in the existence of a supernatural.'[7] This implies, among other things, that human personality originates in some non-personal source. Whereas Covenant Theology says that human personality is derived from a personal Creator, the God who enters into covenant with His people, secular humanists must accept that it is derived from the impersonal, plus time, plus chance. Francis Schaeffer expressed the possibilities bluntly: 'The two alternatives are very clear cut. Either there is a personal beginning to everything or one has what the impersonal throws up by chance, out of the time sequence.'[8] As Schaeffer goes on to argue, 'Only some form of mystical jump will allow us to accept that personality comes from impersonality.'[9] How ironical it is that those holding a materialistic world-view are reduced to such a blind leap of 'faith'!

Covenant Theology assures us that the universe and we ourselves have a personal source. We are not cosmic flotsam thrown up by blind chance. Our existence is the result of the wise planning of a Creator and so life is not a meaningless succession of random experiences without rhyme or reason. Life has the meaning and significance conferred upon it by the Lord. We can sing with David the psalmist, 'The earth is the LORD's and everything in it, the world and all who live in it' (Ps. 24:1). As we will see in a later chapter, it is here that we find the foundation for human dignity: human beings are the image-bearers of a personal God who made them to have a covenant relationship with Himself.

If this is not the case, then even human thought, the product of a mind resulting from chance and blind evolution, is not to be trusted. Why should a more developed version of an ape's brain be thought to give access to any kind of ultimate truth? This road, if followed consistently, leads to the extinction of thought and to complete nihilism. But scarcely anyone could live by such a creed. In practice, most will at some point opt, without any rational justification, to act on beliefs which they profess to deny, for example, belief that the universe makes sense.

It is only in personal covenant fellowship with God that the meaning and significance of life can be found. This is life as human beings were created to live it. Such was the life lived by Adam and Eve in Eden before the Fall. Such is the life granted to repentant sinners by the Lord Jesus Christ, who said, 'I have come that they may have life, and have it to the full' (John 10:10).

We must not forget, however, that belief in a personal source for the whole universe entails responsibility towards the Creator. It was clear to Adam and Eve that they were to obey God, even though His requirements were summed up in a single prohibition regarding the tree of the knowledge of good and evil (Gen. 2:17). As they quickly discovered once they had disobeyed, they were accountable to God for their actions. In this regard nothing has changed: the whole human race is accountable to God. As 2 Corinthians 5:10 states, 'We must all appear before the judgment seat of Christ, that each one may receive what is due to him for the things done while in the body, whether good or bad.' This reality is portrayed graphically in the judgment scene of Revelation 20:11-15:

> Then I saw a great white throne and him who was seated on it. Earth and sky fled from his presence, and there was no place for them. And I saw the dead, great and small, standing before the throne, and books were opened. Another book was opened, which is the book of life. The dead were judged according to what they had done as re-corded in the books. The sea gave up the dead that were in it, and death and Hades gave up the dead that were in them, and each per-son was judged according to what he had done. Then death and Hades were thrown into the lake of fire. The lake of fire is the second death. If anyone's name was not found written in the book of life, he was thrown into the lake of fire.

Only two outcomes of that final accounting are possible. Either one will stand before Christ's judgment seat as a breaker of the Covenant of Works ('in Adam') or one will stand there as a sharer in the Covenant of Grace ('in Christ'). The outcome will therefore be either eternal punishment or eternal blessedness, the alternatives set out in Matthew 25:46 ('Then they will go away to eternal punishment, but the righteous to eternal life'). The final blessedness of the people of God is described in terms of the fundamental covenant promise in Revelation 21:3: 'Now the dwelling of God is with men, and he will live with them. They will be his people, and God himself will be with them and be their God.'

Given contemporary interest in environmental issues, it is important to note that human accountability includes our use or misuse of the material creation. As God's covenant partner, Adam was placed in Eden 'to work it and take care of it' (Gen. 2:15). The dominion granted to the human race by God (Gen. 1:26) must therefore be seen in terms of stewardship. The creation suffers as a result of human sin (Gen. 3:17: 'cursed is the ground because of you...') and now it may be described in Paul's words as in 'bondage to decay' (Rom. 8:21). Even in this condition, however, it is to be treated with respect as God's handiwork, not selfishly exploited for human enjoyment that damages the creation. This is reflected in some of the provisions of the Mosaic Law, as, for example, when fruit trees are to be spared when seeking wood for siege works (Deut. 20:19). Of greatest importance is the promise that the material creation will be renewed, not destroyed, and will share in 'the glorious freedom of the children of God' at the last day (Rom. 8:21). The consummation of the work of Christ in the Covenant of Grace will have a profound impact on the whole creation. It is in Covenant Theology that we find the necessary elements for environmental ethics and action.

Light from the East?
The emphasis of Covenant Theology on God as personal, and as the source of all that is personal in His universe, is a necessary antidote to all the attempts to depersonalize God. Looking back in history, we see that this was the (perhaps unintended) outcome of Deism in the eighteenth century in Europe. Whilst Deists

accepted that God had created the universe, they argued that
He had left it to run according to its own laws and powers, and
consequently He was not involved in any way in its day to day
progress. Whilst it may appear that the 'god' of the Deists is
personal, apologist James Sire is correct in his observation that
'he is really not a *he*, though the personal pronoun remains in
the language used about him... He has no 'personal' relation to
[his creation] at all.'[10] At the popular level, it may be said that
Deism is alive and well, since many people operate with such a
vague idea of a God who is less than fully personal.

In the modern societies of the West, however, ideas of an
impersonal God more often than not can be traced back to the
influence of Eastern ways of thinking, for example, in Hinduism
and Buddhism. Both religions, which historically are closely
related, offer a kind of supermarket of beliefs from which the
devotee can select a range of items to construct a tailor-made
religion or philosophy of life. Some strands of Hinduism believe
in a personal god, found for example in a work which has
become popular in the West, the *Bhagavad-Gita*. Most Hindus,
however, including those who believe in many gods and
goddesses, believe in 'an all-embracing, all-pervading,
omnipresent God',[11] a view which may be termed 'pantheism'.

We should not be misled by the reference to 'theism' in
pantheism. The 'god' of pantheism is ultimately an impersonal
force, with nature and human beings as elements of its being.
The divine is all-inclusive, with nothing having an independent
existence. That is why one Indian writer can refer to 'the
emanation of the world's innumerable forms from the divine'.[12]
No one can have a real personal relationship with such a god,
whatever deities may figure in one's religious activities. In fact,
in such a philosophy personality is an illusion and the goal of
life becomes absorption into the divine and the extinction of
individuality. As the Hindu strives by various means to attain
moksha, so the Buddhist of whatever school seeks *nirvana*.

Such ideas have gained a hearing in the West less through
overtly Hindu or Buddhist channels than through the influence

of the New Age Movement (NAM).[13] The title New Age Movement embraces a vast range of ideas drawn from many sources all of which claim to be means of raising human beings to higher levels of consciousness and, in general, making life better.[14] Prominent influences include Eastern religions such as Buddhism and Hinduism, along with ancient Gnosticism.

Although many of these belief systems have undergone subtle changes to make them more palatable to Western tastes, for example, giving much more prominence to the individual, the 'god' of the New Age is generally described in impersonal terms. Thus one of the pioneers of New Age thinking, Marilyn Ferguson, speaks of the 'Radical Centre' and says:

> God is experienced as flow, wholeness, the infinite kaleidoscope of life and death, Ultimate Cause, the ground of being, what Alan Watts called 'the silence out of which all sound comes'.... God is the organizing matrix we can experience but not tell, that which enlivens matter.[15]

This is not a God who loves and who may be loved. At best this is the 'God Source' described by actress and New Ager Shirley MacLaine, which comes to 'personalization' in us as our Higher Self, the Divine Centre.[16] Whatever the language used, this is not a deity with whom one can have a personal relationship. Indeed a few years earlier MacLaine had followed such a pantheistic philosophy to its logical conclusion as she exhorted her readers, with arrogant blasphemy, 'Know that you are God, know that you are the universe.'[17]

Many who opt for New Age ideas are searching for a way to fill the spiritual void created by man's alienation from God on account of sin. How sad it is to find intelligent and often highly educated people settling for such a spiritual experience as this:

> when I touched and connected with my Higher Self, I suddenly touched the personalized interface with that God Source within, and the experience changed my life.[18]

Whatever precisely that experience may be, it cannot begin to compare with the delight God's people find in daily covenant communion with the Lord. It is for this reason that the Christian can testify, 'Better is one day in your courts than a thousand elsewhere' (Ps. 84:10).

A Triune God

When Covenant Theology speaks of God as 'personal' we must not forget that a unique kind of 'personhood' is in view. The God of the Covenants has revealed Himself to be a Trinity – one God in three Persons. He is personal in a sense that cannot be applied to any of His creatures.

As Alister McGrath has noted, 'To many people, the doctrine of the Trinity is a piece of celestial mathematics – and bad mathematics at that!'[19] Certainly this is a doctrine which far exceeds the comprehension of finite human minds, but if it is a truth that God has revealed about Himself then it must be accepted in humble faith. We do not have space to expound and defend the doctrine of the Trinity here, but that is done thoroughly in the standard textbooks of Reformed Theology.[20] We may sum it up, however, in the words of Calvin that 'Father and Son and Spirit are one God, yet the Son is not the Father, nor the Spirit the Son, but ... they are differentiated by a peculiar quality.'[21]

Human reasoning eventually breaks down in examining the doctrine of the Trinity. It is not logically contradictory to say that God is both one and three, since He is not one in the same way that He is three. In the traditional language of theology He is one in 'substance' or 'essence', whilst three in 'persons'. The real difficulty arises when it has to be asserted on the basis of Scripture that each Person is fully God yet there is only one God. Only by faith can such a statement be accepted. It should not surprise us at all, however, that when thinking about an infinite God our intellectual capacities are soon exceeded.

How are we to deal with the term 'person' in this context? Although the term is not used in the Bible, orthodox theologians have generally used it in the absence of anything more satisfactory. An alternative suggested by Calvin, namely, 'subsistence' has not generally been adopted, perhaps because of its rather abstract sound. To try to be as simple as possible, we may say that a 'person' in the Trinity is 'a distinct centre of self-consciousness'.[22] Thus in the Trinity there is one who can say, 'I am the Father. I am not the Son or the Holy Spirit.' The same can be applied to the Son and to the Holy Spirit, and in Scripture the Persons are portrayed as addressing each other in the second person singular (see e.g. Ps. 110:1; John 17:1ff.). Although most theologians have had some reservations about the term 'person' in this context, it is the best term that has been found thus far to express the 'three-ness' of the Trinity.

The biblical revelation of the God of the Covenants as a Trinity is of great importance for Covenant Theology. This God within His own being is *relational*. Before anyone at all had been created, God enjoyed loving personal relationships within His triune being. When He created, it was not because of any lack within Himself: He did not need to produce another being with whom to have a relationship.

The relationships between the Persons of the Trinity cannot in general be termed 'covenantal' since a covenant requires an agreement, and that is not an accurate way to describe relationships that exist by nature. A human example would be the relationship between parents and children. Within the Trinity, Father, Son and Holy Spirit did not have to agree on how they relate to one another: that is how they exist eternally.

As we have noted already, however, there is one exception, namely, the Covenant of Redemption, established primarily between the Father and the Son. Man's hope of salvation and eternal glory rests upon a covenant within the Trinity, a covenant in which each party is fully God. Redemption is a divine work from start to finish. It should fill believers with awe and with rejoicing to think that their salvation has such an amazing and wonderful origin. How different this is from any other religion or any philosophy which at best can offer only a means by which men and women may accomplish their own salvation. Covenant Theology is rightly characterized by the words of Jonah: 'Salvation comes from the LORD' (Jon. 2:9).

We can now see that by means of the Covenant of Grace sinners are brought into a living relationship with the Triune God and thus with each of the three Persons. Of course that does not mean that any human being is absorbed into the Trinity. The rest of Scripture shows that such a thing is not implied, even by 2 Peter 1:4, which is generally translated as 'participate in the divine nature' or something similar. The line between Creator and creature is never erased. Indeed one Reformed writer has argued at length that 2 Peter 1:4 should be translated '[covenant] partners of the Deity'.[23]

The people of God are, however, brought into real covenant fellowship with each Person of the Trinity. This precious truth was examined at considerable length and in great detail by the outstanding Puritan theologian John Owen in his 1657 treatise *Of Communion with God the Father, Son and Holy Ghost, Each Person Distinctly, in Love, Grace and Consolation*.[24] He shows, for example, that the gifts and graces which God bestows on the saints are ascribed by the apostle Paul 'distinctly, in respect of the fountain of their communication, unto the distinct persons',[25] citing, as an example, 1 Corinthians 12:4-6.

Not only is this so in God's gifts to us, but as Owen argues, 'in all our approaches unto God, is the same distinction observed.'[26] This is apparent in Ephesians 2:18, 'For through [Christ] we both have access to the Father by one Spirit.' Owen makes reference also to such texts as 1 John 1:3, John 14:23, 1 Corinthians 1:9, Revelation 3:20 and 2 Corinthians 13:14, noting that all three Persons are not necessarily mentioned every time.

A trinitarian understanding of the fellowship conferred by the Lord in the Covenant of Grace enriches our conception of the wonder of God's grace and, if taken to heart and acted upon, deepens and strengthens our spiritual life. New aspects of communion with the Trinity are constantly coming to our attention as we meditate on and appropriate the truths of

Scripture. This is a personal relationship which is to grow and develop, and the possibilities are infinite. Believers will literally have eternity to cultivate their fellowship with Father, Son and Holy Spirit, and beyond this present life there will be none of the hindrances now caused by the sin that remains in each believer. Once again the believer's response should be to exclaim, 'Oh, the depths of the riches of the wisdom and knowledge of God!' (Rom. 11:33).

Covenant conversation
To speak of fellowship and communion with God raises the subject of prayer, which may also be understood in covenant terms. If a covenant establishes a personal relationship, that relationship must be two-way if it is to be worthy of the name at all. Under the Covenant of Works there was face to face communion between God and Adam and Eve. On a number of occasions God addresses Adam, e.g. Genesis 2:16-17, and in Genesis 3:8 God is described as 'walking in the garden in the cool of the day' and subsequently confronts Adam and Eve with their sin. If we take these chapters seriously as history, they portray a mutual relationship between God and man.

The relationship established between God and His redeemed people by the Covenant of Grace is no less mutual. Those who belong to the Lord enjoy communion with Him. His Holy Spirit indwells, empowers and instructs them, bringing home the truth of God to their hearts, leading and guiding them according to the Lord's will. It is by the Holy Spirit's working that the Lord's promise is fulfilled: 'My Father will love him, and we will come to him and make our home with him' (John 14:23).

The people of God, as they enjoy covenant fellowship with the Lord, address Him in prayer. Scripture makes it abundantly clear that the people of God are to be praying people. Many of the psalms are cast in the form of prayers which cover the whole range of human experience, including joy, depression, sorrow, doubt, confidence and thanksgiving. Other parts of Scripture record some of the great prayers of the saints offered on

important occasions, such as Nehemiah's prayer when he heard
of the sad state of Jerusalem (Neh. 1:5-11). Biblical commands
to pray are frequent: 'pray continually' (1 Thess. 5:17), 'in
everything, by prayer and petition, with thanksgiving, present
your requests to God' (Phil. 4:6).

But why pray? A sovereign, omniscient God knows better
than we do what are our real needs. 'Before a word is on my
tongue you know it completely' (Ps. 139:4): prayer cannot be a
matter of providing the Lord with information he would not
otherwise possess. Nevertheless prayer is vitally important for
believers, not for any changes it brings about in God, but rather
for the blessings it brings to those who pray. Prayer really is a
means of grace within the Covenant of Grace. We might term it
'covenant conversation'. Many answers can be given to the
question 'Why pray?'. Calvin in his *Institutes* suggested six
answers,[27] but we will consider only three possibilities here.

(i) Prayer expresses our trust in God, and indeed strengthens
that trust. As those who have been saved by grace and who are
members of the Covenant of Grace, believers recognize their
dependence on God for everything they need, both at the
beginning of their new life and also all the way through to final
glory. 'What do you have that you did not receive?' Paul asks
those who were inclined to pride and self-satisfaction (1 Cor.
4:7). Believers must come daily in trust to the Lord, confident
that He will fulfil His promises and supply their every need
'according to his glorious riches in Christ Jesus' (Phil. 4:19).
As the promises are fulfilled, so the believer's trust grows. In
countless ways he experiences the truth of Hebrews 13:5: 'Never
will I leave you; never will I forsake you.'

(ii) Prayer strengthens our fellowship with the Lord. The
believer is drawn closer to God as he prays. This is especially
true when time is spent in adoration – turning over in the mind
some of the perfections of God, such as His love, wisdom,
goodness and power. Prayer is not only petition, otherwise it
rapidly deteriorates into presenting a 'wants list' to the Almighty.

The more we adore God for who He is, the warmer will be our fellowship with Him.

It is also true that fellowship is strengthened as we confess our sins to the Lord and experience the joy of renewed forgiveness. Such an experience is to be found, for example, in Psalm 32, as David joyfully proclaims, 'Blessed is he whose transgressions are forgiven, whose sins are covered' (v. 1). The same is true when petitions are brought to the Lord and we receive His infinitely wise answers which show Him to be better than any parent on earth (Luke 11:9-13).

(iii) In prayer God grants us the privilege of sharing in the unfolding of His purpose in the world. Believers' prayers are effective because they have been included in God's sovereign decrees, along with His answers. The prayers of believers are thus an element in the fulfilment of God's plans, and when His people pray, the work of the kingdom is advanced. Again and again the prayers of God's people are a means of blessing for others. Scripture records the intercessions of people such as Abraham and Moses for our instruction and encouragement.

It is a mark of the value God places on His covenant people that they should be permitted to occupy such a position in the outworking of His plans.

No relationship can be healthy if one partner is continually silent. Those who have a place in the Covenant of Grace must talk to God regularly, or their relationship with Him will wither and their hearts will grow cold. Prayer is a God-given means of grace which we dare not neglect.

How do we know?
In everything that has been said so far, we have made one huge assumption, namely, that it is possible to have knowledge of God and of the covenants He has established. This is, however, a thoroughly well-founded assumption. One aspect of the personhood of the God of the Covenants is that He actively reveals Himself, so that men and women can have accurate

knowledge about Him and, by His grace, can enter into a personal relationship with Him.

Revelation is a personal activity on the part of God. He is not simply 'found' by those who on their own initiative search for Him. He is not an impersonal force that somehow unconsciously 'becomes known' to people. God takes a conscious initiative to make Himself known. As Hebrews 1:1 says, 'In the past God spoke to our forefathers through the prophets at many times and in various ways.'

God has chosen a variety of ways of revealing Himself. He is to be seen in every single aspect of the creation (Ps. 19:1-6; Rom. 1:18-23). Men have only to open their eyes to be confronted with God's self-revelation. As Robert Sheehan has put it, 'Creation is God's autobiography. Every day in nature's round is a new page of divine self-revelation.'[28] God has also implanted a revelation of Himself in the very nature of human beings, as Romans 2:12-16 shows, a revelation which has not been extinguished by the Fall.

The means of revelation which we have noted so far are usually termed 'general revelation' since they come to every person. God also uses other means of revelation which are termed 'special revelation' since the circle of recipients is more limited in each case. Special revelation includes actual manifestations of God in some visible form, technically termed 'theophanies'. Examples would be His appearance as one of the men who visited Abraham (Gen. 18) and also the dramatic manifestations to Israel at Sinai (Exod. 19). The figure of 'the angel of the LORD' in the Old Testament is also a revelation of God, since He speaks as God and accepts worship (Gen. 22:12; Judg. 6:24). On occasion God also spoke in an audible voice (Deut. 4:12-13, 15). Some of these means were used in Eden, under the Covenant of Works, as well as under the Covenant of Grace.

We should also note that all of history reveals God since it is all guided by His sovereign providence and is an expression of His eternal decree. This applies not only to 'salvation history' (events such as the Exodus, the incarnation, the death and resurrection of Christ), but also to all other historical events. All through Scripture His sovereignty over the affairs of all nations is made clear. As Amos 9:7 states, 'Did I not bring Israel up from Egypt, the Philistines from Caphtor and the Arameans from Kir?'

Events on their own, however, are insufficient as a means of revelation. Anyone who has studied even a single period of history knows how varied are the accounts and interpretations offered by different historians. If the revelation provided by God in history is to be understood, authoritative propositional explanations from God Himself are necessary, and such explanations have been provided. The God of the Covenants is a God who acts *and* who speaks.

The self-revelation of God thus includes what He revealed in propositional form to His authorized spokesmen, chiefly the prophets of the Old Testament and the apostles of the New. Explanations of His mighty acts were provided sometimes before, sometimes during and sometimes after the events. Sufficient verbal revelation is provided to enable people to understand what is happening. The supreme example is of course the earthly ministry of Christ: for centuries the prophets foretold what would happen, during His ministry Christ explained what was happening, and after His ascension the apostles further explained what had happened.

This verbal, propositional revelation was then recorded in written form so that later generations would have reliable access to it. How would people know about the covenants and the God who made them? They can turn to the infallible record of Scripture written under the inspiration of God the Holy Spirit. 'All Scripture is God-breathed' (2 Tim. 3:16). 'For prophecy never had its origin in the will of man, but men spoke from God as they were carried along by the Holy Spirit' (2 Pet. 1:21). Without suppressing the faculties and gifts of the writers, in fact by making use of them to the full, the Holy Spirit ensured that what was written was the very word of God, without error in everything it records and teaches.

It is vital to hold on to the truth that Scripture is the word of
our covenant Lord. Many modern theologians argue that
revelation (if they believe in such a thing) is purely in actions.
People are then left to produce their own explanations, which
may contain all sorts of errors, both accidental and deliberate.
On this view Scripture can only ever be the word of man. Thus
one of the biggest names in twentieth century theology, Karl
Barth (1886-1968), held that the word of God is 'event' and
hence 'what we have in the Bible are ... human attempts to repeat
and reproduce the Word of God in human words and thoughts
and in specific human situations.'[29] Such views leave us to sort
through the Bible, trying to sift truth from error. No sure
foundation for faith or life remains. How different is the Bible's
own testimony to its origins in the speech of the Lord. 'Thus
says the Lord' is its constant appeal. We know about God and
about the covenants because He has told us. As Alister McGrath
says of the doctrine that is grounded in Scripture, 'God, it
affirms, has permitted – has authorised – us to speak about him
in this way.'[30]

Notes

1. Christopher B. Kaiser, *The Doctrine of God* (London, 1982), p. 3.
2. A growing number of books examine trends in contemporary 'spirituality'
   and expose their dangers from a biblical perspective. See e.g. *In the Face
   of God* by Michael Horton (Dallas, 1996).
3. The expression is used by the outstanding Christian apologist Cornelius
   Van Til in *The Defence of the Faith*, 2nd edition (Philadelphia, 1963), p.
   12.
4. ibid.
5. See Stephen W. Hawking, *A Brief History of Time* (London, 1988).
6. Carl Sagan, *Cosmos* (London, 1981), p. 20.
7. *Humanist Manifestos I and II* (New York, 1973), p. 16.
8. Francis A. Schaeffer, *The God Who is There* (London, 1968), p. 87.
9. *ibid.*
10. James Sire, *The Universe Next Door*, 2nd edition (Leicester, 1988), p.
    51.

11. K. M. Sen, *Hinduism* (Harmondsworth, 1961), p. 35.

12. Eknath Easwaran, *The Upanishads* (London, 1988) p. 155.

13. A useful survey is provided by James Sire, op. cit., ch. 8.

14. For critical introductions see *A Crash Course in the New Age Movement* by Elliot Miller (Eastbourne, 1989) and two books by Douglas Groothuis, *Unmasking the New Age* (Downers Grove, 1986) and *Confronting the New Age* (Downers Grove, 1988).

15. Marilyn Ferguson, *The Aquarian Conspiracy* (London, 1982), p. 420.

16. Shirley MacLaine, *Going Within* (New York, 1989), pp. 82ff.

17. Shirley MacLaine, *Dancing in the Light* (New York, 1985), p. 350.

18. Shirley MacLaine, *Going Within*, p. 84.

19. Alister McGrath, *Understanding the Trinity* (Eastbourne, 1987), p. 110.

20. A very recent treatment of the subject is to be found in *A New Systematic Theology of the Christian Faith* by Robert L. Raymond (Nashville, 1998), ch. 8.

21. John Calvin, *Institutes of the Christian Religion*, 1559 edition, translated by Ford Lewis Battles (Philadelphia, 1960), I.xiii.5.

22. John Murray, *Collected Writings of John Murray* (Edinburgh, 1982), 4.278.

23. Al Wolters, 'Partners of the Deity: A Covenantal Reading of 2 Peter 1:4' in *Calvin Theological Journal*, volume 25, number 1, April 1990, pp. 28ff.

24. John Owen, *The Works of John Owen*, edited by William H. Goold, 1850-53 edition (Edinburgh, 1965), volume 2.

25. Owen, *Works*, 2.10

26. ibid.

27. John Calvin, *Institutes*, III.xx.3.

28. Robert J. Sheehan, *The Word of Truth* (Darlington, 1998), p. 32.

29. Karl Barth, *Church Dogmatics* (New York & Edinburgh, 1936-69), I/1, p. 113.

30. Alister McGrath, *Understanding Doctrine* (London, 1990), p. 16.

3

A Loving Lord

There is probably no easier way to start a theological argument than by mentioning 'predestination'. Debates about the subject by theologians in the course of the Church's history have been long, complex and often highly charged emotionally. Such is the reputation acquired by predestination that many earnest Christians take it as a mark of wisdom and maturity to avoid discussion of the subject altogether.

That is understandable, perhaps, but sad. At the heart of predestination as it applies to the people of God (when it is usually termed 'election') are two precious truths about God: He is sovereign and He is loving. It is in Covenant Theology that these truths are set out in their biblical harmony. The God of the covenants is a loving Lord, absolutely sovereign and perfectly loving.

God is sovereign

The God of the covenants is the God 'who works out everything in conformity with the purpose of his will' (Eph. 1:11). The glorious salvation which the Apostle Paul describes so magnificently in this chapter is but a demonstration of the sovereignty of God which governs all things. As Charles Hodge comments on this verse, 'Every thing is comprehended in his purpose, and everything is ordered by his efficient control.'[1]

The whole of the Bible provides abundant support for Paul's statement, from the first moment of creation in Genesis to the descent of the New Jerusalem in Revelation.

The sovereignty of God is fundamental to the biblical doctrine of the covenants. We noted this earlier when we demonstrated the place of God's promise in any covenant that He makes. It is always God who lays down the terms of the covenant: they are not the product of negotiation or bargaining. The gulf between Creator and creature is made clear in God's establishing the terms upon which men and women may enter into a relationship with Him, and yet it is by this means that He provides a bridge across that gulf! Covenanting is a free sovereign act on the part of almighty God. This is how the seventeenth century Scottish Covenanter Samuel Rutherford expressed it, in his own inimitable style: 'The Lord is debtor to neither person nor things. He as Lord commands, but it is condescension that he commands Covenant-wayes, with promise of a reward to "the obeyer".'[2]

God's sovereignty is clearly evident in the Covenant of Works which He made with Adam in Eden. Adam is not consulted regarding the terms of his relationship with God. It is God who confers on man the freedom to enjoy all the pleasures the Garden offered; it is God who lays down the penalty that will be imposed for disobedience. In his sinless state Adam willingly accepts these covenantal arrangements to which he makes no contribution.

The sovereignty of God is also clearly and beautifully seen in the Covenant of Grace by which He provides for the salvation of a people for Himself. The very first gospel promise in Genesis 3:15 is sufficient to illustrate this truth. It is God who states what will take place: 'And *I will put enmity* between you and the woman, and between your offspring and hers; *he will crush* your head, and you will strike his heel.' There is no doubt or question that the Lord will accomplish redemption in the way He has planned and will thereby raise up a covenant people for Himself. It almost goes without saying that Adam and Eve have no contribution to make to the divine ordering of redemption.

That God is absolutely sovereign in the salvation of sinners is further confirmed when we take into account the Covenant of Redemption established in eternity within the Trinity. Here is the source of every blessing enjoyed by the covenant people of God, and it was all settled 'before the foundation of the world' (Eph. 1:4, NASB), when nothing else existed, least of all a human being. The covenant arrangements for salvation were made entirely by God, within the councils of the Trinity. It therefore comes as no surprise that the outworking of the divine plan in time and space in the Covenant of Grace rests entirely in God's hands. Each link in the 'golden chain' of salvation described in Romans 8:29-30, from foreknowledge to glorification, is the work of God.

The connection, or, in the view of some, the contradiction, between absolute divine sovereignty and human responsibility has been the cause of much debate and spilled ink within the Church and beyond. Space does not allow a detailed examination of the subject here, and there are plenty of other works that set out the biblical view.[3]

Suffice it to say that we believe absolute divine sovereignty to be entirely compatible with significant human freedom. Both are taught throughout Scripture, often in the same passages, and, whilst many of the details of how they fit together are not provided, the assumption everywhere is that they do fit.

Biblically speaking, human beings are free agents in the sense that they are free to act in accordance with the nature they possess. That is the case whether a person's nature is unfallen (in Eden), fallen or regenerate (in this life) or confirmed eternally in sin or holiness (in the life to come). Thus in the absence of external compelling factors, such as physical force, a man's actions are freely carried out in conformity with the nature he possesses. An unregenerate man therefore is free only to commit sin, a saint in glory free only to perform righteousness.

None of what has been said regarding human freedom conflicts with the sovereignty of God nor with the fact that we are responsible for our actions. There can be no clearer illustration of this than the crucifixion of Christ. In Peter's Pentecost sermon he says that Christ was executed by the Jews 'by the hands of godless men' (Acts 2:23, NASB), an action unparalleled in its wickedness, yet at the same time Jesus 'was handed over to you by God's set purpose and foreknowledge'. In the same way, the Church recognises that Herod, Pilate and all those responsible for the Lord's death 'did what [God's] power and will had decided beforehand should happen' (Acts 4:28). Divine sovereignty and human responsibility are unashamedly set side by side.

The compatibility of these apparent opposites is important for Covenant Theology in at least two ways. On the one hand it reinforces the fact that men and women are responsible for their sin as covenant breakers (it cannot be blamed on God) and for obeying the requirements of God in both the Covenant of Works and the Covenant of Grace. On the other hand, there is now no problem in accepting that God can enable sinners to respond to the gospel call and to all His commands by regenerating them and giving them a new nature. As 2 Corinthians 5:17 puts it, 'if anyone is in Christ, he is a new creation.' With a new nature the regenerate sinner is able to make the covenant response called for by his sovereign God.

It is natural for the sinner to want to manufacture his own way to come to God. His pride is left intact and God is placed in a comfortably subordinate position. We can see this being played out in our contemporary world with its 'smorgasbord' approach to religion: selecting a variety of 'ingredients' from the vast range on offer and combining them into something that 'works' for you. This is precisely the outlook of the New Age Movement and of postmodernism, with its denial of the possibility of absolute truth. Whatever label is attached, the product is the same: man is presuming to devise his own way to God. Even who God is (one, many, personal, impersonal) is to be decided by autonomous man.

The God of the covenants, however, is not at any man's beck and call. He may not be defined in any way we choose: He is who He says He is in His revelation. More than that, He may be approached only in the way He lays down. The terms of His covenant are for acceptance, not negotiation. Sinners enter a covenant relationship with the Lord on His terms or not at all. Covenant Theology thus acknowledges God's supremacy and assigns to man his proper place of subordination. Human pretensions are humbled, something our fallen nature rebels against, yet, without such humbling, salvation will never be ours. A culture which in many ways exalts human powers and potential will not want to hear such a message, yet the Church is not faithful to her covenant Lord if any other gospel is preached. We know too that our sovereign God is able to change the human heart so that such a message is accepted willingly.

A sovereign who is love

The God who establishes covenant relationships is not only sovereign, He is perfectly and infinitely loving. 'God is love' (1 John 4:16). Indeed it is the love of God, along with zeal for the glory of His name, that has resulted in His raising up a covenant people for Himself. In the Covenant of Works, God's love for Adam is evident in every blessing that He provided. In the Covenant of Redemption the mutual love of the Persons of the Trinity is clearly demonstrated as God lays the foundations for the salvation of sinners. In the Covenant of Grace God's redemptive love for a people chosen in eternity is central. In the covenants sovereignty and love meet in perfect harmony, as they are always in harmony within the Trinity.

We find this truth well stated by William Hendriksen in his comments on Ephesians 1:11: 'although everything is included in God's universe-embracing plan and in its effectuation in the course of history, there is nothing in this that should scare any of the children of God. Quite the contrary, for the words clearly imply that the only true God, who in Christ loves his own with a love that passes all understanding, acts with divine deliberation and wisdom.'[4]

The God of the covenants *is* love, and the Bible shows that the most wonderful characteristic of that love is that it is lavished on sinners, on the totally undeserving. Indeed the objects of God's love are worse than undeserving: they are positively deserving of eternal punishment on account of their sins. The wages they have earned are death (Rom. 3:23; 6:23), and yet we read in Romans 5:8 the amazing statement, 'God demonstrates his own love for us in this: While we were still sinners, Christ died for us.' No human mind could have imagined such love.

Such goodness and love directed to those who deserve only punishment is termed 'grace' and the covenant which brings salvation to sinners is rightly called the Covenant of Grace. The Lord is 'the God of all grace' (1 Pet. 5:10). All through the Bible the grace of God is a freely-given gift. Nowhere is this brought out more clearly than in Paul's descriptions of salvation, particularly of justification. Thus we read in Romans 3:24 that God's people are 'justified freely by his grace through the redemption that came by Christ Jesus.' We will have more to say about this chapter 7, but at this point we should emphasize that God's sovereignty is evident in His showing grace to sinners. In Exodus 33:19 God says, 'I will have mercy on whom I will have mercy, and I will have compassion on whom I will have compassion.' Paul quotes these words in Romans 9:15. The grace of God cannot be earned or bought: it flows from the sovereign love of God.

Election: love before time

In the minds of many people election, God's choice of sinners to be His people, is a cold, hard doctrine. They think of election as having as much personal involvement on God's part as rolling a dice or tossing a coin. If that were really the case, we would not be surprised by the hostility that election evokes.

Election as it is portrayed in the Bible, however, is best thought of as 'love before time'. It is God's setting His love on particular sinners, who deserved nothing but condemnation, and decreeing that these would be made His covenant people as the result of the redemptive work of the Son. Far from being the outcome of a random impersonal lottery, election is the fruit of the sovereign love of the Triune God.

Thus we read in Ephesians 1:4-5: 'He chose us in [Christ] before the foundation of the world, that we would be holy and blameless before Him. In love He predestined us to adoption as sons through Jesus Christ to Himself, according to the kind intention of His will' (NASB).[5]

Sovereignty and love are brought into a seamless unity. Election is rooted in the divine love exercised even before the work of creation began. The Covenant of Grace is rooted in the love of God.

The election of God's covenant people is entirely apart from any perceived merit in them. Scripture makes it abundantly clear that sinners can have no merit of any kind that would attract God's love. 'There is no-one righteous, not even one; there is no-one who understands, no-one who seeks God' (Rom. 3:10-11, quoting Pss. 14 and 53). Equally election is not on the basis of God's foreseeing whether or not a person on his own initiative would believe in Christ.[6] Such 'election' would be little more than a divine rubber-stamping of human decisions, and does not fit with what the Bible says about God's election or about human faith. It is clear that sinners believe in Christ only as a result of God's enabling (Acts 16:14; Eph. 2:8-9). Indeed in Acts 13:48 we are told that after Paul's preaching in Antioch 'all who were appointed for eternal life believed'. Luke's statement is emptied of significance if it in fact means 'all whom God foresaw would believe did believe'.

It is clear that election is by the sovereign love of God apart from human merit or effort. As the Shorter Catechism expresses it, God 'out of his mere good pleasure, from all eternity, elected some to everlasting life' (Question 20).

This view receives further support from Paul's reference to God's 'foreknowing' His people, the first link in the 'golden chain' of Romans 8:29-30. Thus we read, 'For those God *foreknew* he also predestined to be conformed to the likeness of his Son.' If 'foreknowing' is not 'knowing in advance what they would do', what does it mean? There is no doubt that God does know in advance what they will do, but much more is intended here.

Many scholars, not all of them by any means covenant theologians, argue that 'foreknowledge' in this context means 'decision in advance', and that is certainly consistent with the biblical view of God's sovereignty. Nevertheless, there is a great deal to be said for the view held by eminent commentators such as Charles Hodge and John Murray, namely that 'foreknew' is equivalent to 'foreloved'. Note that the text in question refers to God foreknowing *people*, not certain facts. Add to this the Bible's use of the verb 'to know', which often implies a relationship. Thus in Genesis 4:1 'Adam knew Eve his wife' (AV), and in many texts God is said to 'know' His people, for example in Genesis 18:19; Exodus 2:25; 1 Corinthians 8:3; Galatians 4:9 and 2 Timothy 2:19. Such texts indicate far more than a knowledge of certain facts: a relationship is indicated. Murray's conclusion is that it 'is used in a sense practically synonymous with "love", to set regard upon, to know with peculiar interest, delight, affection and action'.[7]

The same ideas of love and relationship can be seen in the 'foreknowledge' of God in Romans 8:29. The phrase 'whom he foreknew' therefore means 'whom he set regard upon' or 'whom he knew from eternity with distinguishing affection and delight' and is virtually equivalent to 'whom he foreloved'.[8] It is on the basis of this sovereign love freely bestowed by God that He predestines, calls, justifies and glorifies. The election by which sinners find a place in the Covenant of Grace is the very opposite of cold and impersonal. It is rather an expression of the infinite love of God. Election is warm and throbbing with divine love. It is something that should fill the hearts of believers with humble joy, moving them to worship their covenant Lord and to ascribe all the glory for their salvation and its accompanying blessings to Him alone. Human pride has no place in the equation. All the praise and glory belongs to the Lord.

Christ and election
We cannot speak about election, love and covenant without considering the role played by the Lord Jesus Christ in relation to these doctrines. Some in the past have regarded election as a

cold, harsh doctrine and believed that a focus on the love of
Christ provided a kinder, warmer theology. We do not have to
accept their caricature of election (or of Covenant Theology as
a whole) to acknowledge the central place that must be given to
Christ in our consideration of these great themes.

In the words of Jesus Christ, just as in the rest of Scripture,
we find clear references to divine electing love. Thus in John
6:37 he says, 'All that the Father gives me will come to me.'
Throughout the Gospel records it is evident that Christ had a
powerful awareness of having been given a people by His Father,
for whom He had come to do a great redemptive work. This
awareness is at the forefront of His thought in John 17, often
termed the 'high priestly prayer' of the Saviour. Note for
example verse 2: 'you granted [your Son] authority over all
people that he might give eternal life to all those you have given
him.' His prayer is very specifically for those whom the Father
had given Him out of the world.

Covenant Theology describes this giving in terms of the
Covenant of Redemption. In the eternal councils of the Trinity
specific sinners were given to the Son to be the beneficiaries of
His redemptive work. Thus they can be said to have been
'chosen' in him 'before the creation of the world' (Eph. 1:4). It
is they who will enjoy the saving benefits of the Covenant of
Grace. As Joseph was told, 'you are to give him the name Jesus,
because he will save *his people* from their sins' (Matt. 1:21).
This fact lies behind Jesus' statement in Matthew 22:14, 'many
are invited, but few are chosen', contrasting the outward
summons which all kinds of people hear with the fact of election
which guarantees an inward response on the part of some.

Alongside the reality of sovereign authority exercised in
election, we must stress that nowhere is divine love more
powerfully demonstrated than in the redemptive work of Christ
upon which the Covenant of Grace is founded. The Apostle Paul
speaks with awe and joy of 'the Son of God, who loved me and
gave himself for me' (Gal. 2:20). That infinite yet gloriously
personal love is displayed perfectly at the cross. 'Having loved

His own who were in the world, He loved them to the end'
(John 13:1 NASB),[9] the cross being the immediate prospect that
He faced.

The love of our Covenant Head is a subject about which
Christians can never know too much. In Ephesians 3:18-19 Paul
prays that his readers 'may have power, together with all the
saints, to grasp how wide and long and high and deep is the
love of Christ, and to know this love that surpasses knowledge'.
A most helpful exposition of this text is provided by John
Bunyan in *The Saint's Knowledge of Christ's Love* (1692).[10]
Bunyan considers each of the four dimensions in turn, showing
for example that Christ's love is broad enough to cover the whole
spread of our sins and deep enough to reach believers in the
depths of their miseries and troubles. In fine Puritan style
Bunyan analyses a host of aspects of the Saviour's love, bursting
out at one point, 'I never saw love like the love of Christ, who
as a giant, and bridegroom coming out of his chamber, and as a
strong man, *rejoiceth to run his race* (Ps. 19:5). Loving higher
and higher, stronger and stronger, I mean as to the lettings out
of love, for he reserveth the best wine even till the last (John
2:10).'[11] These are thoughts to thrill the heart of any believer,
and Bunyan's work provides great practical help in cultivating
such a mind-set.

We should perhaps at this point mention John Calvin's
reference to Christ as 'the mirror of our election'. He uses this
image in both his *Institutes* and his 1552 treatise *Concerning
the Eternal Predestination of God*.[12] Calvin is dealing in the
relevant passages of these works with the question that is often
raised as to how one may know if he is among the elect. Calvin's
response is clear and uncompromising: it is only by fixing our
attention on Christ and considering our relationship with Him
that we may know that we are among the elect. As he says in
the *Institutes*, 'if we have been chosen in him, we shall not find
assurance of election in ourselves; and not even in God the
Father, if we conceive him as severed from his Son.'[13] In
practical terms, the question that must be asked is, 'Am I in

communion with Christ?' If the answer is affirmative, Calvin argues that 'we have a sufficiently clear and firm testimony that we have been inscribed in the book of life' (citing Rev. 21:27).[14] On this basis Calvin states, 'Christ then is the mirror wherein we must, and without self-deception may, contemplate our own election.'[15]

Dealing with the same issue, which is so important for assurance of salvation, in *Eternal Predestination*, Calvin points out the scriptural testimonies that all who believe in God's only-begotten Son are sons and heirs of God. Hence Christ 'is for us the bright mirror of the eternal and hidden election of God, and also the earnest and pledge'.[16] As a believer realizes that he has faith in Christ, he is able to conclude that he is among the elect: 'election is prior to faith, but is learnt by faith.'[17] As Calvin says, 'we contemplate by faith the life which God represents to us in this mirror',[18] something which is fully in accord with the Father's plan, since 'He will have us begin with Christ so that we may know that we are reckoned among His peculiar people.'[19] The implications of this view for assurance will be considered more fully in chapter 7.

We should also take note of the influential views of Karl Barth on the relationship between Christ and election, views which diverge radically from what we have presented as the biblical position. For Barth, 'The doctrine of election is the sum of the Gospel because of all words that can be said or heard it is the best.'[20] Although he claims to be following Calvin and the Reformers, and he does stress the sovereignty of God's grace to totally undeserving men and women, Barth has changed the view of election held by the Reformers in a radical way. As Colin Brown puts it: 'What has changed it is the way Barth has rearranged it to fit the thesis that all God's dealings with men are effected in and through the person of Jesus Christ. He has become both the electing God and the elected man.'[21] Barth denies any election apart from the election of mankind – all mankind – in Christ. As he says: 'Jesus Christ reveals to us our election as an election which is made by Him, by His will which is also the will of God. He tells us that He Himself is the One who elects us.'[22] Barth has no time for talk of absolute divine decrees or the Father's giving people to Christ. All centres on Christ Himself.

Barth goes on to argue that since all God's dealings with man flow through Christ, He is the one who is *both* elect *and* reprobate on behalf of all men. Christ bears the 'No' of God's rejection and as a result only the 'Yes' of acceptance is spoken to man by God. All men are elect in Christ; none is reprobate. God has ascribed to man 'election, salvation and life', while choosing for Himself 'reprobation, perdition and death' in Christ.[23] In spite of Barth's numerous references to Scripture, his critics have clearly demonstrated the complete lack of biblical support for his radical reinterpretation of election.[24]

The consequence of Barth's view of election is that all men are to be viewed as elect. Although people may try to live a godless life, rejecting God, nevertheless 'their desire and undertaking were nullified [by God] before the world began... What is laid up for man is eternal life in fellowship with God.'[25] Although Barth denied that he taught universalism, it would seem that his doctrine of election leads inescapably to universal salvation. Thus he can counsel the Church not to take the opposition between believers and unbelievers too seriously: 'We cannot ... regard their opposition as absolute. For all its distinctive sharpness, the opposition between them can only be relative, because both are in the one absolute hand of God.'[26] We must agree with Fred Klooster's assessment: '[Barth's] view simply calls for informing men who are universally involved in what Christ has done. Hence the urgency of preaching is gone, and the biblical significance of the call to repentance and faith loses its relevance.'[27]

A sovereign tyrant

Attacks on what we have set out as the biblical view of election by a sovereign God have been many and various. Often it is said that a God who is absolutely sovereign is little more than a cosmic tyrant who deprives human beings of any significant freedom. Some argue that any concept of divine control over the world is simply outdated and unacceptable. Thus the former Anglican cleric, Anthony Freeman, in expounding his 'Christian Humanism', states that the world has changed so much in recent centuries that biblical concepts of divine kingship, as found for example in the 1662 *Book of Common Prayer*, are now meaningless. 'Like his earthly counterpart, [God] was formerly thought of as wielding absolute power ... He had direct and personal control, not only over the hearts of kings and queens, but over the whole physical universe. We no longer live in a world where such an idea has any place.'[28] Freeman's philosophy, however, entirely removes any place for a personal God, a supernatural dimension to the universe or indeed 'anything beyond what human senses can perceive'. Such thoroughgoing Naturalism has no claim to the adjective 'Christian'.

The biblical view of divine sovereignty has also received short shrift from the growing number of feminist theologians. A description of God as an all-powerful absolute monarch is said to be the product of patriarchal cultures in which the biblical records were produced, and is often blamed for legitimizing the oppression of women. As Sallie McFague states, 'It is a powerful imaginative picture and a very dangerous one.'[29] McFague goes on to argue that the view she is criticizing removes God from genuine interaction with the world, rendering the world a Godless place and making God a worldless deity. In her view, 'in this picture, God can be God only if we are nothing.'[30]

Vigorous criticism of what may be termed the 'traditional' view of God's sovereignty has also come in recent years from theologians who would regard themselves as being within the 'evangelical' camp. Among them are the proponents of what is called 'the open view of God'. This view has been expounded and defended by theologians and philosophers such as Clark Pinnock and William Hasker in the 1994 collection of essays entitled *The Openness of God*.[31] These writers reject what they understand to be 'the traditional understanding of God' and opt instead for a God who is within time, is ignorant of the future and, although almighty, does not exercise control over all things.

Taking Clark Pinnock as a representative of this view, here is how he expresses his understanding of God: 'The all-powerful God delegates power to the creature, making himself vulnerable. In giving us dominion over the earth, God shares power with the creature. The fact of sin in history reveals the adverse effect that disobedience has on God's purpose. God allows the world to be affected by the power of the creature and takes risks accompanying genuine relatedness.'[32] Omnipotence, according to Pinnock, means that God can deal with any circumstance that can arise, like an infinitely skilful chess player. It does not mean that nothing contrary to God's will can take place. In his opinion, 'The idea that it means a divine decree and total control is an alarming concept and contrary to Scripture.'[33]

There are many points at which the 'open' view of God may be answered on the basis of Scripture, but space permits us to make only one vital point in response. As Covenant Theology demonstrates, an absolutely sovereign God is not a cosmic tyrant who has no significant relationship with His creatures. Rather He is a God of infinite overflowing love, providing in the Covenant of Works a rich abundance of blessings for man in his unfallen state, and providing in the Covenant of Redemption and the Covenant of Grace a complete salvation and a glorious inheritance for 'a great multitude that no-one could count' (Rev. 7:9). He is a God, as we have seen, who enters into a genuine loving relationship with His people, yet this does not in any way compromise His sovereignty (or the free agency of men and women, who act in accordance with the nature they possess).

All of God's perfections, including His sovereignty and His love, are always in perfect harmony: He is entirely sovereign and He is entirely loving. Sovereign election and redemptive love are seen in harmony, for example, in the biblical concept of 'grace' by which sinners are saved. Grace is sovereign, based on nothing in man. (See for example Eph. 2:8-9). Grace is also an expression of the loving heart of God. Thus Robert Reymond, in considering Paul's presentation of these issues in Romans 9, says 'We also learn from Romans 9:11-13 that the *elective* principle in God's eternal purpose serves and alone comports with the *grace* principle which governs all true salvation.'[34] Geerhardus Vos is correct to point out that, 'Election is intended to bring out the *gratuitous* character of grace.'[35] We cannot think of a covenant between God and man apart from grace, and as Samuel Rutherford stated three and a half centuries ago, 'In all pactions between the Lord and man, even in a Law-Covenant, there is some outbreakings of Grace.'[36]

The absence from history of absolute rulers who could also be designated 'loving' is no barrier to accepting that the God of the Covenants is such a monarch, one who loves His subjects with an eternal love.

True love?
Although we have spoken frequently of the love of God, there are those, particularly in recent years, who have argued that the traditional view of God, as exemplified in Covenant Theology, in fact eviscerates the term 'love' of much of its content. This, they claim, is especially so in regard to the emotional content of love. Among those who have made such a claim are the proponents of 'the openness view of God' whom we had to consider in the last section.

What is the basis for these theologians' assault on the traditional view of God? Central to their case is the claim that certain ideas about God which form the core of the traditional view in fact were derived from pagan Greek philosophers, particularly from Plato.[37] The Greeks' belief in the unchangeableness of God, it is generally agreed, resulted in a view of God which rendered Him free from suffering and from any kind of emotion. According to John Sanders, this outlook filtered into Christian theology through the Jewish philosopher Philo and gave rise to what he terms the 'biblical-classical synthesis'. This synthesis depicts God as the Unmoved Mover, utterly free from any change and so also free from all emotions. Could such a deity be said to 'love' His creatures in any significant sense?

It is not our task to defend every covenant theologian of the past, and we may freely admit that the issue of suffering and emotions in God has caused problems for many theologians of widely differing viewpoints. Undoubtedly Greek thinking has exercised more influence than it should have done.[38] Nevertheless we believe that Covenant Theology has the resources necessary for dealing with this issue and for showing that in the highest sense the love of God is 'true love'.

In a multitude of passages the Bible speaks of God having feelings: He delights in His people (Ps. 149:4), He has compassion (Jer. 31:20), He longs for the restoration of the wayward (Hos. 11), He is angry with sinners (Ps. 7:11). Although there is more than emotion involved in, for example, love and wrath, there is normally an emotional dimension involved, at least in the human subjects. Human emotions, however, are very variable and sometimes out of control. How could God be envisaged in such terms?

Leaving aside the matter of emotions ascribed to the Lord Jesus Christ, which have traditionally been regarded as located only in His human nature, emotions ascribed to God have usually been explained in terms of 'anthropopathisms', i.e. using human emotions to describe God. This is analogous to 'anthropomorphisms' which describe God in human form, such that speaking about God's 'arms' is a way of describing His strength and action in the creation. No one supposes God literally has arms. Likewise it is not suggested that God has literal human emotions: the language is metaphorical.

It must be remembered, however, that an anthropomorphism refers to something that does actually exist in God, such as strength. If that were not the case the anthropomorphism would be empty and meaningless. By the same token, an anthropopathism must refer to something that actually exists in

God. There must be an actuality to which the metaphor refers or, again, it is empty and meaningless.

We can therefore argue that there exists in God something analogous to human emotions, something best described by the language of human emotions. Such divine 'emotions' will certainly be free from the imperfections of human emotions. He is not fickle or unpredictable, and He is never a prisoner of His emotions. His 'emotions' must be entirely consistent with all that we know of His nature.

Such an approach is taken by the nineteenth century American covenant theologian Charles Hodge, one of the great figures of Princeton Seminary. In considering the love of God Hodge dissents from what others have written on the subject and argues, 'If love in God is only a name for that which accounts for the rational universe; if God is love simply because He develops Himself in thinking and conscious beings, then the word has for us no definite meaning.'[39] Hodge's view is that 'Love of necessity involves feeling, and if there be no feeling in God, there can be no love'.[40] Scripture must be followed, whatever philosophy may say, and Hodge contends, 'We must believe that God is love in the sense in which that word comes home to every human heart.'[41] He supports this, for example, by citing 1 John 4:7-11, where God's love is illustrated in the sending of His Son and is given for the imitation of believers. As Hodge concludes, 'God is love; and love in Him is, in all that is essential to its nature, what love is in us.'[42]

The God of Covenant Theology, the God of the Bible, is a God who loves with a pure, intense, unchanging love. He is not controlled by emotion or by anything outside Himself, and a good case can be made for this interpretation of the statement of the Westminster Confession that God is 'without ... passions' (II.1). His love, however, is real and precious to His people. The covenants are full of the love of God and provide the only true and lasting answer to the loneliness of the human heart which is so evident in contemporary society. The restless heart finds rest only in a covenant Lord.

Contemplation of the love of God, particularly as expressed in the Covenant of Redemption, carried the older covenant theologians to their greatest heights of eloquence. Brief quotations from two of them will provide a fitting conclusion to this chapter. First, John Flavel in *The Fountain of Life*:

> judge the antiquity of the love of God to believers; what an ancient Friend he hath been to us; who loved us, provided for us, and continued all our happiness, before we were, yea before the world was. We reap the fruits of this covenant now, the seed whereof was sown in eternity.[43]

Finally, from the Dutch tradition, Wilhelmus à Brakel:

> this covenant reveals a love which is unparalleled, exceeding all comprehension. How blessed and what a wonder it is to have been considered and known in this covenant, to have been given by the Father to the Son, by the Son to have been written in his Book, and to have been the object of the eternal, mutual delight of the Father and the Son to save you.[44]

Notes

1. Charles Hodge, *Commentary on the Epistle to the Ephesians*, 1856 edition (Grand Rapids, 1980), p. 58.

2. Samuel Rutherford, *The Covenant of Life Opened* (Edinburgh, 1655), part 1, ch. 6, p. 15.

3. e.g. Robert L. Reymond, *A New Systematic Theology of the Christian Faith* (Nashville, 1998), chapter 10, 'The Eternal Decree of God'.

4. William Hendriksen, *Ephesians* (Edinburgh, 1972), pp. 88-9.

5. Translations such as the AV, NKJV and NRSV include 'in love' with 'before Him' in verse 4. We prefer the NASB reading, including the words with 'He predestined', which is also found in the NIV and RSV.

6. A very thorough rebuttal of this view of election is provided by Francis Turretin in his *Institutes of Elenctic Theology*, Translated by G. M. Giger (Phillipsburg, 1992). Locus 4, Q11 (1.355-64).

7. John Murray, *The Epistle to the Romans* (London, 1967), p. 317.

8. Murray, op. cit., p. 317.

9. This is the NASB translation. Other possible translations include 'to the uttermost' and 'eternally'. NIV reads, 'he now showed them the full extent of his love'.

10. Recently republished by the Banner of Truth Trust under the title *All Loves Excelling* (Edinburgh, 1998).

11. John Bunyan, *All Loves Excelling*, p. 97.

12. John Calvin, *Institutes of the Christian Religion*, 1559 edition, translated by Ford Lewis Battles (Philadelphia, 1960) and *Concerning the Eternal Predestination of God*, translated by J. K. S. Reid (London, 1961).

13. John Calvin, *Institutes*, III.xxiv.5.

14. ibid.

15. ibid.

16. John Calvin, *Eternal Predestination*, viii.6.

17. ibid.

18. ibid.

19. ibid.

20. Karl Barth, *Church Dogmatics* (New York and Edinburgh, 1936-39), II/2, p. 3.

21. Colin Brown, *Karl Barth and the Christian Message* (London, 1967), p. 104.

22. Barth, op. cit., II/2, p. 115.

23. Barth, op. cit., II/2, p. 163.

24. e.g. Colin Brown, op. cit., pp. 106-08. Also useful are *The Significance of Barth's Theology* by Fred H. Klooster (Grand Rapids, 1961), chapter 2; and *Christianity and Barthianism* by Cornelius Van Til (Philadelphia, 1962), pp. 30ff.

25. Barth, op. cit., II/2, p. 319.

26. Barth, op. cit., II/2, p. 350.

27. Klooster, op. cit., p. 71.

28. Anthony Freeman, *God in Us* (London, 1993), p. 3.

29. Sallie McFague, *Models of God* (London, 1987), p. 64.

30. ibid.

31. Clark Pinnock et al., *The Openness of God* (Downers Grove/Carlisle, 1994). Key elements of this book have been subjected to a penetrating critique by Gerald Bray in *The Personal God* (Carlisle, 1998).

32. *Openness*, p. 115.

33. *Openness*, p. 114.

34. Reymond, *Systematic Theology*, p. 368.

35. Geerhardus Vos, *Biblical Theology* (Grand Rapids, 1948), p. 108.

36. Rutherford, *Covenant of Life*, part 1, ch. 7, p. 35.

37. The historical argument is set out by John Sanders in his essay 'Historical Considerations' in *Openness*, pp. 59-100.

38. See, however, the comments of Gerald Bray, *The Personal God*, pp. 29-54.

39. Charles Hodge, *Systematic Theology*, 1871-73 edition (Grand Rapids, 1977), 1.428.

40. Hodge, *Systematic Theology*, 1.428-9.

41. ibid.

42. ibid.

43. John Flavel, *The Fountain of Life*, 1671 edition (Grand Rapids, 1977), ch. 3, p. 39.

44. Wilhelmus à Brakel, *The Christian's Reasonable Service*, 1700 edition, translated by Bartel Elshout (Ligonier, 1992), vol. 1, ch. 7, p. 263.

4

Dignity and Depravity

Racism, poverty, oppression, war, abortion, euthanasia, genetic therapy, cloning: the list of ethical problems to be faced in the modern world is almost endless, and the range of opinions offered is bewildering. It may seem at times that a solution to any one of these problems is utterly impossible. Underlying such ethical diversity is the general rejection of God's truth revealed in Scripture, particularly in many of these issues the truth about the nature of the human race. A thoroughly biblical view of man has been obscured or lost even in many Christian circles and urgently needs to be recovered by the Church. The biblical view of man expressed in Covenant Theology provides an antidote both to the excessive exaltation of man and also to the dangerous debasing of man characteristic of various strands of modern thought.

A unique dignity
The fundamental truth about the human race as created by God which is revealed in the biblical record is that these creatures uniquely were made to be covenant partners with the Triune Lord. In the opening chapter of this study we sought to establish that there was indeed a covenant between God and Adam in the Garden of Eden and we considered the terms of this Covenant of Works. We must now draw out some of the implications of this fact for our understanding of man's nature and calling.

It is a humbling thought that the God who enjoyed perfect loving fellowship within His own triune being should create man to share in a covenant relationship with Him, yet that is what He did. It is a mark of the infinite and overflowing love of God that He should do this. No higher dignity could be conferred on a creature.

That man is to be fundamentally different from all other creatures is evident even before Adam draws his first breath. Man's creation is preceded by a special divine council, which was not the case at any other point in the six days of God's creative work. 'Let us make man...' (Gen. 1:26). Thus far God commanded: now He portrays Himself as deliberating. Calvin is exactly right when he comments:

> God certainly might here command by his bare word what he wished to be done: but he chose to give this tribute to the excellency of man, that he would, in a manner, enter into consultation concerning his creation. This is the highest honour with which he has dignified us.[1]

Various explanations have been offered for the plural 'Let us', such as, for example, the speculation that God is addressing the angels. The best interpretation, however, is that this is an early indication of plurality within the being of God, and the full light of the New Testament shows that this is trinitarian in form. The Triune God is making a creature with whom He will enter into covenant, a special relationship which no other creature enjoys. Such a covenant perspective sheds considerable light on another element of man's uniqueness, namely his creation in the image of God.

God's image bearer

The meaning of the phrase 'in our image, according to our likeness' has provoked considerable debate even among covenant theologians. Among theologians in general three broad types of view regarding the image of God have been held:[2] substantive views, identifying a particular quality in man, such as rationality, as the image of God; relational views, which describe the image in terms of interpersonal relationships; and functional views, which regard the image as being a task that man carries out, most often the exercise of dominion spoken of in Genesis 1:26.

Covenant theologians have usually opted for some version of the substantive approach to the image of God, often concentrating on man's rational, moral or spiritual capacities, with varying emphasis on each element. Calvin's focus, for example, is on the original integrity of man's nature, seen in true knowledge, righteousness and holiness.[3] He can also think of the image in a broad sense as extending to 'the whole excellence by which man's nature towers over all the kinds of living creatures'.[4] Calvin's view finds confessional endorsement in the Westminster Confession of Faith where, we are told, God 'created man, male and female, with reasonable and immortal souls, endued with knowledge, righteousness and true holiness, after His own image' (IV.2). Similar ideas are expressed by the Dutch theologian Herman Witsius, using the scholastic categories common in his day:

> 1st *Antecedently*, that it consists in the spiritual and immortal nature of the soul, and in the faculties of understanding and will. 2ndly *Formally* and principally, in these enduements, or qualities of the soul, *viz.* righteousness and holiness. 3rdly *Consequentially*, in the immortality of the whole man, and his dominion over the creatures.[5]

All these elements must be taken into account when considering man as God's image bearer, but a clearer and more unified understanding is possible if the issue is viewed from a covenantal perspective. It is perhaps surprising that covenant theologians have not generally made this connection between covenant and divine image, but it is a fruitful line of thought.

As already noted, man was made to be the covenant partner of God. This was true by virtue of creation, in the Covenant of Works before the Fall, and also by gracious re-creation, in the Covenant of Grace after the Fall. If we ask what kind of being man is, the obvious conclusion is that he is a being fitted for covenant fellowship with God. In whose image is man made? In the image of the God who is a Trinity, one God in three Persons who enjoy loving personal relationships among Themselves. Thus man made in the image of God is man made with a capacity for a relationship with God (and also with other personal beings), expressed by God's design in a covenant.[6]

Covenant and divine image are to be thought of as inextricably linked. Something of this is reflected in Witsius' description of man 'just from the hands of his Maker' as possessing 'whatever contributed to the acquiring an intimate and immediate union with [God]; delighting in the communion of his God; which was now allowed him, panting after further communion...'.[7]

The God who said, 'Let *us* make man in *our* image', delights to have covenant fellowship with man.

This relational capacity with which man was created has implications for every aspect of man's being. Essentially we are asking what kind of creature man must be in order to fulfil his calling as God's covenant partner. The following can be thought of as elements of the divine image which equip human beings for covenant life:

(i) spiritual elements
As well as having a physical body, man has an immaterial soul by means of which he can relate to God in, for example, worship and prayer. The divine gift of immortality makes possible an eternal relationship with God.

(ii) mental elements
Man has a capacity for reasoning, for abstract logical thinking, which is not shared with any other creature. Linked with this is a capacity for language use on the part of human beings which is essential for relationships with one another as well as with God. We might include here man's aesthetic capacities which enable him to enjoy and create beauty (for example, in art, music and literature) and which reflect the creativity of God and enhance covenant living.

(iii) moral elements
Man was created with a capacity to know right and wrong and hence is morally accountable to God. Adam was created in a state of moral perfection, with a positive inclination to holiness. He possessed what is termed 'original righteousness', having a

knowledge of God's righteous requirements, a will conformed to God's holy will and a desire for what is pure and good.[8] Destroyed by the Fall, this element is restored through the Covenant of Grace. All men have an inbuilt sense of right and wrong, even while sinners, and an awareness of God's moral standards expressed in conscience (see Rom. 2:15: 'the requirements of the law are written on their hearts'). It has to be kept in mind, however, that because of sin conscience is not an infallible guide and must be educated by biblical revelation.

(iv) relational elements
In addition to enjoying a relationship with God, Adam was made for community. This is indicated by the Lord's statement, 'It is not good for the man to be alone. I will make a helper suitable for him' (Gen. 2:18). God's immediate response was to create Eve, with whom Adam entered into the covenant relationship of marriage. Apart from marriage, man is made for a wide range of relationships, in families, in society and in the Church, which express the community dimension of the divine image he bears.

Important information about the image of God in man can also be derived from what the New Testament says about the restoration of that image in the Covenant of Grace through the Lord Jesus Christ. A significant text is Colossians 3:10, where Paul speaks of the 'new self' (i.e. believers' new nature) 'being renewed in *knowledge* in the image of its Creator'. The word 'knowledge' here indicates more than the possession of certain information about God. It is a relational word. When God is said to 'know' His people (John 10:14; 2 Tim. 2:19), this indicates that He has entered into a relationship with them. Their increasing 'knowledge' of Him implies a growing relationship with the Lord which results in an ever greater likeness to Him. Such a transformation is spoken of in Romans 8:29 ('conformed to the likeness of his Son') and 2 Corinthians 3:18 ('transformed into his likeness'). At the last day believers will 'be like him, for we shall see him as he is' (1 John 3:2). No sin of any kind will mar the relationship.

Human dignity denied

The unique dignity of human beings as God's covenant partners and His image bearers is under attack from many directions. We have space to examine only two of the most significant contemporary threats.

(i) evolutionary theory

Although there are many Christians who try to marry Darwinian evolutionary theory and biblical Christianity,[9] the basic thrust of Darwinism is anti-Christian, since it is an attempt to explain the universe without appeal to a Creator. Thus the Oxford zoologist Richard Dawkins proclaims that 'Darwinism made it possible to be an intellectually fulfilled atheist.'[10] Dawkins is much closer to the spirit of Darwinism than are Christian 'theistic evolutionists'.

Philosopher James Rachels in his 1990 book *Created from Animals*, subtitled 'The moral implications of Darwinism', makes very clear the significance of Darwinian theory for our understanding of human beings. He argues that 'if Darwinism is taken seriously the brand of theism that supports the image of God thesis is no longer a reasonable option.'[11] As a result, he says, 'the traditional supports for the idea of human dignity are gone',[12] and evolutionary theory shows that no alternative supports exist. The final chapter of the book is, not surprisingly, entitled 'Morality without the Idea that Humans are Special'.

One ethicist who is not afraid to spell out the practical results of such a view is the controversial Australian academic Peter Singer. Like Rachels and others, Singer concludes on the basis of Darwinian evolutionary theory that human beings are of no greater ethical significance than any other animal species. There is nothing, according to Singer, that sets human beings apart in an ethically relevant way from other animals. The only criterion of ethical significance is taken by Singer to be 'sentience', which is, he says, 'shorthand for the capacity to suffer or experience enjoyment or happiness'.[13] To give a place in ethical thinking to factors such as intelligence or rationality would, he argues, be to make an arbitrary decision.

As a consequence of this approach, Singer claims that equal suffering should be given equal consideration, whatever kind of being is suffering.

> No matter what the nature of the being, the principle of equality requires that the suffering be counted equally with the like suffering – in so far as rough comparisons can be made – of any other being.[14]

To give greater weight to the interests of one's own species is, in Singer's terminology, 'speciesist'. Whilst he accepts, for example, that a human cancer victim normally suffers more than a nonhuman victim, where the suffering is equal, the same ethical significance must be accorded to each one, whether man, ape or mouse.

The biblical view of man expressed in Covenant Theology is denied completely by such a Darwinian approach. No unique dignity or ethical significance is left to human beings in the pursuit of 'non-speciesist' equality.

(ii) the computer revolution

The latter part of the twentieth century saw amazing progress in the development of computer technology and artificial intelligence. Computers are now able to accomplish tasks in seconds which once required days of human labour, or were even beyond human capacities. Few areas of life are untouched by such technology and, like it or not, we have to come to terms with contemporary 'cyberculture'.

As with most technological developments, there are positives and negatives in the computer revolution. Many tasks can be performed by machines, but what of the human unemployment that may result? Endless quantities of information are now available, but how many know what to do with even a fraction of it? In particular these developments have raised profound questions about what, if anything, distinguishes human beings and human minds from machines.[15] If a computer were to duplicate all the functions of a human brain, would we have to conclude that a 'mind' has been created? Does cyberculture have room for concepts such as 'soul'? Radical speculation on the fringes of cyberculture considers the possibilities of constructing 'cyborgs' (man/machine hybrids) and 'androids' (entirely artificial people). The character of Data, the android in *Star Trek: The Next Generation*, raises all kinds of profound theological and philosophical questions. A recent symposium in the journal *21-C* considered the question, 'Will androids dream of electric sheep?'[16]

Even if the more extreme theorists are disregarded (at least until they become the mainstream), there is much in the computer revolution that undermines human dignity. From being specially created as God's covenant partner, man is reduced to being a not terribly efficient set of microprocessors who thus far outperforms other computers in certain limited areas. At times in the past man has been regarded as a type of machine,[17] and the advent of computer technology has given new life to such mechanistic views of human nature. Electronic reductionism leaves no basis for asserting human dignity.

Thinking God's thoughts

As God's covenant partner and image bearer in Eden, it was Adam's duty and privilege to submit every aspect of his life to the will of God. The specific commands given in the Covenant of Works regarding subduing the earth and not eating from a specific tree were part of a call to comprehensive covenant obedience. An essential element of that obedience was Adam's submission of his mind to the Lord. God the Omniscient is the source of all knowledge and if Adam was to know anything truly he had, in effect, to 'think God's thoughts after Him'. If Adam was to interpret the world in which he had been placed, he had to depend on what God revealed to him through nature and His word, and as an unfallen image bearer of God he was able to make good use of God's revelation. In this way, man's knowledge was to be a reflection of the knowledge of his covenant Lord.

What revelation did Adam have in Eden? The first element was the truth available from the world and from man himself. As apologist Greg Bahnsen expresses it, human beings 'are already conditioned to recognize their Maker as He is revealed in the world around them and in their intellectual and moral constitution.'[18] This is the truth stated by Paul in Romans 1:20, leading to the conclusion that 'men are without excuse'. In addition, Adam had a verbal revelation of God in His commands and prohibitions. Every fact in the universe spoke to Adam of his God and could not be understood properly without reference to Him.

Adam's covenant response involved receiving the information that God had revealed, and, using the intellectual capacities with which God had endowed him, to understand and exercise dominion over the created order for the glory of the Creator. Each facet of the world was to be interpreted in such a way that it harmonized with the rest of God's revelation. Adam's task may be summed up in this way:

> Man was to gather up in his consciousness all the meaning that God had deposited in the universe and be the reflector of it all. The revelation of God was deposited in the whole creation, but it was in the mind of man alone that this revelation was to come to self-conscious re-interpretation. Man was to be God's re-interpreter, that is, God's prophet on earth.[19]

What a privilege and what an awesome responsibility!

The entrance of sin into the world has not changed that responsibility. Certainly the mind of the sinner, unlike that of Adam before the Fall, is profoundly affected by sin. Romans 1:21 states that 'their thinking became futile and their foolish hearts were darkened', and with reference to the mind controlled by corrupt human nature Paul says, 'It does not submit to God's law, nor can it do so' (Rom. 8:7). Such inability, however, does not abolish the sinner's responsibility to interpret all things by the light of God's revelation.

It is those who have been brought into the Covenant of Grace by the mighty working of the Holy Spirit who are again able to submit their minds to God. Covenant obedience still includes thinking God's thoughts after Him. Those thoughts are now more fully revealed in writing with the completion of the canon of Scripture. All that the people of God need to fulfil their calling has been provided. With the Holy Spirit's assistance, God's covenant partners are able to bring every aspect of life, including the intellectual, into submission to their Lord. To interpret any part of the universe correctly, it is necessary to presuppose the existence of the God who has made all things and who has revealed Himself to us. On this foundation can be built God-honouring science, arts, technology and every other human endeavour. Although sin will continue to exercise a blinding and corrupting effect, both in the gaining and in the interpreting of information, the goal of the believer is to 'take captive every thought to make it obedient to Christ' (2 Cor. 10:5).

Exercising dominion

In Eden God's covenant partner had work to do. As à Brakel puts it, 'The consequence of the image of God is the exercise of dominion over the entire earth.'[20] This is clear in Genesis 1:26, 'Let us make man in our image, after our likeness: and let them have dominion over the fish of the sea...' (AV), and is reinforced in verse 28, 'Be fruitful and increase in number; fill the earth and subdue it.' Man is placed in the creation as a steward, with authority over all things, yet answerable for his actions to his Creator and covenant Lord.

Adam was not given a mandate for selfish exploitation of the creation, leading to its destruction. There is no justification here for human activities which destroy the environment, although some have tried to lay the blame for the world's ecological crisis at the door of Christianity.[21] The kind of work Adam was to do is illustrated in Genesis 2:15: 'The LORD God took the man and put him in the Garden of Eden to work it and take care of it.' As Ron Elsdon correctly observed, 'Here two activities are held in tension – development and conservation.'[22] Using all his God-given faculties Adam, along with his wife, is to develop the potential of the creation in a way that does not harm it. All kinds of cultural, scientific and technological enterprises were to feature in man's covenant obedience before the Fall. In naming the animals (Gen. 2:19-20), for example, Adam demonstrates his understanding of nature and also his position of authority over it.

The advent of sin has resulted in man's misuse of his faculties to abuse the creation for his own selfish ends, leading to all kinds of environmental damage on a worldwide scale. Nevertheless, the mandate to exercise dominion over the creation has not been abrogated. Restored to fellowship with the Lord in the Covenant of Grace, God's people respond to His commands in loving obedience, whether it be the command to make disciples of all nations or that to subdue the earth. These two are complementary aspects of covenant obedience which can be carried out only by the grace of God and the power of the Holy Spirit. All of life is to be lived in willing submission to the Lord.

The biblical understanding of dominion must be maintained and defended against a range of attacks in the contemporary world. Mention has already been made of philosophers such as Rachels and Singer who deny any significant distinction between human beings and animals. If such were in fact the case, talk of 'dominion' on the part of one species would be unacceptable. Similar views are expressed by theologians who seek to combine feminist and ecological concerns in their thinking. Hierarchical societies dominated by males who believe they have a biblically justified licence to dominate woman and the rest of creation are, in the view of such writers, the culprits for many of the woes of the world. One feminist answer provided by theologians like Anne Primavesi[23] involves a 'non-hierarchical' reading of Genesis which reinterprets the texts to conform with an alien philosophical system. A clear grasp of Covenant Theology provides the basis for rebutting such views.

The Covenant broken

In spite of all the blessings provided by God under the Covenant
of Works, the record in Genesis 3 shows that the human race
did not continue in a state of original righteousness. Although
the origins of sin in God's good creation are shrouded in mystery,
in Genesis 3 Satan, the fallen angel, working through the serpent,
presents a temptation to Eve which she fails to resist and which
soon engulfs her husband. As the Westminster Confession of
Faith states:

> Our first parents, being seduced by the subtilty and temptation of
> Satan, sinned, in eating the forbidden fruit. This their sin, God was
> pleased, according to His wise and holy counsel, to permit, having
> purposed to order it to His own glory (VI.1).

What was the precise nature of the first sin? Francis Turretin
is correct to say that 'here is, as it were, a complicated disease
and a total aggregate of various acts.'[24] Many factors are
involved in the failure in Eden. Often it has been argued,
particularly by Roman Catholic theologians, that the basic sin
was that of pride. Without denying the presence of pride,
Reformed theologians have generally argued that the first stage
in man's fall into sin is to be attributed to unbelief, since the
first downward step was a rejection of the threat, 'in the day
you eat of it, you will surely die.' Coupled with this, we might
add, was a failure to believe that the Lord would ensure that
His covenant partner received every necessary blessing.

Of particular concern for our study is the way in which
Adam's actions constituted a breaking of the covenant which
God had established with him. It could be argued that covenant-
breaking is the fundamental category for understanding the Fall.
Such a view is expressed by the English Puritan William Ames
in his famous work *The Marrow of Theology*:

> Therefore the gravity of this sin, containing not only pride, ingratitude
> and unfaithfulness, but also a violation of a most sacred oath showed,
> as it were, a general profession of disobedience and contempt for the
> whole covenant.[25]

Representing a later generation of continental covenant theologians, Herman Witsius describes the first sin in these terms:

> the covenant in its whole constitution was violated by that transgression; the law of the covenant was trampled upon, when man, as if he had been his own Lord, lay hold on what was not his property, and throw [sic] off the yoke of obedience that was due to God.[26]

By his actions Adam was refusing to respond to God's love with covenant obedience. Instead of submitting every thought to God's revelation, Adam was asserting the autonomy of his own thinking and in the depths of his being was rebelling against his covenant Lord. This is well summed up by Van Til:

> When man fell it was therefore his attempt to do without God in every respect. Man sought his ideals of truth, goodness and beauty somewhere beyond God, either directly within himself or in the universe about him.[27]

Refusing to accept God's kingship over him, man attempted to make himself king, although in fact he was pledging his allegiance to the dominion of Satan.

The consequences of Adam's covenant breaking were immediate and devastating. There comes upon them at once a profound sense of guilt and shame – 'they realised that they were naked' (Gen. 3:7). What had not been an issue in their unfallen state (Gen. 2:25) is now the cause of discomfort and embarrassment. God's image bearers, made for relationships with others, find their every relationship shattered. When the Lord approaches, Adam and Eve hide from his presence (Gen. 3:8). In place of love and joy, there is now fear and hostility. The marriage covenant too is affected as loving unity is replaced by anger and blame shifting: 'The woman you put here with me...' (Gen. 3:12). The damage done is ever clearer as the divine sentence unfolds in Genesis 3:16. Adam's God-given authority will be twisted into self-centred domination, whilst Eve will attempt to usurp his legitimate position. Even their relationship with the rest of creation is disrupted. A curse rests on the ground, such that it will resist man's attempts to cultivate it. A land producing 'thorns and thistles' will cause man 'painful toil' (Gen. 3:17-18). As Calvin says, 'The whole order of nature was subverted by the sin of man.'[28]

Adam reaped what he had sown. The penalty attached to eating from the tree and breaking the Covenant of Works, namely, 'for when you eat of it, you will surely die' (Gen. 2:17), was implemented in full. The relationship of Adam and Eve with God was broken and thus they immediately experienced spiritual death. Separated from God, they stood under the curse of the broken covenant, and so they may also be described as judicially dead. The process of bodily deterioration also began immediately, leading to physical death: 'dust you are and to dust you will return' (Gen. 3:19). If their sin is not dealt with, they will ultimately experience eternal death, the 'second death' of Revelation 20:14. The effects of covenant breaking could not be greater, either in comprehensiveness or in intensity.

Unity in Adam

When Adam fell, disaster ensued for the whole human race descended from him. The Shorter Catechism presents in its usual concise way Covenant Theology's understanding of that disaster:

> The covenant being made with Adam, not only for himself, but for his posterity; all mankind, descending from him by ordinary generation, sinned in him, and fell with him in his first transgression (Q16).

Adam occupied a representative position: he was, as the Larger Catechism puts it, 'a publick person' (Q22). In the words of the Puritan commentator on the Shorter Catechism, Thomas Watson, 'Adam being a representative person, while he stood, we stood; when he fell, we fell.'[29]

The link between Adam and the rest of the human race is an essential element in a biblical understanding of sin. That such a link exists is made unmistakably clear in texts such as 1 Corinthians 15:22 ('as in Adam all die, so in Christ all will be made alive') and Romans 5:12-19. As already noted in chapter one of this study, the heart of Paul's argument in Romans 5 is to be found in verse 19: 'through the disobedience of the one man the many were made sinners.' Adam's sin affects all his descendants in the most deadly way, as verse 12 indicates, 'sin entered the world through one man, and death through sin, and in this way death came to all men, because all sinned.' John Murray explains the plight of all men according to Paul in these terms:

> Not only did death rule over them, not only did they come under the sentence of condemnation, but sinnership itself became theirs by reason of the sin of Adam.[30]

Why should Adam's sin have such devastating effects on those who were not present in Eden? Some theologians, including some of the Reformed, have sought the connection in physical descent from Adam. Thus W. G. T. Shedd argues that human nature forms a numerical unity and so all of Adam's descendants were 'really' present with him in Eden and actually sinned that sin.[31] Such a view raises considerable problems, for example, in explaining why only the first sin of Adam affects his descendants and why an individual does not inherit the sins of all his ancestors. The link between Adam and his descendants must be understood covenantally.

The view of most Reformed theologians is that Adam's descendants share in his sin because he stood as their representative head in the Covenant of Works. This is the case even when it is accepted that Adam's descendants were really present in him. Thus James Henley Thornwell concludes, 'federal representation is the ground of benefit or injury from the success of failure of our head.'[32] This is the view which is most in harmony with the New Testament passages cited above and also the view embodied in the Westminster Catechisms.

The question remains, however, as to how precisely Adam's sin affects his descendants. The answer given by Covenant Theology is that the sin of Adam was 'imputed' to those descended from him in the ordinary way (thus exempting the Lord Jesus Christ from any guilt). The sin of Adam was 'charged to their account', we might say. The exact nature of this imputation has been a matter of debate among theologians equally committed to Covenant Theology. All agree that every human being is born with a corrupt sinful nature because of his covenantal link with Adam. Some argue that man's guilt before God is the result of that inborn corruption (the view known as 'mediate imputation'), whilst others argue that the guilt of Adam's sin is directly charged to his descendants' account and therefore they are born corrupt (the view known as 'immediate imputation'). The fact that godly men differ on this issue should make us careful about unduly dogmatic pronouncements, but it seems to us that John Murray's characteristically painstaking examination of the biblical evidence has shown that immediate imputation is to be preferred.[33] Man's corrupt sinful condition is based on his legal standing before God as a covenant breaker, guilty in Adam. When Paul states in Romans 5:19, 'through the disobedience of the one man the many *were made sinners* [a Greek aorist tense], ' he is referring to that one act of rebellion which brought disaster on the whole race.

The human condition
To understand the post-Fall condition it is necessary to look beyond individual sinful actions to the sin that is now rooted in human nature. All men and women enter the world guilty and corrupt, covenant breakers liable to the wrath of God. The human condition may be described as one of 'original sin'. In the Westminster Standards and in some covenant theologians this term includes both guilt and corruption (see, for example, Larger Catechism Q25 and Shorter Catechism Q18), [34] whilst others

such as Calvin and Turretin refer it only to inherent corruption.[35] The precise term used is less important than the description of human nature in terms of guilt and pollution/corruption.

It is clear from Scripture that all men are born guilty sinners. Psalm 51:5 can be applied to every individual: 'Surely I was sinful at birth, sinful from the time my mother conceived me.' Paul's verdict expressed in Ephesians 2:3 is emphatic: 'Like the rest, we were by nature objects of wrath.' Not only is there 'original guilt' inherited from Adam, there is also comprehensive 'original pollution'. Gone is the original righteousness possessed by Adam and Eve in Eden, and in its place is a positive evil which inclines each person inevitably towards sin. The gravity of the human condition is well expressed by Herman Bavinck:

> The original sin in which man is conceived and born is not a dormant, passive quality, but a root, rather, from which all kinds of sin come up, an unholy fountain from which sin continuously wells up, a force which is always impelling the heart of man in the wrong direction – away from God and from communion with Him and towards corruption and decay.[36]

Sin is not merely a disease of the soul, a sickness requiring spiritual medicine: it is spiritual deadness, pervading the whole person. It is in this sense that Covenant Theology speaks of 'total depravity'. The meaning of the term is not that man is in every respect as evil as he could be, but rather that in every respect he is ruled by sin so that everything he does is tainted. As Paul says in Romans 7:18: 'I know that nothing good dwells in me, that is, in my flesh' (NASB), 'flesh' being fallen human nature (see Gal. 5:19-21). 'Total' refers to the extent, not the degree, of depravity.

A corollary of total depravity is 'total inability'. Sinners are completely unable to do anything that meets with the approval of God, they cannot change their basic preference for sin and self, they cannot come to God in their own strength. Thus we read in Romans 8:7-8: 'the mind set on the flesh is hostile toward God; for it does not subject itself to the law of God, for it is not even able to do so, and those who are in the flesh cannot please God' (NASB). Christ Himself states precisely the same facts: 'No-one can enter the kingdom of God unless he is born of water and the Spirit' (John 3:5); 'everyone who sins is a slave to sin' (John 8:34). In general covenant theologians do not deny that, in relation to their fellow men, sinners can do many praiseworthy things, and indeed they would be worse sinners if they did not do them, but there is a fatal flaw in everything sinners do. Nothing that a sinner does is for the glory of God or out of love for God. He is totally unable to do any spiritual good.

Does anything of the image of God remain in fallen man? A number of covenant theologians speak of the image being entirely destroyed. It has to be kept in mind, however, that often they are referring to the image in a 'narrow' sense of moral uprightness. Such an image is destroyed, but the image in a 'wider' sense (usually defined as man's rational capacities) remains. More consistent with Scripture, however, is the view that the image remains, albeit greatly defaced. James, for example, speaks of 'men who have been made in God's likeness' (Jas. 3:9), without suggesting that only Christians are in view. Man is still made for relationships, especially with God, but the necessary capacities have been warped and crippled. Only by grace can the necessary repairs be effected and a living covenant relationship with God established. In Calvin's powerful description, the image was 'so vitiated and almost blotted out that nothing remains after the ruin except what is confused, mutilated and disease-ridden'.[37]

Who am I?

Contemporary culture offers few resources to enable the individual to establish a fixed identity. The influence of the movement known as Postmodernism undermines all absolutes and leaves each one to formulate a 'world and life view' that suits him, regardless of issues of truth.[38] The cyberworld of the Internet allows participants to adopt any persona they wish, and personal identity becomes fluid and unstable.[39] The sense of alienation and meaninglessness that many experience thus comes as no surprise.

Only the biblical view of man can provide a true answer to the question, 'Who am I?' To be told that he is a covenant-breaker, a prisoner of sin standing under the wrath of God and deserving eternal death is, however, the kind of humbling experience from which the sinful heart recoils. Much more soothing is the optimism of some evolutionists who, although in one way they rob man of dignity, paradoxically also exalt him inordinately. In this vein Daniel Dennett, in his influential book *Darwin's Dangerous Idea*, argues that 'we have the mind-tools we need to design and redesign ourselves, ever searching for better solutions to the problems we create for ourselves and others.'[40]

Such belief in human potential has now received a new twist in the writings of various thinkers within the New Age Movement. Convinced of the innate goodness of human beings, NAM adherents seek ways of releasing the god-like capacities in everyone. One popular work is James Redfield's *The Celestine Prophecy*, a 'novel' based on New Age thinking. Its climax has people who are sufficiently enlightened passing over into a higher spiritual realm, allegedly following the example of Jesus. The hope is then held out, 'At some point everyone will vibrate highly enough so that we can walk into heaven, in our same form.'[41]

However unpalatable Covenant Theology's view of man may be, it is the only true anthropology, since based on divine revelation. It is also the only view which paves the way for a proper understanding of the answer to the human condition which the God of the Covenant has provided. When a man sees himself as a covenant-breaker under God's wrath, he will understand his need for the grace of God in Jesus Christ, the Mediator of the Covenant of Grace. As Wayne Spear says of the Covenant of Works: 'we must know that we are under its penalty before we will be ready to throw ourselves upon the mercy of God in Christ Jesus.'[42] A doctrine that seemed to offer

only black despair in fact opens a door of hope, as Thomas
Boston saw clearly. Note well his words in *A View of the
Covenant of Grace*:

> Ye are apt to think light of the sin ye were born in, and the corruption
> cleaving to your nature; but know that God does not think light of
> these. It behoved to be an article of the covenant, that Christ should
> be born holy, and retain the holiness of human nature in him to the
> end; else the unholy birth and corrupt nature we derived from Adam,
> would have staked us all down eternally under the curse.[43]

Notes

1. John Calvin, *Commentaries on the First Book of Moses called Genesis*,
   translated by John King (Grand Rapids, 1948), 1.91.

2. A useful survey is provided by Millard J. Erickson in *Christian Theology*,
   2nd edition (Grand Rapids, 1998), pp. 520-31.

3. John Calvin, *Institutes of the Christian Religion*, 1559 edition, translated
   by Ford Lewis Battles (Philadelphia, 1960), I.xv.3-4.

4. John Calvin, *Institutes*, I.xv.3

5. Herman Witsius, *The Economy of the Covenants Between God and Man*,
   1677 edition, translated by William Crookshank (Escondido, 1990),
   I.2.11.

6. This is not another version of the 'relational' views already described,
   since they locate the divine image in the relationship itself (e.g. between
   male and female in Karl Barth's view). The view we are setting out locates
   the image in the constitution of man. As Millard Erickson says, 'The
   image is something in the very nature of humans, in the way in which
   they are made. It refers to something a human *is* rather than something a
   human *has* or *does*.' (*Christian Theology*, p. 532).

7. Herman Witsius, *Economy*, I.2.4.

8. This is helpfully explained by Thomas Boston in *Human Nature in its
   Fourfold State*, 1850 edition (London, 1964), pp. 40-3. Boston was the
   outstanding covenant theologian in Scotland in the eighteenth century.

9. British geneticist R. J. Berry claims 'there is no viable scientific alternative
   to Darwinian evolution for understanding nature' (*God and Evolution*,
   London, 1988, p. 88).

10. Richard Dawkins, *The Blind Watchmaker* (London, 1986), p. 7.

11. James Rachels, *Created from Animals* (Oxford, 1990), p. 171.

12. ibid.

13. Peter Singer, *Practical Ethics*, 2nd edition (Cambridge, 1993), p. 58.

14. Singer, *Practical Ethics*, p. 57.

15. Some of these issues are considered in *The Invasion of the Computer Culture* by Allen Emerson and Cheryl Forbes (Leicester, 1989). Although the technical information is inevitably dated, the discussion is still valuable.

16. Alex Burns, 'Will androids dream of electric sheep?', *21-C*, 1.97, pp. 22-7.

17. For example in 1747 the philosopher Julien Offray de La Mettrie published a book entitled *L'Homme Machine* ('Man as Machine').

18. Greg Bahnsen, *Van Til's Apologetic* (Phillipsburg, 1998), p. 222.

19. Cornelius Van Til, *Introduction to Systematic Theology* (Phillipsburg, 1978), pp. 69-70.

20. Wilhelmus à Brakel, *The Christian's Reasonable Service*, 1700 edition, translated by Bartel Elshout (Ligonier, 1992), vol 1, ch. 10, p. 325.

21. This is the accusation of historian Lynn White in 'The Historical Roots of our Ecologic Crisis' (*Science*, March 10, 1967, vol. 155, pp. 1203-7), and many have followed his lead.

22. Ron Elsdon, *Greenhouse Theology* (Tunbridge Wells, 1992), p. 65.

23. Anne Primavesi, *From Apocalypse to Genesis* (Tunbridge Wells, 1991), Part 4.

24. Francis Turretin, *Institutes of Elenctic Theology*, translated by G. M. Giger (Phillipsburg, 1992), Locus 9, Q6 (1.604).

25. William Ames, *The Marrow of Theology*, translated from the third Latin edition, 1629, and edited by John D. Eusden (Durham, N.C., 1983), 1.xi.8.

26. Herman Witsius, *Economy*, 1.8.1.

27. Cornelius Van Til, *The Defense of the Faith*, 3rd edition (Philadelphia, 1976), p. 15.

28. John Calvin, *Commentaries on the First Book of Moses called Genesis*, 1.177, on Genesis 1:19.

29. Thomas Watson, *A Body of Divinity*, 1692 edition (Edinburgh, 1965), p. 142.

30. John Murray, *The Epistle to the Romans* (Grand Rapids, 1968), 1.204, on Romans 5:19. Murray's comments on the whole passage are most helpful.

31. W. G. T. Shedd, *Dogmatic Theology*, 1889 edition (Nashville, 1980), 2.168ff.

32. James Henley Thornwell, *Collected Writings*, 1875 edition (Edinburgh, 1974), 1.273.

33. John Murray, *The Imputation of Adam's Sin* (Grand Rapids, 1959).

34. 'Original sin consists of imputed guilt and inherent pollution.' Wilhelmus à Brakel, *Reasonable Service*, vol 1, ch. 14, p. 382.

35. John Calvin, *Institutes*, II.i.8; Francis Turretin, *Institutes*, Locus 9, Q10 (1.629-30).

36. Herman Bavinck, *Our Reasonable Faith*, translated by Henry Zylstra (Grand Rapids, 1956), p. 246.

37. John Calvin, *Institutes*, I.xv.4.

38. See e.g. *Guide to Contemporary Culture* by Gene Edward Veith (Leicester, 1994), ch. 4.

39. See e.g. *The Soul in Cyberspace* by Douglas Groothuis (Grand Rapids, 1997), ch. 1.

40. Daniel Dennett, *Darwin's Dangerous Idea* (Harmondsworth, 1995), p. 510.

41. James Redfield, *The Celestine Prophecy* (London, 1994), p. 277.

42. Wayne Spear, 'Rediscovering the Foundations', *Covenanter Witness*, July/August 1999, p. 5.

43. Thomas Boston, *A View of the Covenant of Grace*, 1734 edition (Lewes, 1990), pp. 80-1.

5

A Great Saviour

Many terms are used in the Bible to describe the redemptive work of the Lord Jesus Christ, such is the richness of that work. If we think about redemption in covenant terms, the key designation applied to Christ is 'Mediator'. As 1 Timothy 2:5 states, 'there is one God and one mediator between God and men, the man Christ Jesus.' In addition, in three passages in Hebrews Christ is said to be 'mediator' of a new covenant which is better than the one established through Moses at Sinai. As covenant theologians have consistently noted, to speak of Christ as Mediator is to penetrate to the very heart of His saving work, and is also to speak covenant language.

The Mediator appointed
Since the Fall in Eden, every member of the human race stands before God as a covenant breaker, a rebel, a sinner. All are liable to punishment: 'the wages of sin is death' (Rom. 6:23), including eternal death if sin is not dealt with. Not only must the punishment of past sins be borne, but perfect obedience to God's law is owed in the present and the future. Such obedience, however, is impossible for fallen human beings since 'the mind set on the flesh is hostile toward God ... those who are in the flesh cannot please God' (Rom. 8:7-8, NASB). Covenant fellowship between God and man has been destroyed and its restoration is impossible by human effort.

If there is to be any hope for such covenant breakers, help must come from outside the ranks of Adam's sinful descendants. Indeed, help must come from God Himself. It is through the provisions of the Covenant of Redemption and consequently of the Covenant of Grace that the Triune God, in His infinite love, provides redemption for helpless sinners. That redemption centres on a person, one who can stand in the middle, to bring God and sinners together, one who therefore is rightly called a 'Mediator'. The depth of the divine love is demonstrated in the fact that God did not send someone else to act as Mediator: no one else could have fulfilled the role. He came himself in the person of His Son.

The work accepted by the Son of God in the Covenant of Redemption is that of bringing elect sinners into covenant fellowship with God. The whole focus of redemption is on Him, so much so that He may be designated 'a covenant', since He is its whole content. Thus in Isaiah 42:6 the Lord says, 'I will make you to be a covenant for the people.' Anything that takes the central place in redemption away from the Son of God is misrepresenting the biblical way of salvation.

Each member of the Trinity is fully involved in all the divine works, but in Scripture it is the Father in particular who is said to send the Mediator. As 1 John 4:14 says, 'the Father has sent his Son to be the Saviour of the world.' The same truth is highlighted in one of the most famous verses in the whole Bible, John 3:16, 'God so loved the world that He gave His one and only Son....' This sending by the Father has its parallel in the Son's sense of being 'sent' with a mission to fulfil. In John 6:38, for example, Christ says, 'For I have come down from heaven, not to do my will but to do the will of him who sent me.' John's description of the Saviour emphasises this awareness of being sent by the Father.

The divine appointment of the Mediator is also reflected in the title 'Messiah' which is applied to Him. The Hebrew term *mashiah* (Greek *christos*) means 'anointed' and could be applied to any who were consecrated to God's service by the application of anointing oil. As the Old Testament scholar Barton Payne states, however, 'this title comes at an early point to be applied in particular to the person of Israel's future Deliverer, to the One who would confirm the testament [i.e. the covenant].'[1] The Messiah will be the One appointed by the Lord to re-establish covenant fellowship between God and His people. It therefore comes as no surprise when Jesus in the synagogue in Nazareth reads Isaiah 61:1 ('The Spirit of the Sovereign Lord is on me, because the LORD has anointed me to preach good news to the poor ...') and proceeds to apply the prophet's words to His own ministry (Luke 4:18). Indeed 'Jesus of Nazareth believed Himself to be the unique and final embodiment of that messianic vision.'[2] The witness of the New Testament is summed up in Peter's confession 'You are the Christ' (Mark 8:29).

The Mediator, then, is provided by the Covenant of Redemption. Duly appointed by the Father, He is promised all that He requires to perform His covenant work. John Owen in *The Death of Death*, one of the greatest studies of the work of Christ ever written, speaks of two promises made by the Father to the Son:

> First, His promise to protect and assist Him in the accomplishment and perfect fulfilling of the whole business and dispensation about which He was employed, or which He was to undertake... Secondly, [His promise] of success, or a good issue out of all His sufferings, and a happy accomplishment and attainment of the end of His great undertaking.[3]

Who is the Mediator?

The covenant context in which the Bible places redemption emphasizes that it is the work of God. Only He can provide the necessary means of salvation since all men are held fast in bondage to sin. Not only does God provide the Mediator: He *is* the Mediator. If sinners are to be saved, it is essential that the Mediator should be God. Only thus can His work have the value necessary to redeem a vast multitude of sinners.

From this we can see the importance of insisting on the full deity of Christ. A Mediator who is less than God cannot save us. The 'Christ' presented by many modern theologies and by the cults cannot deal with the plight of sinners. A single righteous man could not address the need of even a single sinner. A 'Saviour' who is not fully God is not a Saviour at all.

With Scripture, however, we must also insist that the Mediator is also fully man, identical to us in every way, with the single exception of His sinlessness. The Book of Hebrews explains why this is the case. 'Since the children have flesh and blood, he too shared in their humanity,' we are told in Hebrews 2:14, the reason being 'that by his death he might destroy him who holds the power of death – that is, the devil – and free those who all their lives were held in slavery by their fear of death' (vv. 14-15). The necessity for the incarnation of the Son of God is then stated with perfect clarity in verse 17: 'For this reason he had to be made like his brothers in every way, in order that he might become a merciful and faithful high priest in service to God, and that he might make atonement for the sins of the people.' He had to be identified fully with those He came to save, even in respect of the battle with temptation which, uniquely, He never lost (Heb. 4:15: 'tempted in every way, just as we are – yet was without sin').

The Mediator had to be without sin. Had He been a sinner, He would have had to atone for His own sin and could have been no help to anyone else. Because Jesus was conceived by the power of the Holy Spirit, in a virgin, without a human father (Luke 1:35), the line of descent from Adam was in part interrupted, and so He was born without inheriting the guilt of the broken Covenant of Works and the corrupt human nature that resulted from the Fall. As Wayne Grudem says, 'The virgin birth ... makes possible Christ's true humanity without inherited sin.'[4] We do not have to understand precisely how this was the case, and the Bible does not explain in detail, but the sinlessness of Christ is an essential part of the biblical view of the Mediator.

The Mediator is both God and man. No human mind can plumb the depths of John 1:14 ('The Word became flesh'), but we may understand enough to stand in awe before such a miracle. The Mediator had to be, and is, God incarnate. On the necessity of the incarnation James Henley Thornwell comments:

Had Jesus been God alone, He could not have been the representative of man; He could have been only the just Judge and the righteous Governor, upholding the insulted majesty of His law and visiting its vengeance upon the heads of transgressors. Had He been man alone, He would have been utterly incompetent to sustain the load of human guilt and to make satisfaction for the sins of His people; but by combining the two natures in one mysterious personality, He is qualified by His participation in our flesh to be our representative and head, and abundantly able to do the office of a kinsman.'[5]

The last Adam

We have already noted the parallels which Scripture draws between Adam and Christ in Romans 5:12-19 and in 1 Corinthians 15:22. It is most significant that in 1 Corinthians 15:45 Christ is referred to as 'the last Adam'. In its immediate context the verse is dealing with the victorious resurrection of Christ and the eternal life which He is consequently able to confer on His people. As verse 22 shows, the death which Adam's sin brought upon all his descendants ('in Adam all die') is reversed by the work of Christ on behalf of His people ('in Christ all will be made alive'). The two covenant representatives are placed side by side in comparison and contrast. Adam, the head of his people in the Covenant of Works, brought about the rupture of fellowship with God. Christ, the head of His people in the Covenant of Grace, restores that fellowship and surpasses what was provided in Adam. The last Adam reverses the damage wrought by the first Adam.

In order to redeem His people, the Mediator had to assume their legal liabilities – to make satisfaction for their sins and to render perfect obedience to God's Law. Neither obligation could be fulfilled by the sinner who is dead in sin, but Christ takes the obligations of His people fully on Himself. Thus we read, for example, in 2 Corinthians 5:21: 'God made him who had no sin to be sin for us, so that in him we might become the righteousness of God.' The Mediator took upon Himself the obligations of others. That explains why He insisted on receiving John's baptism for repentant sinners, even though He had no

sin that required forgiveness. As He said to John, 'Let it be so
now; it is proper for us to do this to fulfil all righteousness'
(Matt. 3:15). It is this willing acceptance of His people's
obligations that leads to His being termed the 'surety' or
'guarantee' of the covenant in Hebrews 7:22 ('Jesus has become
the guarantee of a better covenant').

The identification between Adam and Christ and their
respective covenant peoples is extremely close. George Smeaton
expresses it in these words:

> So fully are all the individuals represented by that one man, that we
> may say there have been but two persons in the world, and but two
> great facts in human history.[6]

For Christians, those who are 'in Christ', this close
identification with the Mediator should be a very precious thing.
To think of the sinless Son of God willingly identifying with
covenant breakers who hated and rejected Him, even to the point
of taking the burden of their sin and guilt on Himself should
move us to worship and thanksgiving. We should never lose a
sense of wonder in reading of 'the Son of God, who loved *me*
and gave himself for *me*' (Gal. 2:20). That personal dimension
is a powerful incentive to obedience and growth in grace on the
part of Christ's covenant people.

A 'better' covenant?

We should perhaps at this point say something more concerning
what may seem to be a problem in Hebrews 7:22, where Christ
is said to be the surety of 'a better covenant'. What precisely
does the writer to the Hebrews mean? What is this 'better'
covenant? How does such a concept fit into the scheme of
Covenant Theology?

One thing that this reference to a better covenant underlines
is the historical nature of the Covenant of Grace. In order to
save sinners the infinite, eternal, unchangeable God acts in
history. Such saving action is part of His sovereign working in
providence by which He directs all things in creation for the

fulfilment of His holy will. Philosophers may debate *how* God acts in history: *that* He so acts is the testimony of every part of the Bible.

As biblical history unfolds, God makes His covenant, for example, with Abraham and with David, and Jeremiah 31 looks forward to the making of a 'new covenant'. As we noted in the first chapter of this study, the same promise underlies each of these covenants, namely, 'I will be your God and you will be My people.' Covenant theologians have noted this continuity and have stressed that there is one God-ordained Covenant of Grace throughout history. That is why Paul in his letter to the Galatians can speak of believers in Christ as 'Abraham's seed and heirs according to the promise' (Gal. 3:29). As Leon Morris says, 'We are included in the covenant with Abraham, a covenant of grace and faith and freedom.'[7] Beneath the surface differences between the covenants, a deeper unity has been discerned by covenant theologians. Let Herman Witsius speak for them all:

> If we view *the substance* of the covenant, it is but only *one*, nor is it possible it should be otherwise. There is no other way worthy of God, in which salvation can be bestowed on sinners, but that discovered in the Gospel.[8]

Such unity of substance must be set alongside the diversity of administration of each of the covenants. There are obvious differences, for example, between the covenant with Abraham, promising numerous descendants and instituting circumcision, and the covenant with David, promising an eternal King from the Davidic line. Thus Witsius comments, 'But if we attend to the circumstances of the covenant, it was dispensed at sundry times and in divers manners, under various economies.'[9]

This diversity in no way undermines the unity of the covenants, with their focus on Christ and His redemptive work. Only He could provide salvation, only He could offer the sacrifice that would make forgiveness of sin available. All previous covenants look forward to the New Covenant sealed with the blood of Christ (see Luke 22:20), and it is on the basis of His sacrifice that the Old Testament people of God were forgiven. Leon Morris sums the situation up accurately when He comments: 'The coming of Christ did not mean the end of the covenant with Abraham. On the contrary, it is the way the covenant with Abraham is brought to its consummation.'[10] All the covenant promises find their fulfilment in Christ, including the promise of a Davidic King.

It is the covenant with Israel at Sinai that is particularly associated with the giving of the Law, along with all the regulations for worship and social life which came through Moses. The book of Hebrews makes it clear that this Mosaic system has reached its goal with the coming of Christ and so is no longer binding. God's moral requirements have not changed, but the Mosaic pattern of worship has been superseded. The key to this change is the priestly, sacrificial work of Christ: 'He has appeared once for all at the end of the ages to do away with sin by the sacrifice of himself ' (Heb. 9:26). There is a completeness about the New Covenant which was not possible before the coming of the Messiah.

The 'old' covenant which is contrasted with the 'new' in Hebrews is clearly the Mosaic system established by the Sinai Covenant. The need for a new covenant arose from the sinful hearts of the people, which no law could change. Thus we read in Hebrews 8:8 that God found fault with the people. Something was needed that could change and cleanse sinners' hearts: the Old Testament sacrifices could not accomplish that (see Heb. 10:1ff.). The necessary cleansing is accomplished by Christ's sacrifice. Hence Hebrews 7:22 refers to His being Surety of 'a better covenant', better in comparison to the Mosaic system. Contrasting Christ with the Old Testament High Priests, Hebrews 8:6 states that 'the ministry Jesus has received is as superior to theirs as the covenant of which he is mediator is superior to the old one, and it is founded on better promises'. The promises above all relate to complete forgiveness provided by the shedding of the blood of the Mediator of the covenant, together with the writing of God's Law on the heart (Jer. 31:33, quoted in Heb. 8:10).[11] The Mosaic system was another stage in the unfolding of the Covenant of Grace which led to Calvary, and those who were saved while that system was in force were saved by the sacrifice of Christ.

The historical unfolding of the Covenant of Grace must be taken very seriously, and much modern writing on biblical covenants takes a historical approach.[12] This should not, however, obscure the equally biblical unity of the Covenant of Grace which is centred upon Christ.[13] 'There are not therefore two covenants of grace, differing in substance, but one and the same, under various dispensations' (Westminster Confession of Faith, VII.6). We will return to this subject in the Appendix dealing with Dispensationalism.

A threefold office

In order to save sinners and, ultimately, to glorify the triune covenant God, the Son willingly undertook the role of Mediator, with all the costs that this work would entail. He gladly submitted Himself to His Father's will, fulfilling the declaration of Psalm 40:8 ('I desire to do your will, O my God'), applied to Christ in Hebrews 10:7. Such submission in no way compromised the Son's equality with the Father but was rather a 'functional subordination'[14] of Son to Father.

Of the mediatorial work of Christ Calvin says: 'the office enjoined upon Christ by the Father consists of three parts. For He was given to be prophet, king and priest.'[15] This threefold division of prophet, king and priest became the universally accepted pattern for considering the mediatorial work of Christ in Covenant Theology. Typical is the statement of the Shorter Catechism Q. 23: 'Christ, as our Redeemer, executeth the offices of a prophet, of a priest and of a king, both in His estates of humiliation and exaltation.'

Such a pattern is not the product of the imaginations of covenant theologians, but is firmly grounded in Scripture. In J. I. Packer's estimation, 'This view of Christ's ministry derives

directly from the Epistle to the Hebrews, the fullest analysis of
His mediation that the New Testament contains.'[16] Thus in
Hebrews 1:3 the risen Christ is seated as King 'at the right hand
of the Majesty in heaven'. In Hebrews 1:2 He is shown to be
the final perfect Revealer of God. In Hebrews 5:6 He is termed
'a priest for ever in the order of Melchizedek' and throughout
the epistle His priestly work is described. These three categories
of Prophet, Priest and King will shape our further consideration
of the work of Christ.

The promised Prophet

In Deuteronomy 18:15 Moses conveys to Israel the divine
promise of a prophet: 'The LORD your God will raise up for you
a prophet like me from among your own brothers. You must
listen to him.' It is the Lord Jesus Christ who ultimately fulfils
that promise, bringing a complete revelation such as no previous
prophet could bring. The finality of Christ's role is brought out
clearly in Hebrews 1:1-2, 'In the past God spoke to our forefathers through the prophets ... in these last days he has spoken
to us by his Son'. In summing up Jesus' public ministry, Robert
Letham correctly observes: 'Jesus, while he did not specifically
claim to be a prophet, nevertheless affirmed his divine identity
and the ultimate authority of his teaching and so placed himself
in a unique category.'[17] Not only did Jesus speak the word of
God, He was the Word incarnate (John 1), the one who could
reveal God perfectly.

The Shorter Catechism Q. 24 provides a concise definition
of the Mediator's prophetic office: 'Christ executeth the office
of a prophet, in revealing to us, by His word and Spirit, the will
of God for our salvation.' The focus of His revelation is the
divine provision by which sinners will be restored to covenant
fellowship with God. All that needs to be known is revealed
through the ministry of the supreme Prophet, including the plight
of sinners, the redemptive work of the Mediator, the response
required from sinners and the life to be lived by the redeemed.
Not only is the truth presented, but by the illuminating work of

the Holy Spirit it is brought home effectively to the hearts of those whom the Lord will save. 1 Corinthians 2:14 reminds us that 'the man without the Spirit does not accept the things that come from the Spirit of God'. The sinner's heart must be changed by the power of God, and hence 'Christ teaches these sacred mysteries inwardly, by the Spirit.'[18]

Although no longer physically present on earth, Christ continues His work as Prophet through the Scriptures which He has provided for His Church. The apostles, (who had to be eyewitnesses of the risen Christ, Acts 1:22), were His chosen agents to convey to the Church those truths which could not be given during His earthly ministry: 'I have much more to say to you, more than you can now bear. But when he, the Spirit of truth, comes, he will guide you into all truth' (John 16:12-13). Under the inspiration of the Holy Spirit, the apostles complete the revelation of Christ the Prophet in the written Scriptures of the New Testament. As that same Spirit grants illumination to those who read, it may rightly be said that Christ continues His prophetic ministry. The word of Scripture (Old and New Testaments) is Christ's word to us and requires our submission.

A priest and a sacrifice

As so often, the Shorter Catechism packs a great deal of biblical truth into a single sentence: 'Christ executeth the office of a priest, in His once offering up of himself a sacrifice to satisfy divine justice, and reconcile us to God; and in making continual intercession for us' (25). In fulfilling God's plan of salvation, the Mediator of the Covenant of Grace was both the Priest and the sacrifice, a fact that immediately shows the uniqueness of His work. A consideration of Christ's priestly office raises a number of important issues.

(i) the necessity for an atonement to be made

In other words, did Christ have to die? There have been covenant theologians who have argued that God could have provided salvation by some other means and that He chose the atoning death of Christ as the best of the available options. Such a view can claim the support of a theologian of the stature of Samuel Rutherford. Nevertheless most covenant theologians have concluded that the biblical evidence points to the death of Christ as the only means by which salvation could be provided. Thus Francis Turretin argues 'that God not only has not willed to remit our sins without satisfaction, but could not do so on account of His justice'.[19]

The modern covenant theologian John Murray defends this view of the necessity of the atonement[20] by citing various texts which indicate, for example, that the alternative to the giving of God's only-begotten Son is the eternal perdition of all people (John 3:14-16) and that the efficacy of Christ's work depends upon the unique constitution of His person (Heb. 1:1-2; 2:9-18; 9:9-14, 22-28). He goes on to point out that the cross is the supreme demonstration of God's love (Rom. 5:8; 1 John 4:10) and questions whether this could be so if there were no necessity for such a costly sacrifice. He argues too, as we would expect, that the atonement was required to satisfy the justice of God. From his six lines of argument Murray concludes:

> If we keep in view the gravity of sin and the exigencies arising from the holiness of God which must be met in salvation from it, then the doctrine of indispensible necessity makes Calvary intelligible to us and enhances the incomprehensible marvel of both Calvary itself and the sovereign purpose of love which Calvary fulfilled.[21]

It is important to note these references to the love of God by Murray, references which could be duplicated from a host of covenant theologians. These theologians see no conflict between the love of God and the requirement that His justice be satisfied. This needs to be stressed, since theological voices are raised to make the claim that thinking about the work of Christ in terms of law and satisfying justice has obscured the love of God. Thus Clark Pinnock and Robert Brow have recently written: 'Theologians like Anselm and Calvin have led us astray when they have interpreted salvation in heavily formal and legal terms.'[22] Pinnock and Brow claim that such mistaken views lead people to believe that God has to be placated before He can love us. Their claim is that 'seeing God as a parent is more fundamental than seeing him as a judge.'[23]

It is, however, a mistake to think of one description as 'more fundamental' than another. God is described in the Bible as a parent, a judge and many more things. Scripture (and Covenant Theology) sees no conflict between any of them: Pinnock and Brow are setting up an imaginary tension. It must also be said that no one could read Calvin, or his theological successors, and conclude fairly that they believed God had to be placated in order to be loving. Much more consistent with Scripture is John Murray's conclusion: 'The more we emphasize the inflexible demands of justice and holiness the more marvellous become the love of God and its provisions.'[24] Atonement is the fruit of love.

(ii) the obedience of Christ

'Obedience' is the fundamental category for understanding Christ's mediatorial, priestly work. For example Romans 5:19 states that 'through the obedience of the one man the many will be made righteous.' It is not only Christ's death on the cross that is to be thought of in terms of obedience, reflecting His role in the Covenant of Redemption. As Robert Reymond puts it, 'His obedience is the "umbrella" overarching His work in its several biblical characterizations.'[25]

The obedience of the Mediator has reference to the covenantal Law of God, His requirements of those who would enjoy fellowship with Him. As covenant breakers, sinners need both a means of forgiveness of sin and a source of positive righteousness, and both these needs are addressed by the obedience of Christ. As the representative of His people in the Covenent of Grace, He rendered obedience on their behalf, so that His obedience can be termed 'vicarious' (substitutionary).

The first aspect of His obedience, usually termed His 'active' obedience, refers to His keeping of God's Law perfectly throughout His life. As well as His own obligation to obey the Law perfectly, He took upon Himself the covenant obligations of His people. What Adam and his descendants had failed to render, Christ rendered in their place. This means that as a result of Christ's work, His people do not only have their sins forgiven (leaving them in a kind of moral neutrality), but they are constituted *positively righteous* before God. Believers receive 'that which is through faith in Christ – the righteousness that comes from God and is by faith' (Phil. 3:9). Believers can speak of Christ as 'our righteousness' (1 Cor. 1:30) and they are made 'the righteousness of God in Him' (2 Cor. 5:21 NASB).

Sinners' breaking of the Law of God must, however, be dealt with, and this Christ does for His people in His atoning death on the cross. This is traditionally termed His 'passive' obedience, but the term is misleading, since Christ was never a passive victim but actively chose to lay down His life (John 10:18). A better term suggested by some is 'penal' obedience, since at the cross Christ bore the penalty due to the sins of His people. The sufferings that Christ endured were not simply the natural outcome of His course in life: they were a judicial penalty imposed by God and willingly assumed by the Mediator for His people. Thus we read in 2 Corinthians 5:21: 'God made him who had no sin to be sin for us.' It is on this aspect of His obedience that we now focus.

(iii) the atonement at Calvary

The link between the death of Christ and the Covenant of Grace is made explicit in Luke 22:20: 'This cup is the new covenant in my blood, which is poured out for you.' The shedding of the blood of the Mediator is necessary if there is to be a covenant people since, as Hebrews 9:22 states, 'without the shedding of blood there is no forgiveness.' There is no way to remove from the biblical record the truth that Christ shed His blood to bear the penalty due to the sins of others – the view known as 'penal substitution'.[26] Scholars who have denied this view have been able to do so only by denying elements of scriptural teaching.

Throughout the epistle to the Hebrews Christ is portrayed as a priest. Indeed in Hebrews 7:26-27 and 9:11-14 His work is described as that of a high priest entering the Most Holy Place with the blood of the sacrifice that makes atonement for sins. Christ's offering, however, had to be made only once since it truly dealt with man's sin. The Old Testament priesthood, like the Old Testament sacrifices, looked forward to and found its fulfilment in Christ. Important also is Hugh Martin's reminder that, 'Priesthood and all its direct and immediate actings are directly and immediately towards God.'[27] The cross was not designed to move sinners to change themselves but to address the holiness and justice of God.

A whole book would be required to begin to do justice to the work of Christ on the cross, and many such works have been produced by covenant theologians.[28] We have space here only to indicate something of the richness of the biblical descriptions of that work.

Christ died as a *sacrifice* to deal with the sin and guilt of His people. Sin cuts the guilty off from covenant fellowship with a holy God and makes them liable to punishment. As Hebrews 10:4 states, 'it is impossible for the blood of bulls and goats to take away sins', but the blood of Christ does perform that task. Christ is described as 'the Lamb of God who takes away the sin of the world' (John 1:29) and sacrificial language is common in the New Testament with reference to Christ (e.g. Eph. 5:2; Heb. 9:26; 1 Pet. 1:19; Rev. 5:8-9). 'The priestly office belongs to Christ alone because by the sacrifice of His death He blotted out our own guilt and made satisfaction for our sins.'[29]

The death of Christ also was a *propitiation*, turning away the righteous wrath of God. The term 'propitiation' is used in Romans 3:25, 1 John 2:2 and 4:10, with the related verb occurring in Hebrews 2:17. In spite of the efforts of scholars such as C. H. Dodd earlier last century to remove the idea of wrath, it is clear from linguistic and contextual considerations that the term refers to a sacrifice that turns away divine wrath.[30] Wrath is what covenant breakers deserve, the wrath of Father,

Son and Holy Spirit, yet it is God who in Christ provides the means of averting that wrath. The Mediator bears that wrath. We must of course rid our minds of any ideas of God as a vindictive tyrant who loses His temper: His wrath is the response of His holiness to covenant breaking and rebellion, His 'steady, unrelenting, unremitting, uncompromising antagonism to evil in all its forms and manifestations'.[31] That is what Christ in His love has borne for His people.

As a consequence, the work of Christ effects *reconciliation*, dealing with the alienation between God and sinners which inevitably results from the latter's transgressions. Significant New Testament passages on this theme include Romans 5:10-11; 2 Corinthians 5:17-21; Ephesians 2:14-17 and Colossians 1:19-22. In Robert Letham's words, 'Christ has brought us out of a state of enmity with God into friendship. The original fellowship that Adam enjoyed with God before the fall has been restored.'[32] It is vital to stress that it is primarily *God's* enmity towards sinners that is dealt with by the Mediator. In a careful study of the use of 'reconciliation' terminology in the New Testament, John Murray has shown that in the first instance Christ removes the ground of God's alienation from us (namely, our sin) and as a result peaceful relations may be restored, so that we are reconciled to God.[33] We may rightly conclude, 'The change in attitude on our side is in fact the consequence of a reconciliation that God himself has undergone.'[34] Enmity is replaced by covenant fellowship.

The work of Christ may also be described in the language of *redemption*, indicating that sinners are bought back out of bondage to sin. Jesus said in John 8:34: 'I tell you the truth, everyone who sins is a slave to sin.' In order to free sinners from bondage the Mediator must pay a price, a ransom. Thus He speaks of giving His life 'a ransom for many' (Mark 10:45) and Peter indicates that believers were 'redeemed ... with the precious blood of Christ, a lamb without blemish or defect' (1 Pet. 1:18-19). To take only one more example, in Revelation 5:9 the Lamb is said to be worthy because 'You were slain, and with your blood you purchased men for God from every tribe and language and people and nation'. The price is paid to God, whose holiness and justice were offended by sin, not to Satan, as some theologians in the early Church taught. Christ has paid the price for His covenant people, and consequently they belong to Him (cf. Acts 20:28: 'the church of God, which He purchased with His own blood', NASB).

References to Satan are also a reminder that we must think of Christ's work in terms of *victory* over the powers of evil.[35] Covenant breaking sinners have in effect pledged allegiance to the kingdom of darkness, serving Satan instead of God. Christ, however, appeared to destroy the devil's work (1 John 3:8) and this He accomplished at the cross. In fulfilment of the promise of Genesis 3:15, Christ is the 'offspring of the woman' who crushes the head of the serpent at the cost of injury to His heel. Having resisted Satan's temptations (e.g. in Matt. 4:1ff.), He is able to bind Satan, 'the strong man', and thoroughly plunder His house (Matt. 12:29). Christ is able to rescue His people 'from the dominion of darkness' (Col. 1:13) and His ultimate triumph will *include* the destruction of Satan and His hosts (Heb. 2:14-15; Rev. 20:10). God's people can rejoice that the decisive victory has been won.

(iv) the objects of the atonement
The work of Christ had a specific goal which He accomplished in full, namely, the salvation of His people. As we have seen, He was given a people whom He would redeem, according to the provisions of the Covenant of Redemption. They were chosen in Him before the creation of the world (Eph. 1:4). The design of the work of Christ was specific and hence the atonement He made was specific, namely, for the elect. This traditionally has been termed 'limited' atonement, although a term such as 'definite' would be more suitable. Apart from universalists, all limit the atonement, either in its design or in its application. If we use the illustration of building a bridge between God and man, the Reformed view held by covenant

theologians is that Christ has built a bridge all the way across for a specific number (which may be very large), whilst others believe that a bridge has been built part way across for all, with something additional required for salvation to be accomplished. The scriptural evidence is that Christ died actually to save His people, not merely to make salvation possible, and in this He was gloriously successful.[36]

(v) the priest as intercessor
Because of His atoning work, Christ has been exalted to the highest position, the right hand of the Father (Eph. 1:19ff; Phil. 2:9-11). In raising him up, the Father testified to the acceptance of the atonement He had made. As Puritan Thomas Manton expressed it, the resurrection was a 'token of the acceptance of His purchase, or a solemn acquittance, a full discharge of Christ as our mediator and surety.'[37] There is no doubt that the work has been done.

His work as Priest, however, continues as He makes intercession for His people. Such a ministry is spoken of in Romans 8:34 and Hebrews 7:25, for example. He has gone into the Most Holy Place in heaven with the blood of the covenant (Heb. 9:11ff.) and on the basis of that sacrifice He obtains all necessary graces and blessings for His people from a Father who delights to bless. There Christ is the 'advocate' to plead the cause of His people (1 John 2:1). God's people should derive great comfort and encouragement from knowing of Christ's intercessory work, and He ensures 'the application of the good things procured by His oblation unto all them for whom He was an offering'.[38] We may therefore trust fully in such a promise of provision as Philippians 4:19: 'And my God will meet all your needs according to his glorious riches in Christ Jesus.'

The Mediatorial King
As the second Person of the Trinity, the Son shares fully in God's sovereign direction of His whole creation. With the Father and the Holy Spirit He is Creator and Sustainer of all things.

'God is the King of all the earth' (Ps. 47:7) is rightly applied to the Son. This may be termed His 'essential' kingship since it belongs to His very being as God.

Covenant theologians have also recognized that Scripture attributes a kingship to the Mediator, the Son incarnate, and this may be termed His 'mediatorial kingship'. This kingship is directed particularly towards the glorification of God in the salvation of His covenant people. Covenant theologians have generally spoken of Christ as being King only over the Church and have thought of His activity beyond the Church in terms of subduing the Church's enemies.[39] Thus the Shorter Catechism (26) speaks of Christ 'subduing us to himself, ... ruling and defending us and ... conquering all His and our enemies'. It was argued that Christ could not be King over any for whom He is not also Prophet and Priest, and references to 'the kingdom' in the New Testament are viewed primarily in terms of a realm, a body of people. Closer attention to the New Testament record, however, provides a much richer view of the mediatorial kingship of Christ.

At the beginning of His public ministry Jesus proclaims, 'The time has come. The kingdom of God is near. Repent and believe the good news' (Mark 1:15). It becomes clear as His ministry unfolds that not only is God's kingdom present in a new way, it is present because the King himself is present in human flesh. Thus Jesus can say, 'But if I drive out demons by the finger of God, then the kingdom of God has come to you' (Luke 11:20). The kingdom has come in Jesus and His work. In a measure it is veiled during His earthly ministry in that the King does not yet appear in His full glory, but the emphasis of the Gospels is on the arrival of the kingdom of *God*.[40]

It is very important to note that the Greek word generally translated 'kingdom' (*basileia*) in the New Testament often has the sense of 'reign, kingship'. After noting the possible meanings of 'kingship/reign' and 'kingdom/realm', Herman Ridderbos comments: 'There is no doubt that the former sense, especially that of *dominion* as the exercise of royal dignity, is the most prominent usage of the word in various central pronouncements about the "kingdom of heaven" in the Gospels.'[41] In Christ the dominion of God has come, the royal power of God is at work to carry out His covenant purposes. Christ fulfils the Old Testament pattern of kingship which even the best kings of Israel and Judah had failed to do, and in him the promise of God to David in 2 Samuel 7 is also fulfilled.

The mediatorial kingship of Christ is rooted in His redemptive work. As Priest He paid the price for His elect and trampled Satan underfoot. His victory is a royal victory – the different elements of His mediatorial office should not be artificially separated. It is as a conquering King that He has crushed the head of the serpent (Gen. 3:15). He reigns over a spiritual kingdom into which sinners are brought by the grace and power of God. His authority is not derived from any human source and in this sense His kingdom 'is not of this world' (John 18:36). As His parables, such as those of the growing seed (Mark 4:26-9), the mustard seed (Mark 4:30-2) and the leaven (Matt. 13:33), make clear, His kingdom is not advanced by human effort and there is always an element of mystery about its growth.

Christ is certainly mediatorial King over His Church. Although all ought to submit willingly to Him, only those regenerated by the Holy Spirit do so. 'No-one can see the kingdom of God unless he is born again' (John 3:3). Only they can enjoy the blessings of life under the King's gracious reign and only they willingly serve Him. As Paul says in Romans 14:17, 'the kingdom of God is not a matter of eating and drinking, but of righteousness, peace and joy in the Holy Spirit.' As we will see in chapter 8, the citizens of the kingdom are to render willing obedience to the King's covenant Law. 'If you love me, you will obey what I command' (John 14:15).

Just as the covenant people in Old Testament days had an outward form (the state of Israel) and an inward reality (in those who were regenerate), so do the people of the New Covenant. The working of God's grace takes visible form in the organized Church over which Christ reigns by His Word and Spirit. All who truly belong to Christ are to identify with that Church, which is to be organized according to the pattern He provides. Some of the implications of this will be considered when we look at the nature, structure, worship, sacraments and mission of the Church in later chapters. The presence of hypocrites within the Church does not negate its true nature under Christ.

In Matthew 28:18 Jesus proclaims, 'All authority in heaven and on earth has been given to me.' Here He lays claim to a universal mediatorial dominion. That dominion is exercised to fulfil the divine purpose of salvation: God 'placed all things under his feet and appointed him to be head over everything for the church' (Eph. 1:22). Part of this involves what the Shorter Catechism calls 'restraining and conquering all His and our enemies' (Q. 26). Nothing can frustrate the ingathering of the covenant people.

One conclusion to be drawn from the biblical evidence is that Christ's mediatorial reign includes the nations. Many covenant theologians have been reluctant to speak in these terms, assigning authority over the nations to the eternal Son (with the Father and the Holy Spirit). Some later theologians in the Covenanter tradition, [42] however, have recognized the true import of Scripture and have spoken of the mediatorial kingship of Christ over the nations. Such a view is expounded, for example, by the Scot William Symington in his 1840 work *Messiah the Prince*.[43] He argues forcefully that the Messiah is termed 'Governor among the nations' (Ps. 22:28) and 'King of kings' (Rev. 20:16), and so civil rulers are obliged to submit to Christ in their public capacity and exercise their authority in conformity with His Law. Such a command is issued to rulers in Psalm 2:12 ('Kiss the Son ...'). This view underlies the belief of the Covenanters that nations ought to enter into covenant with God. The implications of such a view, if accepted, are far-reaching for politics and public life in general, as all areas of life are to be brought into conformity to the will of the King revealed in Scripture.

Three stages can be discerned in the exercise of Christ's

mediatorial reign. During His earthly ministry He appeared as a Servant-King, veiling His glory. After the resurrection He reigns in glory in heaven. 'The transition from the cross to the empty tomb marks the great turning point in Christ's kingly ministry from humiliation to exaltation.'[44] The final stage, inaugurated at His return in glory, will occupy our attention in chapter 11.

Which Christ? Which way?

Covenant Theology presents a unique Christ, one who is God and man, one who has provided a unique way of salvation. Submitting itself to the absolute authority of Scripture, it cannot do anything else. Taking a stand for the uniqueness of the Christ of the Bible and for the exclusiveness of the redemption He has accomplished, however, sets Covenant Theology in direct opposition to many currents in contemporary theology and, indeed, in Western culture in general.

Even a limited acquaintance with modern biblical studies will show that there are almost as many portraits of Jesus as there are scholars producing them. A recent survey of 'quests for the historical Jesus' includes views of Jesus which portray him as, for example, an itinerant cynic philosopher, a 'man of the Spirit', an eschatological prophet, a prophet of social change, a sage, a marginal Jew and a Jewish Messiah.[45] These are only the most prominent ideas among contemporary scholars. Many are seeking a 'Jesus' who fits more comfortably into their own culture, whether Asian, African or whatever. Thus books offer, for example, 'Asian faces of Jesus'.[46] Soon we find talk of 'The Buddhist Jesus' and 'The Anonymous Jesus'.[47] There would seem to be no limit to the views of Jesus that can be suggested.

Much of this diversity is symptomatic of the pluralism which increasingly has come to characterize Western culture. Whilst the theories differ, some asserting the equal validity of all religions, others claiming that all religions are fundamentally the same, pluralists are united in dismissing the claim of Christianity to be the only way to God. Many would echo the sentiments of Mahatma Gandhi: 'The soul of religion is one, but it is encased in a multitude of forms. My position is that all the great religions are fundamentally equal.'[48]

From the professedly Christian side, and at a more scholarly level, we may cite the ground-breaking collection of essays entitled *The Myth of Christian Uniqueness*, edited by John Hick and Paul F. Knitter, the papers from a conference held in 1986 in California. According to Knitter the participants were 'exploring the possibilities of a *pluralist* position – a move away from insistence on superiority or finality of Christ and Christianity toward a recognition of the independent validity of other ways. Such a move came to be described by participants in our project as the crossing of a theological Rubicon.'[49]

Since then many have crossed that Rubicon and it has become commonplace to find religions described as different paths to the top of the same mountain or different tributaries flowing into the same river. The views of Roman Catholic theologian Karl Rahner on 'anonymous Christians' have also exercised a powerful influence in many circles. Even some professed evangelicals show sympathy for such views[50] and a clear assertion of the uniqueness of Christianity is offensive to many.

Various responses to pluralism are possible.[51] As evangelical apologist Harold Netland points out, most religions are in fact exclusivist in the sense that each 'maintains that its own central affirmations are true, and that if the claims of another religion appear to be incompatible with its own claims, the former are to be rejected as false.'[52] In addition, careful comparison of the tenets of different belief systems quickly shows that the Christianity expressed in Covenant Theology is absolutely unique. Of course, covenant theologians must exercise great care to ensure that their cultural prejudices do not distort their understanding of Christ and of the way of salvation. When this is done, however, Covenant Theology does have a unique Christ and a unique way of salvation. This is a fact that must be held tenaciously and proclaimed fearlessly in an increasingly hostile environment which exalts tolerance as the supreme virtue.

Covenant Theology has at its heart the God who says, 'I am the
LORD; that is my name! I will not give my glory to another or
my praise to idols' (Isa. 42:8).

Notes

1. J. Barton Payne, *The Theology of the Older Testament* (Grand Rapids,
1962), p. 258. Chapters 20 and 21 of this book provide a thorough
examination of the Old Testament messianic hope. See also *Jesus, Divine
Messiah: The Old Testament Witness* by Robert L. Reymond (Fearn,
1990).

2. Robert L. Reymond, op. cit., p. iii.

3. John Owen, *The Works of John Owen*, edited by William H. Goold, 1850-
53 edition (Edinburgh, 1967), 10.168, 170. *The Death of Death in the
Death of Christ* was published in 1647.

4. Wayne Grudem, *Systematic Theology* (Leicester/Grand Rapids, 1994),
p. 530. The most comprehensive study of the virgin birth is J. Gresham
Machen's 1930 book *The Virgin Birth of Christ* (London, 1958).

5. James Henley Thornwell, *Collected Writings*, 1875 edition (Edinburgh,
1974), 2.322.

6. George Smeaton, *Christ's Doctrine of the Atonement*, 1871 edition
(Edinburgh, 1991), p. 65.

7. Leon Morris, *The Atonement* (Leicester, 1983), p. 38.

8. Herman Witsius, *The Economy of the Covenants Between God and Man*,
1677 edition, translated by William Crookshank (Escondido, 1990),
III.2.2.

9. ibid.

10. Leon Morris, op. cit., p. 37.

11. A comprehensive study of the covenant theme in Hebrews is provided
by Geerhardus Vos in the article 'Hebrews, the Epistle of the Diatheke'
(1915-16), reprinted in *Redemptive History and Biblical Interpretation*,
edited by R. B. Gaffin (Phillipsburg, 1980).

12. See e.g. *Covenant and Creation* by W. J. Dumbrell (Exeter, 1984).

13. This is explained helpfully by O. Palmer Robertson in *The Christ of the
Covenants* (Grand Rapids, 1980).

14. The term is used by Carl Trueman in *The Claims of Truth* (Carlisle,
1998), p. 133.

15. John Calvin, *Institutes of the Christian Religion*, 1559 edition, translated

by Ford Lewis Battles (Philadelphia, 1960), II.xv.1.

16. J. I. Packer, *God's Words* (Leicester, 1981), p. 115.

17. Robert Letham, *The Work of Christ* (Leicester, 1993), p. 94.

18. Thomas Watson, *A Body of Divinity*, 1692 edition (Edinburgh, 1965), p. 166.

19. Francis Turretin, *Institutes of Elenctic Theology*, translated by G. M. Giger (Phillipsburg, 1992), Locus 14, Q10. para 4 (2.418).

20. John Murray, *Redemption Accomplished and Applied* (Grand Rapids, 1955), chapter 1.

21. ibid, p.18.

22. Clark H. Pinnock and Robert C, Brow, *Unbounded Love* (Carlisle/ Downers Grove, 1994), p. 9.

23. ibid.

24. Murray, op. cit., p. 18.

25. Robert L. Reymond, *A New Systematic Theology of the Christian Faith* (Nashville, 1998), p. 630.

26. Leon Morris has some helpful comments on the Greek words used in the New Testament in relation to Christ's atoning work in *The Apostolic Preaching of the Cross* (Leicester, 1965), pp. 62ff.

27. Hugh Martin, *The Atonement* (Edinburgh, 1976), p. 59.

28. These range from John Owen's *The Death of Death* to modern works such as John Murray's *Redemption Accomplished and Applied* and Robert Letham's *The Work of Christ*.

29. John Calvin, *Institutes*, II.xv.6.

30. Leon Morris, *The Atonement*, chapter 7.

31. John Stott, *The Cross of Christ* (Leicester, 1986), p. 173.

32. Letham, op. cit., p. 143.

33. Murray, op. cit., pp. 33-42.

34. Letham, op. cit., p. 146.

35. This is the focus of Gustaf Aulén's study *Christus Victor*, translated by A. G. Hebert (London, 1931).

36. The classic defence of this view of the atonement is John Owen's *The Death of Death*. A useful modern study is *For Whom did Christ die?* by R. B. Kuiper (Grand Rapids, 1959).

37. Thomas Manton, *Complete Works* (Worthington, n.d.), 12.370.

38. John Owen, *Works*, 10.176.

39. These issues are considered in detail particularly with reference to George

Gillespie in *An Ecclesiastical Republic* by W. D. J. McKay (Carlisle, 1997), chapter 2.

40. A most helpful study of these issues is *The Coming of the Kingdom*, by Herman Ridderbos, translated by H. de Jongste (Nutley, 1962).

41. Ridderbos, op. cit., p. 24.

42. Earlier Covenanters such as Gillespie and Rutherford rejected this view, partly from fears that it would allow civil rulers authority in the Church (Erastianism).

43. William Symington, *Messiah the Prince*, 2nd edition (Edinburgh, 1840).

44. Gordon J. Spykman, *Reformational Theology* (Grand Rapids, 1992), p. 415.

45. Ben Witherington III, *The Jesus Quest*, (Downers Grove, 1995).

46. R. S. Sugirtharajah, (ed.), *Asian Faces of Jesus* (London, 1993).

47. Thomas J. J. Altizer, *The Contemporary Jesus* (London, 1998), chapters 9-10.

48. Mahatma Gandhi, *Christian Missions*, (Ahmedabad, 1941), quoted by Bruce Demarest in *General Revelation* (Grand Rapids, 1982), p. 255.

49. John Hick and Paul F. Knitter, (eds.), *The Myth of Christian Uniqueness* (London, 1987), p. viii.

50. See e.g. *A Wideness in God's Mercy*, by Clark Pinnock (Grand Rapids, 1992).

51. A recent helpful study is *Only One Way* by Hywel R. Jones, (London, 1996).

52. Harold A. Netland, *Dissonant Voices. Religious Pluralism and the Question of Truth* (Leicester, 1991), p. 35.

6

The Holy Spirit

Writing in the latter part of the seventeenth century, the great Puritan theologian Thomas Goodwin commented: 'There is a general omission in the saints of God, in their not giving the Holy Ghost that glory that is due to his person, and for his great work of salvation in us, insomuch that we have in our hearts almost lost this third person.'[1] Goodwin and many other covenant theologians have written copiously on the person and work of the Holy Spirit, yet Goodwin's description still seems to apply to many Christians, not least to those who would consider themselves to be Reformed.

It might have been expected that the development of the Charismatic Movement in the latter part of the twentieth century would have remedied such a deficiency. Leaving aside the issue of how biblical the Charismatic view of the gifts of the Spirit actually is, it has to be said that, in general, the result has not been a deeper understanding of the wide-ranging work of the Holy Spirit. The focus has tended to be on a limited set of issues, with experience too often acting as the judge regarding issues of truth, and the result has been that the Holy Spirit has still not been given 'that glory that is due to his person'.

Covenant Theology, however, has to hand rich resources to provide a profound grasp of the person and work of the Spirit. He is involved, as we will see, in every aspect of the work of the Triune God, and His role is indispensable especially in relation to the salvation provided for by the Covenant of Redemption and the Covenant of Grace. When describing the latter covenant, Scottish theologian George Smeaton states: 'The Father and the Son come before us as two contracting parties, the sender and the sent; while the Holy Spirit is a concurring party in the entire provisions of the covenant.'[2] Our study will demonstrate that His role goes far beyond mere passive assent to the work of Father and Son. In keeping with His place as third Person of the Trinity He is constantly active in furthering the divine plan of redemption.

In this connection Hugh Martin, in considering the links between atonement and covenant, demonstrates that the work of Christ is to be understood in covenant terms and then goes on to say: 'The work of the Spirit is spoken of in similar connection with a covenant.'[3] To support this view he quotes Isaiah 59:21 which reads: ' "As for me, this is my covenant with them, " says the LORD. "My Spirit, who is on you and my words that I have put in your mouth will not depart from your mouth, or from the mouths of your children, or from the mouths of their descendants from this time on and for ever, " says the LORD.' It is most significant that even in the Old Testament the Holy Spirit is explicitly linked with God's covenant.

The Holy Spirit and the Trinity
A fundamental principle expressed in the orthodox doctrine of the Trinity is that the three Persons of the Trinity are involved in all the activities of the Trinity which traditionally are designated the *opera ad extra*. These are 'those activities and effects by which the Trinity is manifested outwardly',[4] chiefly creation, providence and redemption.

Father, Son and Holy Spirit each play a part in each of these activities, even though the Bible sometimes ascribes an activity particularly to one Person, for example, the ascription of redemption to the Son. There is no 'independent' action by any Person of the Trinity.

In the language of the early creeds, the Holy Spirit is said to 'proceed' from the Father and the Son.[5] Support for this view is drawn from John 15:26 ('the Spirit of truth who proceeds from the Father' NASB), from Christ's references to His sending the Spirit into the world, and from the way in which the Spirit is designated the Spirit of God and the Spirit of Christ (Rom. 8:9) and the Spirit of the Son (Gal. 4:6). It is always stressed that such 'procession' does not in any way make the Spirit subordinate to Father and Son as far as His being is concerned.

Covenant theologians have generally accepted the traditional terminology regarding the procession of the Holy Spirit, although all have admitted that its precise meaning is beyond human definition or understanding. Calvin, for example, is very restrained in what he says of the subject, seeking as always to avoid unbiblical speculation.[6] Some theologians, such as Robert L. Reymond, have argued that John 15:26 refers only to the Father's sending the Spirit at Pentecost and that 'procession' is not to be applied to eternal relationships within the Trinity. Reymond regards the traditional terminology as dangerously subordinationist and prefers to assert simply that the Holy Spirit is eternally and of himself God.[7] Other contemporary Reformed theologians believe that 'procession' can be understood as indicating a relationship within the being of the Trinity (an 'ontological' relationship) without any suggestion of subordinationism.[8]

However the issue of 'procession' is to be settled, we should heed Calvin's warning not by 'subtly penetrating into the sublime mystery to wander through many evanescent speculations'.[9] Nevertheless the traditional terminology did serve to emphasize that the Holy Spirit is related equally to both Father *and* Son. This is particularly important when we think of the mediatorial work of Christ. The Holy Spirit, as we will see, is involved in every aspect of this work, and hence in every aspect of the Covenant of Redemption and the Covenant of Grace. The Eastern Churches reject the view that the Spirit proceeds *from* the Son (preferring '*through* the Son'), but as Gordon Spykman observes, 'This position resulted in a very tenuous view of the relationship between the incarnate Word and the Spirit', a weakness which Spykman blames for 'allowing ... the development of a rather independent role for the Spirit in Christian living'.[10] The covenant-work of the Spirit needs to be seen as intimately related to that of Father and Son.

A comprehensive work

The work of creation not only expressed the glory of God but provided a suitable environment for man, God's covenant partner. Genesis 1:2 indicates the involvement of the Holy Spirit from the very outset: 'the Spirit of God was hovering over the waters'. It is the Spirit who is described in Scripture as the giver of life, physical as well as spiritual. Thus in Psalm 104:30 we read, 'When you send your Spirit, they are created, and you renew the face of the earth', with reference to all living creatures.

The Spirit thus played an essential role in giving life to Adam and Eve, in sustaining their existence and in producing the rich and beautiful world which they enjoyed in Eden. Clearly much of God's gracious provision for the human race under the Covenant of Works was bestowed by the agency of the Holy Spirit.

Taking account of what has been said about His place in the Trinity, we are not to envisage the Spirit's role simply as the executor of the will of Father and Son. He must be thought of, rather, as standing alongside the other two Persons in the formulation and execution of the Covenant. It is equally His covenant.

The radical changes in the created order resulting from the Fall in no sense mark the end of the Holy Spirit's involvement in the world. He continues to be the giver and sustainer of life, so that apart from his working the human race would cease to exist. Hebrews 1:3 speaks of the Son as the one 'sustaining all things by his powerful word', but this in no way denies the activity of the Spirit. Just as the Son was involved in creation (John 1:3, 10) along with the Spirit (Gen. 1:2), so too in the providential upholding and guiding of all things they work together along with the Father in putting into effect the divine decrees.

The Holy Spirit is thus instrumental in providing the historical arena in which the covenant purpose of God unfolds. The revelation to men and women of that purpose must also be attributed particularly to Him. As noted in chapter two, we know about God's covenants because of the revelation that is contained in the Bible. In it we have, as indicated previously, 'authorised' speech about God. It is through the miraculous work of the Holy Spirit that this 'God-breathed' Scripture (2 Tim. 3:16) is provided. 2 Peter 1:21 emphasises that 'prophecy never had its origin in the will of man', and then indicates the true origin by asserting that 'men spoke from God as they were carried along by the Holy Spirit'. Another significant text is 1 Peter 1:11 which speaks of the Old Testament prophets 'trying to find out the time and circumstances to which the Spirit of Christ in them was pointing when he predicted the sufferings of Christ and the glories that would follow'. God's covenant word, with its focus on the redemptive work of Christ, is conveyed to the human race by the agency of the Holy Spirit.

It is on redemption that we now concentrate attention as we consider the Holy Spirit's ministry in relation to the divine covenants. In speaking of the grace of God, John Owen rightly comments: 'Our actual participation of the fruits of this grace is by the Holy Ghost.'[11]

In expounding God's provision of salvation by means of the covenants, covenant theologians speak much of the roles of Father and Son, as is proper. The Holy Spirit, however, tends to be mentioned only as having been promised to the Son to equip Him for His redemptive work and as being sent to apply redemption.[12]

All of this is perfectly true, but at least runs the risk of portraying the Spirit as a commodity passed from the Father to the Son and hence to the Church. The Holy Spirit who is fully personal and fully God must, however, be thought of as exercising an equally active role in the covenants. Thus in the Covenant of Redemption He freely undertakes to equip the Mediator with all necessary graces and to apply the redemption secured at Calvary, and in the Covenant of Grace He undertakes to regenerate the elect, to sanctify them and endow them with gifts for ministry. The active participation of the Holy Spirit in the divine covenants should not be obscured in any way.

The work of the Holy Spirit must be given due weight in Covenant Theology. In relation to one element of His work, this is well expressed by contemporary Dutch theologian J. van Genderen:

> Viewed in the light of Scripture, the covenant of grace concerns more than simply the reality of the covenant and its promises. Just as important is the realization or fulfilment in our life of the salvation promised in the covenant. The new covenant of which Paul speaks in 2 Corinthians 3 is reality in Christ... But the apostle also speaks of the Holy Spirit's work in applying the benefits of this covenant to the congregation, in order that its riches may be known and experienced.[13]

The Holy Spirit and the Mediator

In the synagogue at Nazareth, at the beginning of his public ministry, Jesus applied to himself the words of Isaiah 61:1: 'The Spirit of the Lord is on me, because he has anointed me to preach good news to the poor.' Before a fascinated audience He claimed to be the promised Messiah, anointed with the Holy Spirit of God (Luke 4:16ff.).

The use of such a text serves to indicate the important role played by the Holy Spirit in the life and work of the one appointed as Mediator *in* the Covenant of Redemption.[14] As our investigation unfolds it will become clear that apart from the Spirit's ministry, Christ's mediatorial work would have been impossible and the Covenant of Redemption, along with the Covenant of Grace, would have foundered.

The Spirit's activity begins at the beginning, at the incarnation of the eternal Son of God. John 1:14 states the most profound truth: 'The Word became flesh.' Only thus could He make atonement for human sin. Although much about that miracle is beyond human understanding, Scripture does indicate that it took place by the working of the Holy Spirit. This is stated, though not explained, in Luke 1:35: 'The Holy Spirit will come upon you, and the power of the Most High will overshadow you.' As a result Mary 'was found to be with child through the

Holy Spirit' (Matt. 1:18). Thus we can conclude that 'the Holy Spirit was the former of Christ's human nature.'[15] It was to this nature that the Son condescended to unite Himself.

The outcome of the Spirit's work was a 'virgin conception', rather than a 'virgin birth', which ensured that the Mediator did not share in the guilt of the broken Covenant of Works, the normal process of descent from Adam having been interrupted. Not only was the Mediator sinless, but He was also indwelt and empowered by the Spirit to a degree unknown to any mere human being. As he is described in John 3:34, to him 'God gives the Spirit without limit'. In the most complete sense Christ was a temple of the Holy Spirit.

This truth regarding the Spirit's anointing of the Mediator has been eloquently expressed by various covenant theologians. George Smeaton notes:

> the soul of Christ, from the first moment of conscious existence, was filled with actual communications of the Spirit for such exercises of trust, and love, and holy affections as were necessary in the experience of Him who came as the second Adam, with the image of God restored in all its fulness.[16]

In a similar vein the great Dutch theologian Abraham Kuyper speaks of Christ:

> to whom ... gifts, powers, and faculties are imparted in such a measure that He never could feel the lack of any gift of the Holy Spirit. He lacked nothing, possessed all; not by virtue of His divine nature, which can not receive anything, being the eternal fulness itself, but by virtue of His human nature, which was endowed with such glorious gifts by the Holy Spirit.[17]

The incarnation did not mean that Christ's human nature shared the attributes of His divine nature. If it had, He would not have needed to grow 'in wisdom and stature' (Luke 2:52), nor would he have confessed ignorance of the time of His second coming (Matt. 24:36). John Owen, among others, argues that the only *immediate* action of the Son on the human nature was His assumption of it at conception. Apart from that, 'all other actions of the Son on the human nature are performed via the Spirit as intermediary'.[18] This is also argued by Smeaton, who states, 'The Godhead dwelling in Him made all due communications to His manhood by the Holy Ghost.'[19] The Spirit's role could not have been more important.

The endowments of the Holy Spirit enjoyed by the Mediator gradually became apparent as He grew and matured. The evidence provided by Luke 2:52 has already been noted.[20] The daily life of Jesus was shaped by 'the Spirit of the LORD ... the Spirit of wisdom and of understanding, the Spirit of counsel and of power, the Spirit of knowledge and of the fear of the LORD' (Isa. 11:2). By the power of the Spirit, He was enabled to obey His Father's will perfectly (His 'active' obedience) and was prepared for His atoning death (His 'passive' obedience). All that was required of the Mediator by the Covenant of Redemption was rendered by the enabling of the Spirit.

If the role of the Holy Spirit is indeed that which we have described, we must conclude that He played a crucial part in the Mediator's self-understanding. Since Jesus passed through the normal stages of human growth from infancy to adulthood, His mental capacities likewise developed and His understanding of His own identity and mission must also have matured. Scripture does not provide detailed evidence for this process, but the Holy Spirit was undoubtedly instrumental in leading the human mind of the Messiah to a full self-understanding. He must, for example, have led Jesus to a realization of the application to Himself of various Old Testament prophecies, such as the Isaiah 61 passage which He quoted in Nazareth.

Douglas MacMillan in *Jesus – Power Without Measure* provides a most helpful study of the Spirit's place in Jesus' self-understanding.[21] He identifies five elements in that self-understanding which we may note briefly. There is first of all Jesus' sense of obedience to the will of His Father in heaven. This is clearly demonstrated when He was found at the age of twelve debating with the theologians in Jerusalem. His response to His parents, 'Did you not know that I had to be in the things of My Father?' (Luke 2:49, literal translation), indicates His love for the Father and His awareness of and commitment to the divine will. He would fulfil the requirements of the Covenant of Redemption.

The second element of Jesus' self-understanding was His sense of sinlessness. He could say without fear of contradiction that He always did His Father's will: 'I always do what pleases him' (John 8:29). He could challenge His hearers, 'Can any of you prove me guilty of sin?' (John 8:46), certain that no reply would be forthcoming. Such sinlessness was essential to His mediatorial work, and indeed He was conscious that sinners would stand before Him as their Judge (Matt. 25:31ff.).

Another aspect of Jesus' self-understanding was His sense of Sonship. He often referred to Himself as 'the Son' and spoke of God as His Father. The relationship indicated by these terms was not one that others shared. Jesus is careful to speak of 'my Father and your Father ... my God and your God' (John 20:17). His is a Sonship by nature: all others are adopted. The mysterious depths of this relationship are hinted at in Matthew 11:27: 'No-one knows the Son except the Father, and no-one knows the Father except the Son, and those to whom the Son chooses to reveal him.'

Closely linked to Sonship is, in the fourth place, Jesus' sense of messiahship. 'He knew he had been given a unique calling and that calling dominated his life.'[22] It is clear that throughout His public ministry Jesus' eye was fixed determinedly on the cross. Thus He can say, 'for this very reason I came to this hour' (John 12:27). He knew the road that He was to walk; He spoke often to His disciples of how He 'must' suffer and die. Although He did not overtly claim to be the Messiah, a claim open to radical misunderstanding on the part of His hearers, Jesus clearly believed that He had come to fulfil the promises of a Redeemer given through the prophets. When asked by John's disciples, 'Are you the one who was to come, or should we expect someone else?' (Matt. 11:3), Jesus does not answer directly but points to the works which demonstrate that He is indeed the Coming One.

MacMillan's final point really sums up the other four, namely, the Holy Spirit and Jesus' sense of uniqueness. The Spirit endowed Jesus with all the gifts and graces necessary for His life as a perfect man. MacMillan observes: 'It was the Spirit's function too to quicken those gifts and graces and bring them into their full exercise as he pursues his redemptive ministry to its ultimate goal.'[23] In Jesus we see a man 'filled to the measure of all the fulness of God' (Eph. 3:19).

In His preparation for His mediatorial work, Jesus' baptism by John at the Jordan plays an important role. His acceptance of baptism although Himself sinless is part of His fulfilling 'all righteousness' (Matt. 3:15). He is taking upon Himself the obligations of His people and is, as it were, entering officially upon His mediatorial work. Smeaton describes this as 'the public inauguration of the Lord Jesus into His office'.[24] In addition to the confirmation of His Sonship and the assurance of His Father's approval conveyed by the voice from heaven, He receives a fresh endowment of the Spirit who descends upon Him in the form of a dove (Matt. 3:16). Outward and inward elements come together in the descent of the Spirit. In a public way Jesus is set apart as the Messiah, whilst inwardly in His human nature He is strengthened and further prepared for the costly mediatorial work which will embrace His whole life. This can be linked with Peter's words in Acts 10:38: 'God anointed Jesus of Nazareth with the Holy Spirit and power.' As Thomas Goodwin comments: 'It was the Holy Ghost *who* had the honour of the consecration of him to be the Christ, and that by anointing him "without" or "above measure", as John the Baptist witnessed, John 3:34.'[25] Alluding to Psalm 45:7 ('God, your God, has set you above your companions by anointing you with the oil of joy'), Goodwin argues that the Holy Spirit is that oil.

At His baptism Jesus did not receive the Spirit for the first time. He was endowed with the Spirit from conception. At the

Jordan He received a fresh empowering for His work as Mediator. Abraham Kuyper explains this by distinguishing 'between the personal and the official life of Jesus'.[26] It is appropriate that the anointed Mediator should immediately be 'led by the Spirit' into the wilderness to engage in warfare with Satan (Matt. 4:1ff.). For one 'full of the Holy Spirit' (Luke 4:1) the outcome was not in doubt.

The Holy Spirit and redemption

When examining the mediatorial work of Christ in the last chapter, we noted that His activity on behalf of sinners may be thought of in terms of the offices of prophet, priest and king. At the Jordan Jesus, by the descent of the Holy Spirit, is anointed to fulfil each of these offices. 'The Spirit given at the baptism was intended to equip Him for the execution of His mediatorial office, as Prophet, Priest, and King'.[27]

In each aspect of the Mediator's work the power of the Holy Spirit is evident. As Prophet Christ revealed God's will for men's salvation, for example in His powerful preaching ministry. It was by the illumination of the Spirit that the human mind of Jesus understood the application of the Old Testament Scriptures to His mission, and it was by the Spirit's working that people who were dead in sin accepted Jesus' message.

Preaching and the ministry of the Spirit are closely linked in Isaiah 61:1, quoted by Jesus in the synagogue at Nazareth: 'The Spirit of the LORD is on me, because he has anointed me to preach good news to the poor.' The Westminster Divines correctly reflected this truth when they wrote: 'Christ executeth the office of a prophet, in revealing to us, by His Word *and Spirit*, the will of God for our salvation' (Shorter Catechism, Q. 24).

Supporting Jesus' proclamation of the good news were the 'signs' of the Kingdom which demonstrated His royal authority and power. Of great importance are the exorcisms, the driving out of the servants of the kingdom of darkness which proved that the rightful King was present in the world binding 'the strong man' and carrying off his possessions (Matt. 12:29). The role of the Holy Spirit is made clear in verse 28: 'But if I drive out demons by the Spirit of God, then the kingdom of God has come upon you.' By the Spirit's power the King sets free those held in bondage by the usurper Satan because of their covenant-breaking. The exorcisms showed that 'the King of a new Kingdom was on the scene and had begun His sway over those who are born of the Spirit'.[28] The other 'signs and wonders' performed by the Mediator serve the same purpose and, as Thomas Goodwin points out: 'The Holy Ghost anointed him with power to do all his miracles and all the good he did.'[29] Acts 10:38 is particularly relevant, when Peter speaks of 'how God anointed Jesus of Nazareth with the Holy Spirit and power, and how he went around doing good and healing all who were under the power of the devil, because God was with him.'

The central requirement of the Covenant of Redemption is the atoning death of the Mediator, His work as High Priest as well as sacrificial offering. Jesus' agony in Gethsemane shows the crushing burden that He took upon Himself as the sin-bearing Lamb of God. It is clear that the Holy Spirit was instrumental in upholding Him all the way through His suffering and death.

The key text in this regard is Hebrews 9:14 which speaks of 'Christ, who through the eternal Spirit offered himself unblemished to God.'[30] As He bore the righteous wrath of the Triune God, He was sustained in every respect so that He could pay the full price of redemption. Though He would cry out, in the words of Psalm 22:1, 'My God, my God, why have you forsaken me?', the Spirit would bring to mind the psalmist's expressions of confidence in God (e.g. vv. 9-10) and the vision of ultimate victory (vv. 25-31). In body and in mind the Saviour was upheld by the indwelling Spirit.

Great significance must be attached not only to the *fact that* Christ offered Himself but also to the *manner in which* He offered Himself. The sacrifice had to be offered with the correct attitude on the Mediator's part: a cold unwilling conformity to the divine requirements would not suffice. Edwin H. Palmer rightly says: 'If Jesus had gone to the cross unwillingly, sullenly, grudgingly, stoically, simply out of a feeling of necessity ... no atonement could have been made.'[31] Neither passive nor active obedience would have been rendered. His blood would not have sealed the Covenant of Grace. By the sustaining ministry of the Holy Spirit, however, Christ was enabled to offer a perfect sacrifice: 'He went to death, knowing its consequences, but willingly, with a faith in God, and with love, trust, and obedience. His attitude was perfect.'[32] John Owen expresses the same truth in a most striking way when he says: 'The willing offering of himself through that Spirit was the eternal fire under this sacrifice, which made it acceptable unto God.'[33]

That acceptance was demonstrated powerfully when Christ rose from the dead. Had He remained in the tomb, the necessary conclusion would have to be that death had won the victory and that there is no hope of salvation. These are the issues that Paul considers in his exposition of Christ's resurrection in 1 Corinthians 15. Again the Holy Spirit must be seen as an essential actor in this phase of the Mediator's work. Having preserved Christ's body from decay (Ps. 16:9-10; Acts 2:31), He was instrumental in the resurrection. In keeping with the biblical revelation of the Trinity, the resurrection is attributed also to the Father and to the Son, but the Spirit also had a role. This would seem to be the best way of understanding 1 Peter 3:18 which speaks of Christ being 'put to death in the body, but made alive by the Spirit'. Also significant is Romans 8:11: 'And if the Spirit of him who raised Jesus from the dead is living in you, he who raised Christ from the dead will also give life to your mortal bodies through his Spirit, who lives in you.' Other relevant Scriptures include Romans 1:4 and 1 Timothy 3:16. It is clear that the work which the Spirit performed in relation to the Mediator He will also perform in all those who have a share in the Covenant of Grace.

A consideration of the work of the Holy Spirit in Christ during His ministry on earth serves to deepen our understanding of redemption and enables us to be more consistently trinitarian in our thinking. It is also a subject full of encouragement for the Lord's covenant people as they consider His redeeming work for them. We begin now to think of the Lord's work *in* his people.

The outpouring of the Spirit at Pentecost

As Acts 2 records, the day of Pentecost saw a mighty and definitive outpouring of the Holy Spirit upon the Church in its New Covenant form. The risen Christ had promised His disciples: 'you will receive power when the Holy Spirit comes on you' (Acts 1:8), a phenomenon that He describes as 'the gift my Father promised' (v. 4). That gift is the Holy Spirit Himself, given to apply the redemption purchased by Christ.

On several occasions Jesus spoke of the Father giving the Spirit, as for example in John 14:16 ('I will ask the Father, and he will give you another Counsellor'). More often, however, it is the Son in particular who sends the Spirit to His Church. Thus in John 16:7 He says, 'Unless I go away, the Counsellor will not come to you; but if I go, I will send him to you.'

Much light is shed on the Pentecostal outpouring of the Spirit if the event is viewed from a covenant perspective. The gift of the Spirit is to be seen as part of the covenantal mediatorial work of Christ. This is made explicit in Peter's sermon at Pentecost. Having spoken of the life, death and resurrection of the Messiah, Peter goes on to say, 'Exalted to the right hand of God, he has received from the Father the promised Holy Spirit and has poured out what you now see and hear' (Acts 2:33). Peter goes on to quote Psalm 110:1 ('The Lord says to my Lord: "Sit at my right hand until I make your enemies a footstool for your feet."'), depicting Christ enthroned as mediatorial King, sending the Spirit to apply the redemption He has purchased. Having fulfilled all that He undertook in the Covenant of Redemption, the Son receives from the Father the gift of the Spirit who will bring sinners into the Covenant of Grace. The Spirit may thus be termed a 'covenantal gift'.

Christ's mediatorial work and the outpouring of the Holy

Spirit cannot be separated. In his writings on the Holy Spirit Richard Gaffin has highlighted this unbreakable bond. He emphasizes that the outpouring (or baptism) of the Spirit at Pentecost is to be thought of as another integral part of Christ's redemptive work, alongside His life of obedience, His suffering, death and resurrection. Gaffin's conclusion is worth quoting at length:

> the gift of the Spirit is nothing less than the gift of Christ himself to the church, the Christ who has become what he is by virtue of his sufferings, death and exaltation. In this sense the gift (baptism, outpouring) of the Spirit is the crowning achievement of Christ's work. It is his coming in exaltation to the church in the power of the Spirit. It completes the once-for-all accomplishment of salvation. It is the apex thus far reached in the unfolding of redemptive history.[34]

This theme of the Spirit as the Mediator's gift could be traced in other parts of the New Testament, but one example must suffice. J. I. Packer notes that in Galatians Paul shows how the mediation of Christ, which brings men out of bondage to sin and the law into 'the glorious liberty of the sons of God', is also the means by which the gifts of justification and the Spirit are bestowed (referring, for example, to Gal. 3:1-14).[35]

Pentecost is clearly a covenantal event. The outpouring of the Spirit is part of the promise of the New Covenant to which the Old Testament prophets looked forward. Thus Peter in his Pentecost sermon quotes from Joel 2:28-32 ('In the last days, God says, I will pour out my Spirit on all people') and demonstrates that such a promise is fulfilled in what is currently taking place (Acts 2:16ff.).

It is vital to emphasize that the Holy Spirit focuses attention not on Himself but on the Mediator. John 15:26 makes this clear: 'When the Counsellor comes, whom I will send to you from the Father, the Spirit of truth who goes out from the Father, he will testify about me.' As the Spirit brings sinners to saving faith and into membership of the Covenant of Grace, it is into union with Christ that they come. As we will note in the next chapter, that is not to deny the reality of believers' fellowship with the Father and the Spirit, but it does maintain a biblical balance.

When the gifts of the Holy Spirit, particularly those of a miraculous nature, are emphasized, as for example in the Charismatic Movement, there is at least the danger that undue attention is given to the Spirit and the focus is moved off Christ. Even in such a wide-ranging study of systematic theology as J. Rodman Williams' *Renewal Theology*,[36] the place given to the gifts of the Spirit is very considerable. At the more popular level a biblical balance is even harder to maintain.

Of even greater concern is the recent exponential growth of interest in 'spirituality', fuelled in large part by the New Age Movement. The term 'Spirit' (or 'spirit') has become almost endlessly elastic, much of what is said about it having nothing to do with biblical truth. In inter-religious dialogue, too, the focus is generally much more on the Spirit than on Christ. The particularity of Christ seems often to be an embarrassment in such a setting, whilst many different traditions can speak of the 'Spirit'. The biblical doctrine of the Holy Spirit held by Covenant Theology, however, makes it clear that the Spirit testifies unwaveringly to the biblical Christ, the Mediator of the Covenant of Grace.

Applying redemption

Much of the Holy Spirit's work in the covenant people of God will be considered in the next chapter. Those who are dead in 'transgressions and sins' (Eph. 2:1) must, however, be made such covenant people. We conclude this chapter by looking at the divine work of regeneration, the beginning point of salvation, effected through the agency of the Holy Spirit. As always, this is a trinitarian work, but in Scripture it is ascribed particularly to the Holy Spirit.

The only sufficient remedy for sinners' spiritual deadness, resulting from the broken Covenant of Works, is the implantation in them of new life. This is made clear by Jesus in

John 3:3, 'I tell you the truth, no-one can see the kingdom of God unless he is born again.' The verb used by Jesus, *gennaō*, can refer to the role of the father ('to beget') or of the mother ('to bear, bring forth'). Thus His words could be translated as 'unless a man is born again' or 'unless a man is begotten again'. The same terminology is found in John 1:13; 3:3, 4, 5, 6, 7, 8; 1 John 2:29; 3:9; 4:7; 5:1, 4, 18. A closely related term, *anagennaō*, is used in 1 Peter 1:3, 23 and indicates the father's role.

What is clear from this language, and related concepts such as 'new creation' in Ephesians 2:10 and 2 Corinthians 5:17, is that regeneration is the work of God alone. No mere creature could perform such a work. Only the God who gives physical life can give spiritual life. Thus 1 John 3:9 speaks of believers as 'born of God/begotten by God'. John 3 makes the Holy Spirit's agency in regeneration clear. Verse 8, for example, refers to those who are 'born of the Spirit'. In verse 5 there is a reference to birth 'of water and the Spirit'. Numerous suggestions have been offered as to the meaning of this phrase.[37] It seems to us that this is best regarded as one birth in which the Spirit works like water to bring cleansing to the sinner, drawing on Old Testament passages such as Ezekiel 36:25-26. Whatever may be the correct view, the essential role of the Spirit is clear. As Thomas Goodwin says: 'He is the author of all the principles or habits of grace, of that whole new creature, of that workmanship created to good works, the spiritual man ...'[38]

The New Testament terminology thus points to regeneration as the work of the Holy Spirit 'by which the principle of the new life is implanted in man, and the governing disposition of the soul is made holy ... and the first holy exercise of this new disposition is secured.'[39] This latter element is particularly termed the 'new birth'. At this point the sinner is enabled by the Holy Spirit to respond to the gospel message, read, heard or remembered. The outward call of the word becomes an inward call in his heart which always receives a positive response. By the 'effectual call' of the Spirit sinners, such as Lydia in Acts

16:14, embrace Christ and become sharers in the Covenant of Grace.

John Calvin in discussing why all who hear the gospel do not accept Christ says, 'reason itself teaches us to climb higher and to examine into the secret energy of the Spirit, by which we come to enjoy Christ and all his benefits.'[40] Any 'technique' of evangelism which replaces the centrality of the regenerating work of the Spirit with humanly-devised methodologies in fact betrays the gospel it claims to advance. An understanding of the covenantal work of the Spirit emphasises the need for total reliance upon Him, while doing everything that Scripture commands by way of presenting Christ. Covenant Theology must regard prayer as a central evangelistic responsibility.

Notes

1. Thomas Goodwin, *The Work of the Holy Spirit in our Salvation* (Edinburgh, 1979), p. 3.

2. George Smeaton, *The Doctrine of the Holy Spirit*, 1889 edition (Edinburgh, 1974), p. 122.

3. Hugh Martin, *The Atonement* (Edinburgh, 1976), p. 32.

4. Louis Berkhof, *Systematic Theology* (Edinburgh, 1958), p. 89.

5. In AD 589 the Council of Toledo added the words 'and from the Son' to the statement of the Niceno-Constantinopolitan Creed that the Holy Spirit 'proceeds from the Father'. The Eastern Churches rejected this addition by the Western Churches and the controversy was one factor in the division between East and West in AD 1052.

6. John Calvin, *Institutes of the Christian Religion*, 1559 edition, translated by Ford Lewis Battles (Philidelphia, 1960), I.xiii.14-20.

7. Robert L. Reymond, *A New Systematic Theology of the Christian Faith* (Nashville, 1998), pp. 331-8.

8. Sinclair Ferguson, *The Holy Spirit* (Leicester, 1996), pp. 72-8.

9. John Calvin, *Institutes*, I.xiii.19.

10. Gordon Spykman, *Reformational Theology* (Grand Rapids, 1992), p. 418.

11. John Owen, *The Works of John Owen*, Edited by William H. Goold, 1850-53 edition (Edinburgh, 1967), 16.341.

12. See e.g. Louis Berkhof, op. cit., p. 270.

13. J. van Genderen, *Covenant and Election* (Neerlandia, 1995), p. 66.

14. A wide-ranging and helpful study of the work of the Holy Spirit in the life of Christ is *Jesus - Power Without Measure* by J. Douglas MacMillan (Bryntirion, 1990).

15. George Smeaton, op. cit., p. 129

16. George Smeaton, op. cit., p. 132.

17. Abraham Kuyper, *The Work of the Holy Spirit*, translated by Henri de Vries. 1900 edition. (Grand Rapids, 1975), p. 95.

18. Carl Trueman, *The Claims of Truth* (Carlisle, 1998), p. 178, citing John Owen, *Works*, 3.160ff.

19. George Smeaton, op. cit., p. 134.

20. Owen cites Luke 1:80, but this probably refers to John the Baptist (*Works*, 10.178). Smeaton follows the AV reading of Luke 2:40 which included the words 'in spirit' and sees this as a reference to the Holy Spirit. Most modern commentators would reject this reading. (Smeaton, op. cit., p. 133).

21. J. Douglas MacMillan, op. cit., chapter 4.

22. J. Douglas MacMillan, op. cit., p. 56

23. J. Douglas MacMillan, op. cit., p. 58.

24. George Smeaton, op. cit., p. 135.

25. Thomas Goodwin, op. cit., p. 11

26. Abraham Kuyper, op. cit., p. 96.

27. George Smeaton, op. cit., p. 138.

28. George Smeaton, op. cit., p. 140.

29. Thomas Goodwin, op. cit., p. 12.

30. A concise rebuttal of the view that 'the eternal Spirit' refers to Christ's divine nature is provided by MacMillan, op. cit., pp. 117-20.

31. Edwin H. Palmer, *The Person and Ministry of the Holy Spirit* (Grand Rapids, 1974), p. 72.

32. ibid.

33. John Owen, *Works*, 10.178.

34. Richard B. Gaffin, Jr., *Perspectives on Pentecost* (Phillipsburg, 1979), p. 20.

35. James I. Packer, *God's Words* (Leicester, 1981), p. 112.

36. J. Rodman Williams, *Renewal Theology. Systematic Theology from a Charismatic Perspective*, 3 volumes (Grand Rapids, 1988-92).

37. A range of views is discussed by D. A. Carson in *The Gospel according to John* (Leicester, 1991), ad.loc. We do not, however, accept his conclusions.

38. Thomas Goodwin, op. cit., p. 17.

39. Louis Berkhof, op. cit., p. 469. An extensive examination of the subject is provided by the Southern Presbyterian theologian C. R. Vaughan in *The Gifts of the Holy Spirit*, 1894 edition (Edinburgh, 1975), pp. 132-207.

40. John Calvin, *Institutes*, III.i.1.

7

Blessings of the Covenant

A fundamental principle of Covenant Theology is the assertion that God provides everything that is needed by sinners for salvation. In the Covenant of Redemption the elect were given to Christ to be His people; the power and the grace of God ensure that all of them will in fact be brought into covenant with the Lord. There is no uncertainty in the outworking of God's covenant decree. Everything necessary, including the free, willing response of sinners, is secured by God, so that from start to finish salvation is His work, and all the glory is to be ascribed to His name.

Every aspect of salvation is to be thought of in terms of God's covenant blessings. This is so, as we are about to see, even with regard to the way in which sinners are brought into the Covenant of Grace. The more we understand about God's work of salvation, the more we marvel at the richness of the grace shown to us in the covenant.

Faith and repentance

'The condition of the covenant is faith', wrote Samuel Rutherford in *The Trial and Triumph of Faith*.[1] No hint of human merit or man-made righteousness attaches to such a statement. As Rutherford vividly puts it, 'faith sendeth a person out of himself, and taketh him off his own bottom, that in Christ he may have his righteousness.'[2] Nothing could be further than this from salvation by human effort or merit. Rutherford, like all covenant theologians, puts great stress on the free grace of God:

> Faith holdeth forth God in Christ, in the most lively and lovely properties of free grace, mercy, love transcendent; hence a believer,

as such cannot possibly glory in himself; all that faith hath, is by
way of receiving and begging-wise.[3]

As Rutherford's sermon develops, it is clear that the faith
which admits sinners to the Covenant of Grace includes godly
sorrow for sin, true biblical repentance. Taken together, faith
and repentance constitute a sinner's proper response to the
gospel call and the means by which he enters into covenant
fellowship with God. The two are inseparable, and it is futile to
ask which comes first. As John Murray rightly observes, 'There
is no priority, the faith that is unto salvation is a penitent faith
and the repentance that is unto life is a believing repentance.'[4]

It is vital to stress the 'gift' nature of faith and repentance.
Both are human actions, yet they are also the fruit of the gracious
working of the Holy Spirit. It is as a result of the regeneration
which the Spirit effects in an elect sinner that he repents and
believes on the Lord Jesus Christ. As Rutherford says, saving
faith 'certainly is an act performed by a regenerate person.'[5]
Covenant Theology's biblical view of sinners as dead in sin
emphasizes that this must be the case. Behind the free response
of the sinner is the working of the Holy Spirit.

Scripture makes abundantly clear that both faith and
repentance are granted by God. In the language of the Shorter
Catechism, they are 'saving graces' (Q86, 87). With reference
to faith, we may note Acts 13:48, where we are told regarding
the response to Paul's preaching in Antioch that 'all who were
appointed for eternal life believed.' Faith flows from the divine
decree and the divine enabling, a truth illustrated in the
conversion of Lydia in Philippi. Acts 16:14 states, 'The Lord
opened her heart to respond to Paul's message.' We may also
note Acts 18:27 which states that Apollos 'was a great help to
those who by grace had believed'. A further striking text is
Ephesians 2:8-9, 'For it is by grace you have been saved, through
faith – and this not from yourselves, it is the gift of God – not
by works.' Whether the 'gift' is faith or the whole of salvation
including faith, the nature of faith as God's gift is clear.[6]

Regarding repentance, we should note Peter's reference in Acts 5:31 to Christ's exaltation as Prince and Saviour 'that he might *give* repentance and forgiveness of sins to Israel'. The same truth is found in the rejoicing of the Jerusalem church over the conversion of Cornelius: 'God has *granted* even the Gentiles repentance unto life' (Acts 11:18). Other relevant texts are 2 Timothy 2:25 ('in the hope that God will *grant* them repentance') and the Old Testament prayers for God to 'turn' sinners (e.g. Ps. 80:3, 7, 19). Apart from God's enabling power, sinners will continue down the broad road that leads to destruction (Matt. 7:13).

We must now consider faith and repentance separately and in more detail.

(i) saving faith

A famous definition of saving faith is provided by the Shorter Catechism: 'Faith in Jesus Christ is a saving grace, whereby we receive and rest upon Him alone for salvation, as He is offered to us in the gospel' (Q86). Similar themes are given fuller expression in Calvin's definition of faith as, 'a firm and certain knowledge of God's benevolence toward us, founded upon the truth of the freely given promise in Christ, both revealed to our minds and sealed upon our hearts through the Holy Spirit.'[7]

Various definitions of faith have been given by covenant theologians, with some seventeenth century writers multiplying the elements to be included in their definitions. All agree, however, that the whole of the sinner's being is involved: his thinking, his emotions, his will. Summing up the views of the Reformed tradition on the subject, Daniel Migliore states, 'The subject of faith is the *whole* person – mind, affections and will – in response to God's goodness, faithfulness and forgiveness of sins in Christ.'[8] Thus Herman Witsius, for example, says that faith 'imparts a change of the whole man, is the spring of the whole spiritual life'.[9]

The commonest, and probably most straightforward, view

of faith among covenant theologians is that it is made up of three elements: knowledge, assent and trust (in Latin, *notitia, assensus* and *fiducia*). This scheme is found as far back as 1597 in Robert Rollock's *A Treatise of God's Effectual Calling*, [10] and has been used by many other writers.

Saving faith must begin with *knowledge*, the mind's understanding of the truths presented in the word of God. In Romans 10:17 Paul insists that 'faith comes from hearing, and hearing by the word of Christ.' (NASB). It is impossible to have biblical saving faith in an object about which one knows little or nothing. Thus the Bible often speaks of believing certain facts – 'believing *that*'.[11] A good example is John 20:31, 'But these are written that you may *believe that* Jesus is the Christ, the Son of God.' The facts proclaimed in the gospel message must be known: 'We *believe that* Jesus died and rose again' (1 Thess. 4:14).

Even at this stage it is clear that saving faith differs fundamentally from what passes for 'faith' in the modern world. In the opinion of many people, it is enough to 'believe' sincerely, regardless of *what* one actually believes. It appears that they are ignoring the fact that one may believe a lie, as many once believed that the world was flat. Sincerity is no defence against the harmful effects of false beliefs.

The faith that saves has specific content. It may be difficult to say precisely how much knowledge is required for salvation, but at the very least it must include the identity of Christ and the nature of his redeeming work. In sharp contrast, the 'faith' of many, shaped by a range of influences such as New Age thinking, is so vague that its content could scarcely be stated.

The second element of saving faith is *assent*, the conviction that the gospel record regarding the person and work of Christ is true and that he is able to meet one's real spiritual needs. Bare knowledge of the facts is insufficient: there are biblical scholars with an encyclopedic knowledge of the facts of Scripture who would laugh at the idea of their needing to be 'saved', and who would deny the historicity of much of the

Gospels. Assent to the truth of what the Bible teaches and recognition of its personal significance are essential. This element of faith is indicated in the New Testament by such texts as John 2:22 ('Then they believed the Scripture and the words that Jesus had spoken') and John 5:46 ('If you believed Moses, you would believe me'). As Rollock puts it, 'For those things which are published in the Gospel are to be understood to be spoken specially of me, and of thee.'[12]

This personal dimension is emphasized in the third necessary element of faith, namely *trust*. This is well described by J. I. Packer as 'a reliant outgoing of the soul in trust and confidence towards the living God and his living Son.'[13] The sinner who exercises true saving faith forsakes any reliance on his own efforts and wholeheartedly puts all reliance for salvation upon Christ the only Mediator. Without such unreserved commitment, 'faith' is not saving faith. As James points out, even the demons hold certain true beliefs about God – in a certain sense their theology is quite accurate – yet they remain God's implacable enemies (Jas. 2:19). The New Testament language of faith emphasizes this movement away from self to 'rest upon' Christ. Thus sinners 'believe in' Him (John 3:15), 'believe upon' Him (Rom. 10:11; Acts 9:42; two different constructions in Greek), and 'believe unto' Him (John 1:12, 2:11, and many more times in this Gospel).

The object of saving faith is in a general sense the word of God, in particular the promises of salvation through Christ that God makes to sinners. The word of course testifies to Christ and it is He who is ultimately the object of faith. To enter the Covenant of Grace, sinners must put their trust in the Mediator whom God has provided. The object of faith is therefore 'Jesus Christ with all his benefits, and even so, as he offereth himself in the Word and Sacraments'.[14]

In the present climate in evangelicalism it is important to stress that sinners in order to be saved must trust in Christ as Saviour *and Lord*. This is how He is 'freely offered to us in the gospel' and that is how He must be received. Thus Witsius says,

'Moreover, when the believer so receives Christ and leans upon him, he not only considers him as a Saviour but also as a Lord.'[15] He goes on to explain, 'For he receives a *whole* Christ, and receiveth him just as he is: but he is no less Lord than a Saviour.'[16] Saving faith, as we will see later in relation to justification, is not itself a work but inevitably leads to good works in joyful obedience to Christ as Covenant Lord.

The view we have stated here has in recent years become known as 'lordship salvation'. In a controversy originating in the USA, some writers of a Dispensational persuasion, such as Zane Hodges and Charles Ryrie, have argued that to preach the need for repentance and receiving Christ as Lord compromises the gospel of free grace.[17] An adequate reply to the 'nonlordship' position cannot be undertaken here,[18] but we may note, as Ernest Reisinger points out,[19] that lordship was the central confession of the whole Christian community (1 Cor. 1:2), the central confession of the New Testament (Phil. 2:9-11), the personal confession of New Testament believers (Rom. 10:9) and a key part of presenting the gospel (2 Pet. 1:11, 2:20). Sadly we must conclude that a 'nonlordship' gospel is a false gospel.

It is also important to stress that it is not, strictly speaking, the sinner's faith in itself that saves, but it is Christ who saves through the sinner's faith in Him. Faith is no more than an instrument which God has granted to the sinner.

The focus in salvation must never be moved from the Mediator of the Covenant of Grace. As John Murray says, 'Faith unites us to Christ in the bonds of abiding attachment and entrustment and it is this union which insures that the saving power, grace and virtue of the Saviour become operative in the believer.'[20]

What warrant does a sinner have for believing in Christ? It cannot be that he knows he is elect: Rutherford and many others have shown the impossibility of such knowledge before we believe.[21] Equally well it cannot be because he discerns evidences of the Holy Spirit's working in him before he believes (e.g. showing he is 'awakened'). The sinner's warrant for believing is instead based on what is revealed in Scripture. *The Sum of Saving Knowledge*, generally printed with the documents of the Westminster Assembly, speaks of the warrants and motives to believe as God's hearty invitation, His earnest request to be reconciled, His command charging all to believe, and the assurance of life given to believers. More concisely, John Murray indicates that the warrant consists of two elements, namely the universal offer of the gospel and the all-sufficiency and suitability of the Saviour.[22] On such a basis a sinner may believe in Christ for salvation.

(ii) repentance unto life

Much of what has been said regarding saving faith applies equally to repentance, which is also a human act resulting from the Holy Spirit's regenerating work. It is, of course, essential that our understanding of repentance should be thoroughly biblical. As so often, the Shorter Catechism definition is most helpful: 'Repentance unto life is a saving grace, whereby a sinner, – out of a true sense of his sin, and apprehension of the mercy of God in Christ, – doth, with grief and hatred of his sin, turn from it unto God, with full purpose of, – and endeavour after, – new obedience.' (Q87).

At the heart of true repentance is sorrow for sin. When speaking of the coming of the Holy Spirit, Jesus said, 'When he comes, he will convict the world of guilt in regard to sin and righteousness and judgment' (John 16:8). The Spirit produces sorrow for, and hatred of, sin. Many people sorrow over their wrongdoing because of the harm it has done themselves and other people; they sorrow because of the punishment that sin may bring. Repentance unto life is fundamentally different in that it has a Godward orientation. As Rollock puts it, it is 'a sorrow for the sin itself, and because of the offence which is committed against God'.[23] Such an outlook is expressed perfectly in David's confession of sin in Psalm 51:4 'Against you, you only, have I sinned and done what is evil in your sight.' This is the 'godly sorrow' which Paul speaks of in 2 Corinthians

7:10, sorrow which 'brings repentance that leads to salvation and leaves no regret'. It is sorrow that results in the forsaking of sin and the pursuit of holiness.

Like saving faith, repentance involves every element of our being. The mind recognizes sin for what it is, an offence against a holy God, and also realizes the hope of cleansing that Christ offers. The emotions are engaged as the sinner grieves over his offences. Such changes of attitude and feeling must be accompanied by action, turning from sin to the Lord. This was exemplified by the believers in Thessalonica, to whom Paul wrote, 'you turned to God from idols to serve the living and true God' (1 Thess. 1:9).

Once again, the necessity of repentance must be stressed in opposition to holders of the 'nonlordship' view of salvation. Zane Hodges, for example, argues that 'Faith alone (not repentance and faith) is the sole condition for justification and eternal life.'[24] If such were the case, we might wonder why Peter's response to those who were anxious about their spiritual welfare after his Pentecost sermon was 'Repent' (Acts 2:38). The Bible knows nothing of salvation without repentance. As Robert Reymond expresses it, 'Such teaching is incredible, for it means that the impenitent can receive eternal life and be saved even though they never forsake their sin or have any fellowship with God!'[25]

Union with Christ

The regenerated sinner begins to experience the wonders of salvation when he is brought into union with Christ. This is reflected in Q30 of the Shorter Catechism: 'The Spirit applieth to us the redemption purchased by Christ, by working faith in us, and thereby uniting us to Christ in our effectual calling.'

Union with Christ is the most basic category for describing the experience of salvation. From this saving union flow numerous blessings such as justification, adoption, sanctification and assurance of salvation.[26] Every benefit that a believer enjoys can be traced back to the union with Christ that the Spirit establishes. We will have more to say about this in a moment.

In harmony with the biblical doctrine of the Trinity, it should be noted that Scripture speaks of a union of the believer with the Father and with the Holy Spirit, depicted in terms of both Persons dwelling with the believer.[27] Thus Jesus can say, 'If anyone loves me, he will obey my teaching. My Father will love him, and *we* will come to him and make our home with him' (John 14:23). In the same chapter Jesus speaks of the outpouring of the Holy Spirit and tells his disciples, 'But you know him, for he lives with you and will be in you' (v. 17).

It is, however, the believer's union with Christ that is the focus of attention in the New Testament.

This union may be thought of as having three elements:

(i) Union begins with election, the giving of a people to Christ in eternity by the Covenant of Redemption. There is therefore a 'legal', covenant union between Christ and His people from eternity. Even before the world was created, elect sinners were in the mind and purpose of God, and always thought of 'in Christ'. Until they actually believe in Christ at a particular point in history, however, they continue to be 'children of wrath even as the rest' (Eph. 2:3 NASB).

(ii) The next stage of union with Christ involves His representative work on behalf of His people as the Mediator of the Covenant of Grace. From birth, through life, to death and beyond, all that Christ did was performed for those given to Him. As 2 Corinthians 5:21 states, 'God made him who had no sin to be sin for us.' This is described in the most personal terms in v. 14 of the same chapter: 'one died for all, and therefore all died.' Similarly, in Romans 6 Paul speaks of dying, being buried and rising with Christ. Before this could be a present personal experience, Christ had to perform the work required of Him for all who are 'in' Him. As A. A. Hoekema says, 'This work must be seen as the meritorious basis for union with Christ. It is only because our Savior did all these things for his people that actual union between Christ and his own has become possible.'[28]

(iii) Believers begin to experience the new life of the

Covenant of Grace when they are actually united to Christ. This is the personal experiential side of what Paul describes in Romans 6:4-11. In a certain sense the Holy Spirit reproduces in believers the death and resurrection of Christ. As Paul says in v. 11, 'count yourselves dead to sin but alive to God in Christ Jesus.'

Covenant theologians rightly stress that this union is a *spiritual* union, not in any sense a physical union. In Boston's words, 'As one soul or spirit actuates both the head and the members in the natural body, so the one Spirit of God dwells in Christ and the Christian'.[29] The New Testament also speaks in terms of Christ's dwelling in his people. Note Galatians 2:20, 'I have been crucified with Christ and I no longer live, but Christ lives in me.' In Colossians 1:27 Paul speaks of 'the glorious riches of this mystery, which is Christ in you, the hope of glory'. The same precious truth is to be found in texts such as Romans 8:10, 2 Corinthians 13:5 and Ephesians 3:17.

The covenant life flowing from union with Christ is thus one of intimate personal communion with the Lord. In John 15 it is described in terms of the life-giving bond between a vine and its branches: there is to be growth and development, always remembering the Lord's warning, 'apart from me you can do nothing' (v. 5). There must always remain much about this union that is mysterious. Human language struggles to express even a little about a living personal union between the infinite eternal Son of God made flesh and His redeemed people. Despite the mysteries, the union is real and the source of all other blessings enjoyed by believers.

Every aspect of salvation and Christian living must be related to this 'in Christ' relationship. At the outset believers are 'created in Christ Jesus to do good works' (Eph. 2:10). The new life we receive continues by virtue of our union with Christ. Thus Paul says in 1 Corinthians 1:5, 'For in him you have been enriched in every way.' All necessary blessings for progress in sanctification are provided. Believers ultimately die in Christ (1 Thess. 4:14, 16), they are never separated from Him and it is in Christ that they will be glorified (Rom. 8:17). As John Murray says of union with Christ, 'It embraces the wide span of salvation, from its ultimate source in the eternal election of God to its final fruition in the glorification of the elect.'[30]

An understanding of this indissoluble union is vital for the spiritual health of believers. They must constantly remember that their spiritual life is dependent from start to finish on Christ and that from Him they are to seek all the grace and strength that they require. It is 'in Christ' that they have been set free from the guilt and dominating power of sin, and on this basis they must seek daily victory over sin and temptation. When these facts are lost from view, inconsistent ungodly conduct is the inevitable result.

Justification

God cannot be in covenant fellowship with those who stand under His righteous wrath and curse. The sins of covenant-breaking rebels must be dealt with, otherwise God would deny His own holiness in receiving them. Thomas Boston states the problem and the solution in this way:

> The elect of God, lying under the breach of the first covenant, were dead in law, as being under the curse. They could not be restored to life in the eye of the law, but upon the fulfilling of the righteousness of the law; the which they not being able to do for themselves, Christ in the covenant undertook to do it for them; and thereupon was made the promise of their justification.[31]

Thus we come to consider the great doctrine of justification by faith alone, one of the crucial evangelical doctrines rediscovered at the Reformation.[32] It is well summarized in the Shorter Catechism Q33, 'Justification is an act of God's free grace, whereby He pardoneth all our sins, and accepteth us as righteous in His sight, only for the righteousness of Christ imputed to us, and received by faith alone.'

Talk of 'justification' takes us into the realm of law courts and legal proceedings. In a typically exhaustive study of the use of 'justification' language in both the Old and New Testaments, [33] John Murray has demonstrated that in the overwhelming majority of cases the action in view is a *declaration* of a person's righteous standing. Thus when God 'justifies' someone, he is not making him righteous but declaring him to be righteous. In a text such as Deuteronomy 25:1 judges deciding a dispute 'justify the righteous and condemn the wicked' (NASB). Clearly the judges do not make either party righteous or wicked, but declare what their legal standing actually is. The nature of justification is also shown by the fact that it stands as the opposite of condemnation. The same contrast is drawn in Proverbs 17:15.

Not only is this the case in the Hebrew of the Old Testament: the same is true in the Greek of the New Testament. Thus we read in Matthew 12:37 'For by your words you will be justified and by your words you will be condemned' (NASB). It is perhaps unfortunate that the NIV uses the translation 'acquit' in these texts, thus losing the clear reference to justification.

Murray's examination of the linguistic evidence shows definitively that when Paul in Romans 8:33 states, 'It is God who justifies', he has in view God's declaration that His people are 'not guilty' in His sight. As Robert Reymond says, 'This biblical evidence makes it clear that justification is a juridical or forensic determination made by a judge.'[34] Justification relates to the standing of a person before God, not to his spiritual condition. In this it contrasts with regeneration, the divinely wrought change in our spiritual deadness. Using Murray's striking analogy, in regeneration God acts like a surgeon to bring healing, whilst in justification He acts as a judge.[35]

More must be said about the nature of justification, however, since it is sometimes claimed that the forensic view of justification amounts to little more than a legal fiction, with God somehow pretending that sinners are really righteous.

If He were to do so He would be acting contrary to His own commandments to human judges in, for example, Proverbs 17:15. How is this problem to be resolved? The solution is to be found in a feature of God's justification of sinners which differs from the action of any human judge and which makes God's act of justification unique.

'The peculiarity of God's action consists in this that he causes to be the righteous state or relation which is declared to be.'[36] God grants to the sinner who has been regenerated and who trusts in Christ a new judicial standing. He constitutes him righteous and thus can in perfect justice declare him to be righteous. We may say that God's act of justification is *constitutive* as well as forensic. This is the significance of Romans 5:19, 'For just as through the disobedience of the one man the many were made sinners, so also through the obedience of the one man the many will be made righteous.' We must link this with verse 17 which speaks of 'the gift of righteousness'. God constitutes His people righteous and then passes the appropriate judicial verdict upon them. Not only are they 'not guilty', but they are positively righteous.

The verses quoted above from Romans 5 show the source of this righteousness and hence the basis for God's justification of the ungodly. The basis cannot be any good thing in the sinner since he is 'dead in transgressions and sins' (Eph. 2:1). Equally well it cannot be because of any efforts the sinner makes since even his best efforts are 'filthy rags' (Isa. 64:6), works not performed out of love for God. As Galatians 2:16 states, justification is 'not by the works of the Law, since by the works of the Law no flesh will be justified' (NASB). Ephesians 2:9 also reminds us that salvation is 'not by works'.

The sinner's righteousness must be provided by another. In His rich grace God has provided that necessary righteousness through the work of Christ as our covenant Surety. We have seen how He took the guilt and punishment of our sins upon Himself (they were 'imputed' to him), and as a consequence of His redemptive work His righteousness is 'imputed' to all those who are united to Him. The righteousness of justification is the righteousness and obedience of Christ, as Romans 5:17-19 shows. Charles Hodge sums it up in these terms: 'By the righteousness of Christ is meant all he became, did and suffered to satisfy the demands of divine justice, and merit for his people the forgiveness of sins and the gift of eternal life.'[37] It is by virtue of their union with Christ that believers have this perfect righteousness imputed to them and so are justified.

In 2 Corinthians 5:21 Paul shows that the consequence of Christ's being 'made sin' for us is 'that *in him* we might become the righteousness of God'. Justification is inextricably bound up with union with Christ.

We cannot stress too strongly that the basis of God's justification of sinners is the righteousness of Christ the Surety and Mediator of the Covenant of Grace. Such is the corruption of the sinful human heart that men constantly seek to find some basis for being declared righteous in themselves or their own efforts. No such basis exists. The only possible hope for sinners is Christ, since, as Francis Turretin states, 'God justifies us because the righteousness of Christ, our surety, is imputed to us.'[38] In the midst of complex theological debates about justification, we should not lose sight of the fact that the heart of the doctrine may be summed up as simply as that.

Imputation of the righteousness of Christ to the elect in the Covenant of Grace parallels the imputation of Adam's sin to his descendants as a result of the broken Covenant of Works. This truth is stated concisely in, for example, Romans 5:16, 'The judgment followed one sin and brought condemnation, but the gift followed many trespasses and brought justification.' The following verse makes clear that the gift is 'the gift of righteousness'. As Adam was, along with his descendants, counted as guilty before God, so those who are 'in Christ' are counted as righteous before God. 'This righteousness, ' says Wilhelmus à Brakel, 'is imputed to the elect, and since Christ, as Surety, has accomplished this in their stead, God considers it as if they themselves had accomplished this.'[39]

Justification is entirely by the free grace of God, as is every element of the salvation provided for in the Covenant of Redemption. Thus Romans 3:24 speaks of being 'justified freely by his grace through the redemption that came by Christ Jesus'. All the glory is due to God's name and there is no room left for human works to make a contribution to justification. Thus when we speak of 'justification *by faith*' we must be most careful to remember that faith is not a 'work', something man works up in himself and presents to God as meriting justification. Faith itself is 'the gift of God' (Eph. 2:8) and is necessary for justification, but it can never be the basis of justification. As we have seen, only the righteousness of Christ can perform that function.

The New Testament language regarding faith makes this conclusion inevitable. We are said to be justified 'by faith' (e.g. Rom. 3:28, 30, two different grammatical constructions), 'through faith' (e.g. Gal. 2:16), 'upon faith' (e.g. Phil. 3:9) and 'according to faith' (e.g. Heb. 11:7). What is never said is that we are justified 'on account of faith' or 'because of faith'. The Holy Spirit, speaking through the New Testament writers, is clearly ruling out any meritorious role for faith.

What then does 'by faith' mean in relation to justification? The phrase indicates that faith plays an *instrumental* role in justification, it is the channel by which we receive this blessing. Strictly speaking, faith does not justify: God justifies graciously on the basis of the atoning work of Christ. To use Calvin's useful illustration, faith is an empty vessel into which God pours His blessings.[40]

The Westminster Confession of Faith reflects this line of thought in its statement that faith 'is the alone instrument of justification' (XI.2). The biblical teaching on the role of faith is well summed up by Robert Reymond:

> Faith in Jesus Christ is simply the regenerated sinner's saving response to God's effectual summons, by means of which the righteousness of Christ – the sole ground of justification – is imputed to him.[41]

Faith is not in any sense meritorious, and when some covenant theologians speak of it as a 'condition' of salvation they do so with the clear understanding that it is a gift of God's grace, not a product of human effort.[42]

The inescapable conclusion to be drawn from what has been said about faith and justification is that justification is 'by faith alone'. Nothing else on man's side can enter into the transaction. Any supposed 'merits' he may claim are of no value, and as Paul emphasizes, grace and works are mutually exclusive in relation to salvation. As Romans 11:6 states, 'if by grace, then it is no longer by works; if it were, grace would no longer be grace.' Covenant theologians have been at one with the Reformers in contending for the 'exclusive instrumentality'[43] of faith for justification.

It also needs to be stressed, however, that such justifying faith 'is not alone in the person justified, but is ever accompanied with all other saving graces, and is no dead faith, but worketh by love.' (Westminster Confession XI.2). True faith is invariably accompanied by good works. Thus in Ephesians 2:10, Paul, having just stated that salvation is by grace through faith apart from works, goes on to say that we are 'created in Christ Jesus to do good works'. Such good works, in joyful obedience to God's Law, are the evidence of living faith. As James says, 'faith without deeds is dead' (Jas. 2:26). Such works do not contribute in any way to justification.

These facts indicate how we are to understand James' assertion that 'a man is justified by works and not by faith alone' (Jas. 2:24, NASB). At first sight this appears to be a flat contradiction of Paul's doctrine of justification by faith, but careful attention to the context of such statements in the whole letter shows that the 'justification' of which James speaks is the believer's *demonstrating* his genuine faith to the surrounding world by his works. Paul deals with how a man may be justified before God; James deals with how he demonstrates that standing to others. The apostles do not conflict in any respect.[44]

The view of justification taught in Scripture and held by covenant theologians conflicts at numerous points with the Roman Catholic doctrine framed by the Council of Trent (1545-

63)[45] and restated in full in the most recent *Catechism of the Catholic Church* (1994).[46] It should be noted that the *Catechism* quotes and reaffirms the position of Trent. However the views of some Roman Catholic theologians may have changed, the official stance of Rome is unchanged. We cannot undertake a full examination and refutation of Rome's position here, but a few significant matters may be noted.[47]

The Roman Catholic documents speak freely of 'grace' in relation to justification and will also indicate belief in justification 'by faith'. So far, so good. What they cannot endorse from their theological perspective is justification 'by faith *alone*'. To begin with, Rome's definition of justification includes actual spiritual renewal of the sinner (i.e. sanctification). In *Catechism* para. 1989 we read that 'Justification is not only the remission of sins, but also the sanctification and renewal of the interior man', a direct quotation from the Tridentine decree. The biblical categories of justification and sanctification are thus confused, making justification not only a change of status but also a change of spiritual condition. Rome replaces the biblical doctrine of *imputed* righteousness with a doctrine of *infused* righteousness.

Of crucial significance is Rome's view that 'Justification is conferred in Baptism, the sacrament of faith' (*Catechism*, para 1992). Indeed when lost, justification can be restored through another sacrament, that of penance (para. 1446). Thus the sacraments replace faith as the instrumental cause of justification. In para. 1227 we read, 'Through the Holy Spirit, Baptism is a bath that purifies, justifies and sanctifies'. Sinners must have faith to be justified, they must cooperate with God in this work, and with the free will which Rome believes they still possess, they may freely prepare themselves to receive God's grace. In the less gentle language of Trent, (Canon IX),

> If anyone saith, that by faith alone the impious is justified, in such wise as to mean, that nothing else is required to co-operate in order to obtaining the grace of Justification, and that it is not in any way necessary, that he be prepared and disposed by the movement of his own will: let him be anathema.

Roman Catholic theology imports a great deal of unbiblical 'baggage' into its doctrine of justification, so much so that the heart of the biblical doctrine is removed, to be replaced by sacramentalism. Even where the language is the same as that used by Protestants, the meaning is sometimes radically different. On these grounds we may question the depth of agreement claimed to have been reached by the Roman Catholic and Evangelical signatories of the recent document *Evangelicals and Catholics Together: The Christian Mission in the Third Millennium* (1994). Some of the language used is (perhaps deliberately) ambiguous and could be read so as to conform to traditional Roman Catholic theology (for example references to 'justification by faith', omitting 'alone'). If the Roman Catholic signatories are true to their tradition, their position is incompatible with biblical teaching, and should be incompatible with Evangelicalism.[48]

The biblical doctrine of justification by grace through faith alone, a declaration of the righteous standing of believers on the basis of the imputed righteousness of Christ, has constantly come under attack. Recently the Anglican theologian Tom Wright, drawing on the work of scholars such as E. P. Sanders, has proposed a radical revision of the traditional doctrine.[49] In his view Paul's polemic in Romans is directed against Jews who in a nationalistic way were seeking to demonstrate their membership of the covenant by their works. Against this background justification is thought to deal with covenant membership, rather than with righteousness before God. As writers such as Philip Eveson have shown, however, such views do not do justice to the biblical material.[50]

Rightly understood, justification is a doctrine full of comfort for those who trust in Christ. The verdict of God the righteous Judge is in effect 'brought forward into the present time and rendered here and now concerning the believing sinner.'[51] In Christ we have been acquitted and accepted as righteous, with our condemnation lifted and no punishment to fear at the last day. We rest on the great covenant work of our Surety, in the knowledge that His work cannot be undone or the verdict of God reversed. Here is a solid foundation for the assurance that will be considered below.

Adoption
The adoption of redeemed sinners by God to be his children is a truth that has not always been accorded sufficient attention by covenant theologians. Some do not mention it in so many words, although they generally mention the believer's 'acceptance' with God as an element of justification, which draws on some of the scriptural material relating to adoption. Too often adoption has been treated as almost an appendage to justification.

Other covenant theologians, following the (somewhat brief) lead of the Westminster Confession, chapter XII, have recognized the importance of adoption in the scheme of salvation and have treated it as a separate covenant blessing. Vital aspects of adoption's links with other aspects of salvation have not been neglected, but adoption has been seen to require particular individual attention.[52]

The Shorter Catechism Q34 provides a brief summary of the biblical meaning of adoption: 'Adoption is an act of God's free grace, whereby we are received into the number, – and have a right to all the privileges – of the sons of God.' In the view of John Murray, 'it is adoption into the family of God as sons and daughters of the Lord God Almighty that accords to the people of God the apex of blessing and privilege.'[53] To use the language of the covenant, God provides for covenant fellowship with His people not as servants or slaves, but as dearly loved children.

The importance to be attached to adoption is apparent from Paul's description of the goal of redemption in Galatians 4:4-5: 'But when the fullness of the time came, God sent forth His Son, born of a woman, born under the Law, so that He might redeem those who were under the Law, that we might receive the adoption as sons' (NASB; the NIV translates the Greek word *huiothesia* as 'the full rights of sons'). The apostle also links the origin of salvation (predestination) with its highest goal (adoption) in Ephesians 1:4-5: 'In love he predestined us to be adopted as his sons through Jesus Christ.' Indeed so prominent is the language of fatherhood, sonship and adoption in Ephesians that one theologian has said of the epistle that it 'in a special sense is Paul's treatise on the Fatherhood of God and the doctrine of adoption'.[54]

The adoptive sonship of which Paul speaks is clearly to be understood in redemptive terms. This is not a standing which sinners naturally possess. Their present status is that of 'foreigners and aliens' (Eph. 2:19). There is a certain sense in which God may be said to be the Father of all people since He is their Creator and they are all descended from Adam, who enjoyed the status of a son of God in Eden. Such a universal Fatherhood would seem to be alluded to in Acts 17:25-29, in Paul's Areopagus address, where he states, for example, 'From one man he made every nation of men, ... "For in him we live and move and have our being".' Such a view was vigorously opposed by Scottish theologian Robert Candlish in his controversial book *The Fatherhood of God*, where he argued that Adam in Eden had the status of a servant and was only potentially a son of God.[55] His case was answered thoroughly, and it appears to us convincingly, by John L. Girardeau.[56] It is a truth, however, that is not prominent in Scripture and must be stated carefully, since it was characteristic of liberal theologians in the nineteenth century to insist on the universal Fatherhood of God and the brotherhood of all men apart from the redemptive work of Christ.

It is in the context of God's redeeming sinners to be His sons and daughters, however, that the Bible generally speaks of the Fatherhood of God. In the Old Testament Israel is viewed as God's 'son', for example in Exodus 4:22 and Hosea 11:1. The New Testament material provided, for example, by Galatians and Ephesians shows that believers are adopted as children of God by virtue of their election in Christ before the foundation of the world and their saving union with Christ in time. The Father's election of a people to be His in the Covenant of Redemption has its outworking in union with Christ and adoption in the Covenant of Grace. As John Murray says, 'Hence union with Christ and adoption are complementary aspects of this amazing grace. Union with Christ reaches its zenith in adoption and adoption has its orbit in union with Christ.'[57]

Adoption is a wonderful demonstration of the Father's love for His people. Even in translation it is easy to hear the amazement of the apostle John when he writes, 'How great is the love the Father has lavished on us, that we should be called children of God! And that is what we are!' (1 John 3:1). Adoption addresses the specific issue of the believer's relationship to God the Father. As with justification, adoption addresses our standing before God, rather than our spiritual condition. Adoption is a forensic, legal act by the Father which constitutes those united to Christ as His children. The status of the Second Person of the Trinity, the eternal Son by nature, is unique and can be shared by no one, but believers are given the status of children adopted into the family of God by grace.[58] The distinction is indicated in Christ's careful choice of words when he says, 'I am returning to my Father and your Father, to my God and your God' (John 20:17). Nevertheless no higher privilege could be granted to sinners.

We should ask at this point what is the relationship between adoption and regeneration. In an article written a few years ago Tim Trumper argued that in the writings of John sonship is described in terms of new birth and new nature, whilst in the writings of Paul it is described in terms of status and freedom. His contention is that Paul's adoption metaphor is unique to the apostle, and concludes, 'The Johannine and Pauline metaphors are best treated separately for the simple reason that as vehicles of discovery they are not compatible.'[59] Each metaphor, he argues, performs a distinct function.

It has to be admitted that some covenant theologians have not distinguished between these two concepts as clearly as they should, and on occasion verses are cited as proof texts for adoption which seem in fact to relate to the new birth. Others, however, have noted the distinction and have sought to make biblically supported connections. Girardeau, for example, argues that

> Regeneration is a *real translation*; adoption a *formal translation*. Regeneration *adapts* us to our place in God's family; adoption *formally introduces* us into it. Regeneration *makes* us God's children; adoption *recognizes* and *treats* us as his children.[60]

Whilst there is truth in what Girardeau says, he does run the risk of reducing the significance of adoption as the gate of entry to the family of God. John Murray's more cautious statement is to be preferred:

> When God adopts men and women into his family he insures that not only may they have the rights and privileges of his sons and daughters but also the nature or disposition consonant with such a status. This he does by regeneration – God never has in his family those who are alien to its atmosphere and spirit and station.[61]

The believer's heart should be filled with rejoicing and thanksgiving when he considers the blessings granted to God's adopted children. So many things that people today are desperately searching for in the philosophies and therapies of the world are provided in abundant measure by the Lord for His covenant children. The Westminster Confession of Faith speaks of 'the liberties and privileges of the children of God' (Chapter XII), but they are so wide-ranging that a complete list could not be drawn up. A helpful and thought-provoking selection of some of our privileges is provided by Wilhelmus à Brakel:

1. God cherishes us with a fatherly love; e.g. Ephesians 2:4
2. God has his eye upon us to keep us from evil; e.g. Psalm 121:3-8

3. He cares for us in all needs of body and soul; e.g. Psalm 23:1, 5-6
4. He has compassion on us in all our ailments; e.g. Psalm 10:14
5. He hears and answers us; e.g. Luke 11:13
6. Since we are his children, we are free from the Covenant of Works, from the old ceremonial administration, from the power of Satan, from the dominion of sin and from eternal punishment
7. We are heirs of all the benefits of the Covenant of Grace.[62]

This final benefit is spoken of in Romans 8:17, 'Now if we are children, then we are heirs – heirs of God and co-heirs with Christ.' This verse serves also to indicate the further blessing that Christ has by grace become our adopted brother.

In Christ we have a brother who loved us from eternity, who gave Himself for us so that we might be brought into the family of God and who is united to us in an indissoluble bond. How precious it is to be able to read in Hebrews 2:11 'Both the one who makes men holy and those who are made holy are of the same family. So Jesus is not ashamed to call them brothers.' Since He knows fully the depths of our sin, we could well understand why He might be ashamed of us, yet He is not. Instead He loves us with an infinite love. Tracing the unfolding of the 'brotherliness' of Jesus, Mark Johnston concludes, 'The final frame in this sequence, so to speak, is the Brother who shares in the joy of the Father who presides over his reunited family and who eternally is the living link between these children and their God.'[63]

This quotation reminds us that adoption has what we may call an 'eschatological' dimension: in other words, its completion is bound up with the return of Christ and the end of the world in its present form. The 'co-heirs' can look forward to receiving the 'inheritance that can never perish, spoil or fade' (1 Pet. 1:4), the full blessings of salvation which our Surety has purchased and which are promised to us in the Covenant of Grace. In particular, the resurrection is linked with adoption in Romans 8:23, 'we ourselves, who have the firstfruits of the

Spirit, groan inwardly as we wait eagerly for our adoption as
sons, the redemption of our bodies.' God's adopted children
will enjoy the glories prepared for them with perfected bodies
as well as perfected souls, as complete people.

Romans 8:23 also reminds us that the role of the Holy Spirit
in adoption should not be overlooked. As always, each Person
of the Trinity fulfils an appropriate role in conferring this
blessing. Thus earlier in Romans 8 we read, 'For you did not
receive a spirit that makes you a slave again to fear, but you
received the Spirit of sonship. And by him we cry "Abba,
Father"' (v. 15). It is the Holy Spirit who stirs in believers an
awareness of their standing as children of God. Paul goes on to
speak of the witness of the Spirit in believers: 'The Spirit himself
testifies with our spirit that we are God's children' (v. 16). The
precise nature of this witness has exercised theologians of all
varieties for centuries. Some covenant theologians have insisted
that the Spirit's role is indirect, enabling believers to discern
marks of grace in their lives and to understand the relevance of
biblical teaching on adoption to themselves. Girardeau, however,
argues convincingly that the witness of the Spirit is 'an
immediate certification made to believers of the fact of their
adoption'[64], a view which he traces back to the Reformers. As
he points out, the Spirit's witness is said to be alongside and
'with' the witness of the believer's own spirit. The Spirit surely
enables God's children to recognize Him as their Father in a
variety of situations – in prayer, in meditating on the promises,
in seeing the fruit of His grace in their lives, indeed in any
situation where a believer enjoys fellowship with His Father.

The role of the Holy Spirit is described in various ways in
the New Testament. In Ephesians 1:14 He is 'a deposit
guaranteeing our inheritance', a further significant use of legal
sonship terminology, and in verse 13 believers are said to be
'sealed' with the Spirit. The same expression is found in
Ephesians 4:30, 'the Holy Spirit of God, with whom you were
sealed for the day of redemption', whilst the Spirit is again
termed the 'deposit guaranteeing what is to come' in 2

Corinthians 5:5. The confirmation of the believer's position and privileges as an adopted child of God is a vital part of the Holy Spirit's ministry.

A well grounded assurance

For many Christians at different points in their lives assurance of salvation can be a significant problem. The Westminster Confession of Faith recognizes that infallible assurance 'doth not so belong to the essence of faith, but that a true believer may wait long and conflict with many difficulties, before he be partaker of it' (XVIII.3). Nevertheless the Confession rightly recognizes that assurance *is* possible.

The truths we have considered in the last two chapters provide a solid foundation for a Christian to have a well grounded assurance of salvation. As 1 John indicates, there is a place in assurance for the recognition of the fruit of God's grace in our lives, particularly in love for God and love for fellow believers (e.g. 1 John 4:16-21). That line of evidence on its own, however, could easily lead to an unhealthy introspection and the destruction of assurance on account of the lack of fruit often apparent in professing Christians. Thus John also emphasizes the need for right belief, concentrating on the identity of Christ (e.g. 1 John 4:2). The subjective tests must be balanced by the objective.

In this respect Covenant Theology is of great assistance. We have considered the work of Christ as our Surety in the Covenant of Redemption and the application of that work in the Covenant of Grace in terms of faith and repentance, union with Christ, justification and adoption. It is on Christ and His covenant-work that the believer seeking assurance should fix his attention. The Confession of Faith alludes to 'the divine truth of the promises of salvation' (XVIII.2) and at the centre of all these promises is Christ. The more fully the believer understands who Christ is and what He has done for His people, the stronger will his assurance be.

The fact that the work of Christ and its application are

covenantal underlines their unshakeable certainty. As Malcolm Watts expresses it, 'covenanted promises guarantee the believer's perseverance in grace and his eternal security.'[65] The same truth is stated in these terms by Puritan theologian John Flavel: 'God's single promise is security enough to our faith, but his covenant of grace adds further security; both these, viewed as the effects and fruits of this covenant of redemption, make all fast and secure.'[66]

As the Holy Spirit bears witness with the believer's spirit (Rom. 8:16) and enables him to grasp the promises with joy and love, his attention will necessarily focus on Christ. Samuel Rutherford understood this well. Referring to the covenant between Father and Son as the Covenant of Suretyship, he says, 'the Covenant of Suretyship is the cause of the stability and firmnesse of the Covenant of Grace'[67], and he concludes, 'faith principally must be fixed upon the most binding Covenant-relation between Jehovah and the Son of God. Eye Christ always in the covenant.'[68] For any child of God that surely is a most precious application of Covenant Theology that he must daily make as he awaits the time when he will see his Covenant Lord face to face.

Notes

1. Samuel Rutherford, *The Trial and Triumph of Faith*, 1645 edition (Glasgow, 1845), p. 87.

2. ibid.

3. ibid.

4. John Murray, *Redemption Accomplished and Applied* (Grand Rapids, 1955), p. 113.

5. Samuel Rutherford, op. cit., p. 94.

6. Various possibilities are examined by Robert L. Reymond in *A New Systematic Theology of the Christian Faith* (Nashville, 1998), p. 732.

7. John Calvin, *Institutes of the Christian Religion*, 1559 edition, translated by Ford Lewis Battles (Philadelphia, 1960), III.ii.7.

8. Daniel L. Migliore, 'Faith' in *Encyclopedia of the Reformed Faith*, edited

by Donald K. McKim and David F. Wright (Louisville and Edinburgh, 1992), p. 133.

9. Herman Witsius, *The Economy of the Covenants Between God and Man*, 1677 edition, translated by William Crookshank (Escondido, 1990), III.7.1.

10. Robert Rollock, *A Treatise of God's Effectual Calling*, 1603 edition, translated by H. Holland, in *Select Works of Robert Rollock* (Edinburgh, 1849), pp. 198-9 (ch. 29).

11. For a helpful discussion of the Greek terms used for 'believing' in the New Testament see Robert L. Reymond, op. cit., pp. 726-9.

12. Robert Rollock, op. cit., p. 199.

13. J. I. Packer, *God's Words* (Leicester, 1981), p. 130.

14. Robert Rollock, op. cit., p. 197.

15. Herman Witsius, op. cit., III.7.23.

16. ibid.

17. See e.g. Zane C. Hodges, *Absolutely Free! A Biblical Reply to Lordship Salvation* (Grand Rapids, 1989), and, from an earlier day, Charles Ryrie, *Balancing the Christian Life* (Chicago, 1969).

18. Thorough responses are to be found in e.g. Ernest C. Reisinger, *Lord and Christ* (Phillipsburg, 1994) and in various works by John F. MacArthur, including *The Gospel according to Jesus*, 2nd edition (Grand Rapids, 1994).

19. Ernest C. Reisinger, op. cit., pp. 48-9.

20. John Murray, op. cit., p. 112.

21. Samuel Rutherford, op. cit., pp. 299ff.

22. John Murray, op. cit., pp. 107-10.

23. Robert Rollock, op. cit., p. 241.

24. Zane C. Hodges, op. cit., p. 144.

25. Robert L. Reymond, op. cit., p. 722, footnote 22.

26. Thomas Boston in *Human Nature in its Fourfold State*, 1850 edition (London, 1964), adds to this list peace, growth in grace, fruitfulness, acceptance of this fruit of holiness before the Lord, establishment (i.e. perseverance), support and the special care of the Husbandman (John 15:1-2).

27. See John Murray, op. cit., pp. 171-2.

28. A. A. Hoekema, *Saved by Grace* (Grand Rapids and Exeter, 1989), p. 59.

29. Thomas Boston, op. cit., p. 254.

30. John Murray, op. cit., p. 165.

31. Thomas Boston, *A View of the Covenant of Grace*, 1734 edition (Lewes, 1990), p. 109.

32. The standard academic history of the doctrine is *Iustitia Dei* by Alister E. McGrath, 2nd edition (Cambridge, 1998). For the Reformation doctrine of justification see also *The Doctrine of Justification* by James Buchanan, 1867 edition (Grand Rapids, 1977), pp. 100-126.

33. John Murray, *The Epistle to the Romans*, 1968 edition (Grand Rapids and Cambridge, 1997), volume 1, appendix A, pp. 336-62.

34. Robert L. Reymond, op. cit., p. 745.

35. John Murray, *Redemption*, p. 121.

36. John Murray, *Redemption*, p. 123.

37. Charles Hodge, *Systematic Theology*, 1871-3 edition (Grand Rapids, 1977), 3.142.

38. Francis Turretin, *Institutes of Elenctic Theology*, translated by G. M. Giger (Phillipsburg, 1992), Locus 16, Q3 (2.647).

39. Wilhelmus à Brakel, *The Christian's Reasonable Service*, 1700 edition, translated by Bartel Elshout (Ligonier, 1992), vol. 2, ch. 34, p. 351.

40. John Calvin, *Institutes*, III.xi.7.

41. Robert L. Reymond, op. cit., p. 745.

42. e.g. Francis Turretin, op. cit., Locus 16, Q7 (2.675).

43. James Buchanan, op. cit., p. 384.

44. See e.g. Robert L. Reymond, op. cit., pp. 748-50.

45. The Canons and Dogmatic Decrees of the Council of Trent can be found in *The Creeds of Christendom*, edited by Philip Schaff, 6th edition, 1931 (Grand Rapids, 1983), 2.77-206. For the Decree on Justification, see pp. 89-118.

46. *Catechism of the Catholic Church* (Dublin, 1994). On justification, see pp. 432-4.

47. This task is performed by Philip H. Eveson, *The Great Exchange* (London, 1996), ch. 7, and by R. C. Sproul, *By Faith Alone* (London, 1995).

48. Consideration of the document is provided by Eveson and by Sproul in the works previously cited.

49. For N. T. Wright's views see e.g. *The Climax of the Covenant* (Edinburgh, 1991).

50. Philip H. Eveson, op. cit., chs. 9-10.

51. Robert L. Reymond, op. cit., p. 743. A few Reformed writers have held

that justification took place in eternity. The biblical view is stated by Samuel Rutherford: 'Justification is a forensical sentence in time pronounced in the gospel, and applied to me now, and never till the instant now that I believe' (*The Trial and Triumph of Faith*), p. 94.

52. An important extended discussion of adoption is John L. Girardeau's paper 'The Doctrine of Adoption' in *Discussions of Theological Questions*, 1905 edition, (Harrisonburg, 1986), pp. 428-521. At a more popular level is Mark Johnston's study *Child of a King* (Fearn, 1997).

53. John Murray, *Redemption*, p. 170.

54. Robert L. Reymond, op. cit., p. 760.

55. Robert S. Candlish, *The Fatherhood of God*, 3rd edition, (Edinburgh, 1866), pp. 103ff.

56. John L. Girardeau, op. cit., pp. 433-72. J. H. Thornwell also held Candlish's view.

57. John Murray, *Redemption*, p. 170.

58. Candlish argued that believers are brought into a relationship with the Father which is essentially the same as that between Father and Son. It is not 'anything less, or anything else, than participation with Christ in his sonship' (op. cit., p. 31).

59. Tim Trumper, 'The Metaphorical Import of Adoption: A Plea for Realisation. I: The Adoption Metaphor in Biblical Usage' in *Scottish Bulletin of Evangelical Theology*, 14:2 (Autumn, 1996), p. 143.

60. John L. Girardeau, op. cit., p. 475.

61. John Murray, *Redemption*, p. 133.

62. Wilhelmus à Brakel, op. cit., pp. 421-7.

63. Mark Johnston, op. cit., p. 80-1.

64. John L. Girardeau, op. cit., p. 499.

65. Malcolm Watts, 'Introduction' to Thomas Boston's *A View of the Covenant of Grace* (Lewes, 1990), no page number.

66. John Flavel, *The Fountain of Life*, 1671 edition (Grand Rapids, 1977), ch. 3, p. 38.

67. Samuel Rutherford, *The Covenant of Life Opened*, (Edinburgh, 1655), part 2, ch. 8, p. 309.

68. ibid.

8

The Way of Holiness

In 1 Thessalonians 4:3 Paul states that 'this is the will of God, your sanctification' (NASB). Holiness is a pervasive theme throughout the Bible. Hebrews 12:14 reminds Christians that 'without holiness no-one will see the Lord', and Peter reminds his readers of God's command, 'Be holy, because I am holy' (1 Peter 1:16, quoting Old Testament texts such as Leviticus 11:44,45). Clearly it is essential the God's covenant people should be holy people.

The reason for this is not difficult to find: those who are in covenant with a holy God must share in his holiness. Although God's eternal covenant love was set upon sinners, he does not and cannot leave them in that condition. In the previous chapter we have seen how the elect, on the basis of the atoning work of Christ, are justified, counted as righteous, in the sight of God. Justification deals with the believer's standing before God; it is a single act by which the guilt and punishment of sin are removed; it is an essential part of our being made holy people. Nevertheless, as Samuel Rutherford points out, justification 'is not an abolition of sin in its real essence and physical indwelling'.[1] Having performed a work *for* us, God must also perform a work *in* us, so that the very presence of sin in God's people is progressively destroyed. Justification must be, and inevitably will be, followed by sanctification.

As we noted in our discussion of justification, Roman Catholicism blurs the distinction between justification and sanctification. They are, however, entirely distinct even though inseparable. In addition to the distinctions already mentioned, Swiss theologian Johannes Wollebius adds that 'in justification the righteousness of Christ is imputed to us, in sanctification a new and inherent righteousness is infused into us'. [2] The former takes place outside the believer, the latter within him and with his co-operation. This chapter examines sanctification and related issues such as the Law of God.

A holy God

Our covenant God is holy: of that there can be no doubt. Throughout the Bible God is described as holy. To take but one example, the prophet Isaiah regularly refers to the Lord as 'the Holy One of Israel' (e.g. Isa. 1:4; 5:19,24), and in Isaiah's vision of the Lord the seraphim cry, 'Holy, holy, holy is the LORD Almighty' (Isa. 6:3). Examples could be multiplied from all parts of Scripture.

What, then, is holiness? In the Old Testament holiness is described by words derived from the verb *qadash*. Often it is said that the basic meaning of the verb is 'to cut' or 'to separate', but the evidence, according to one modern authority, 'makes any positive conclusion in this regard difficult.' [3] What can be said is that holiness is 'the essential nature of that which belongs to the sphere of the sacred and which is thus distinct from the common or profane.' [4] In the New Testament the words derived from the Greek term *hagios* take up and build upon this background. God and all that belongs to him are 'holy'. Thus Jesus is fittingly described as holy, as for example in Luke 1:35: 'So the holy one to be born will be called the Son of God.' As Hebrews 4:15 states, he was 'tempted in every way, just as we are – yet was without sin.' It is, of course, in the New Testament that the ministry of the Holy Spirit comes into clear focus, and Horst Seebass has argued that the 'concept of holiness in the NT is determined rather by the Holy Spirit, the gift of the new Age'. [5]

It is clear that God himself is holy and everything related to him is consequently holy: his name is holy (Lev. 20:3), his word is holy (Ps. 105:42, 'he remembered his holy promise'), his covenant is holy (Dan.11:28). It is the relationship to God that confers holiness on anything. Dutch theologian Herman Bavinck sums this up well when he states that 'people and things are never by nature themselves holy, but can become this only through a definite action which accrues to them. Nor can they sanctify themselves, for all holiness and sanctification proceeds from God. Jehovah is holy, and therefore He wants a holy people, a holy priesthood, a holy temple.'[6]

Since this is so, it is no surprise that in a covenant relationship with God sinners are transformed into holy people, and that the Lord himself is the standard and agent of such sanctification.

What is sanctification?

The word 'sanctification' itself indicates its meaning: it is a *making holy*. Saved sinners are not only given a righteous standing before God (in justification), they are also made actually holy in the gradual process of sanctification. Wollebius defines sanctification in this way:

> It is the free act of God, by which the faithful, who are engrafted into Christ through faith and justified through the Holy Spirit, are progressively set free from their innate sinfulness and restored to his image, so that they may be made fit to glorify him by good works.[7]

We may also turn to the definition given by the Westminster Confession of Faith (XIII.I), where the Divines state that those who have been effectually called and regenerated are 'further sanctified, really and personally, through the virtue of Christ's death and resurrection, by His Word and Spirit dwelling in them: the dominion of the whole body of sin is destroyed, and the several lusts thereof are more and more weakened and mortified; and they more and more quickened and strengthened in all saving graces, to the practice of true holiness, without which no man shall see the Lord.'

Some of these themes will be taken up in the following sections, but it is important to stress at this point that sanctification is something far more profound and radical than the elimination of bad habits (even thoroughly evil habits) and the cultivation of good ones in their place. The latter view betrays a superficial understanding of the nature of the sin that has to be dealt with in believers. In Reformation days heretics such as the Socinians denied the innate depravity of man's nature after the Fall, and it was in answer to such false teaching that Francis Turretin argued that sanctification 'consists in a change and renovation of the nature itself (corrupted by original sin) by which depraved qualities and habits are cast out and good ones infused so that the man desists from evil acts and strives for good.'[8] As our study unfolds, we will see that the radical view of sanctification held by covenant theologians provides the word of hope so urgently needed by believers struggling with temptation and sin. By the grace of our covenant God, victory is possible.

The covenant context of holiness is important. God's people are to live as they do because of their relationship with him. Thus we read in Leviticus 20:26: 'You are to be holy to me because I, the LORD, am holy and I have set you apart from the nations to be my own.' It is on the basis of their being a people in covenant with a holy God that Israelites are to live holy lives. No doubt this verse echoes God's call to his people in Leviticus 19:2: 'Be holy, because I, the LORD your God, am holy.' In dealing with the latter verse, Dutch commentator A. Noordtzij states:

> The continual reminder of the bond that the covenant had established between the Lord and Israel serves notice to the people that they were at all times to bear in mind both the privileges and the obligations that derived from this special relationship. The common basis of these privileges and obligations lies in Israel's calling to manifest the fullness of life that comes from obeying the Lord's law, which forms an expression of the holiness of His divine nature.[9]

Such requirements are not confined to Old Testament Israel. The promise of the New Covenant given in Jeremiah 31 includes the specific promise, 'I will put my law in their minds and write it on their hearts.' The promise is taken up and quoted in, for example, Hebrews 8:10, 10:16 and 13:20-21. Holiness is still vital for the covenant people. As Peter Lillback says, 'The new era in no way diminishes God's demand for a covenant-keeping people. Hence the new covenant itself promises the ability to keep the covenant as one of its greatest benefits.'[10]

Holiness entails faithfulness to God's covenant requirements, and, as we shall see, it is itself one of the blessings of the covenant. When believers are summoned, using the language of the Old Testament, 'Therefore come out from them and be separate. . . . Touch no unclean thing and I will receive you' (2 Cor. 6:17), the context is one of God's covenant with his people and the 'therefore' of verse 17 refers to the covenant promise of verse 16: 'I will live with them and walk among them, and I will be their God and they will be my people.' As we will have occasion to stress when considering the place of God's law in sanctification, covenant grace precedes covenant obedience. To understand sanctification correctly, we must begin with God.

Definitive sanctification

According to Ephesians 1:4 the elect were chosen in Christ by the Father 'to be holy and blameless in his sight'. Election was with a view to holiness. Those given to Christ the Surety in the Covenant are to be made holy people.

Although sanctification is often thought of solely in terms of a *process* that unfolds gradually in the Christian's experience, it is vital to grasp that according to Scripture there is a sense in which every believer *has been sanctified* already. In Romans 6 this is made strikingly clear by Paul's use of the language of death and resurrection: 'We died to sin' (v. 2), 'our old self (or 'the old man') was crucified with him' (v. 6), 'count yourselves dead to sin but alive to God in Christ Jesus' (v. 11). A different image reinforces the same point in verse 18: 'You have been set free from sin and have become slaves to righteousness.' Clearly a fundamental breach with sin has taken place: its dominion has been broken as far as God's covenant people are concerned. A decisive change has taken place which lays the foundation for the gradual process of transformation that will follow. In a profound sense we can say that believers are now sanctified. As Paul says of the Corinthians, 'But you were washed, you were sanctified' (1 Cor. 6:11). We can call this 'definitive sanctification'.

Justification and adoption have already been shown to flow from the believer's union with Christ as his Surety and representative in the Covenant of Grace. In the same way, sanctification is the fruit of union with Christ. Those who are united to Christ in his death and resurrection are delivered from the enslaving power of sin. That is the central thrust of Paul's argument in Romans 6. Union with Christ destroys union with sin: the two cannot coexist. Behind the bondage that sin exercised stands the lordship of Satan who has usurped authority over sinners. By his atoning work Christ has broken the power of Satan over the elect and so Jesus was able to proclaim as he approached the cross: 'Now is the time for judgement on this world; now the prince of this world will be driven out' (John 12:31). Believers experience the power of that victory when the dominion of sin over them is irreversibly destroyed.

After surveying the relevant New Testament evidence, this is how John Murray sums up the precious truth of definitive sanctification:

> We are compelled to reach the conclusion that it is by virtue of our having died with Christ, and our being raised with him in his resurrection from the dead, that the decisive breach with sin in its power, control and defilement has been wrought, and that the reason for this is that Christ in his death and resurrection broke the power of sin, triumphed over the god of this world, the prince of darkness, executed judgement upon the world and its ruler, and by that victory delivered all those who were united to him from the power of darkness, and translated them into his own kingdom. So intimate is the union between Christ and his people, that they were partakers with him in all these triumphal achievements, and therefore died to sin, rose with Christ in the power of his resurrection, and have their fruit unto holiness, and the end everlasting life. [11]

The fatal blow was struck at Calvary, but, as is the case with justification and adoption, the elect do not receive their sanctification until conversion. Until then they are sinners, unholy, 'children of wrath, even as others' (Eph. 2:3, AV).

The apostle Paul expressed the same truth about definitive sanctification in striking terms in Galatians 2:20: 'I have been crucified with Christ and I no longer live, but Christ lives in me.' That which has been crucified is dead. What is termed 'the old man' in Romans 6:6 is dead. So too in Colossians 3:3 Paul says, 'For you died, and your life is now hidden with Christ in God.' It is therefore unhelpful to speak, as some covenant theologians do,[12] of Christians having two natures, a regenerate and an unregenerate, an old and a new. Such statements obscure the decisive nature of what has taken place already by virtue of union with Christ. It is certainly true that sin remains in believers. There is much of the 'old man' that still clings to him, for example in ungodly habits and thought-patterns. He may live in ways that are inconsistent with his being a new creation in Christ (2 Cor. 5:17). His new nature is not perfectly holy as yet, hence the need for growth in holiness. Nevertheless Colossians 3:9-10 describes the true state of affairs, namely, that 'you have taken off your old self with its practices and have put on the new self, which is being renewed in knowledge in the image of its Creator'.

The fact that a Christian has a new nature which has been freed from the bondage of sin should be of great encouragement to every child of God. Even though he struggles with temptation and sin, he knows that the decisive blow has been struck. Romans 6:14 ('For sin shall not be your master') is a promise that should give the believer fresh heart for the battle: the victory has been secured by his Lord. However hard the struggle, he will never return to the prison of sin from which Christ has released him. The challenge of this truth is also evident: when a believer surrenders to temptation, he has no excuse. He has chosen to live as if he were still in bondage. He has all the resources necessary to stand firm from Christ the Mediator of the Covenant of Grace 'who has become for us wisdom from God – that is, our righteousness, holiness and redemption' (1 Cor. 1:30).

Progressive sanctification

Although the dominion of sin has been broken in the lives of God's covenant people, much sin remains in each of them and it must be dealt with ruthlessly. Sin in a Christian is still sin, and indeed it is worse when found in someone who has the privileges and resources that a Christian has. It is a grave matter to sin against your covenant Lord, the one who loved you and gave himself for you (Gal. 2:20). Nevertheless, as the apostle John shows, no believer is free from sin: 'If we claim to be without sin, we deceive ourselves and the truth is not in us' (1 John 1:8). He goes on to show that there is therefore an ongoing need for confession, forgiveness and cleansing by the blood of Christ (v. 9).

We must keep these statements of John in mind when we read later in 1 John 3:6 (NASB): 'No-one who abides in Him sins; no-one who sins has seen Him or knows Him.' This appears to be contradictory of his earlier statements. John cannot be claiming sinless perfection for believers: he repeatedly and emphatically denies such an achievement in this life. The NIV seeks to resolve the problem by translating the present tense Greek verbs (correctly) as continuous: 'No-one who lives in him keeps on sinning. No-one who continues to sin has either seen him or known him.' Such a statement is entirely consistent with what we have said about definitive sanctification. The decisive break with sin has been made: anyone who continues to sin habitually is denying in practice that he has experienced that victory. As Simon Kistemaker comments, John 'knows that the believer is no longer in the grip of sin, for his life is controlled by Christ (compare Gal 2:20).'[13] So it is that John can go on to say, 'No-one who is born of God will continue to sin, because God's seed remains in him; he cannot go on sinning because he has been born of God' (1 John 3:9). Definitive sanctification and progressive sanctification must be held together in biblical harmony.

To commit sin is to break our covenant obligation to be holy people. Such covenant-breaking must be dealt with by the only possible means – the application of the atoning blood of the Mediator. Thus we read in 1 John 1:7 that 'the blood of Jesus, his Son, purifies us from all sin'. As the present tense of the Greek verb shows, that blood 'keeps on' cleansing – continually and repeatedly. Verse 9 of the same chapter reminds us that God is 'faithful and just' and so will forgive. He is 'faithful' to his covenant promises of forgiveness for the repentant; he is 'just' in forgiving sin on the basis of the price paid by the Lord Jesus Christ. The Covenant of Grace provides our hope of cleansing.

More is required, however, than a remedy for believers' sins. A growth in positive holiness is also necessary, and indeed is the heart longing of every child of God. It is a mark of grace when we want to increase in holiness. Our goal must be to reproduce the ethical holiness of God. We recall the summons of 1 Peter 1:16, 'Be holy, because I am holy.' Consequently, on a number of occasions, imitation of God is made the ground for ethical exhortation. Thus in relation to showing mercy, believers are told, 'Be perfect, therefore, as your heavenly Father is perfect' (Matt. 5:48). Note also Ephesians 4:32: 'Be kind and compassionate to one another, forgiving each other, just as in Christ God forgave you.' God's requirements are spelled out in detail in his covenant law, which we will consider futher in a later section.

The goal of the process of sanctification for the covenant people of God can also be stated in another way: we are to become more and more like Christ, the Mediator of the Covenant of Grace. This is brought out clearly in 2 Corinthians 3:18 (NASB) which describes how 'we all, with unveiled face, beholding as in a mirror the glory of the Lord, are being transformed into the same image from glory to glory'. Christ is himself the pattern according to which progressive sanctification unfolds. As John

Murray puts it, 'the goal of the whole redemptive process, as it has respect to the people of God, is conformity to the image of Christ as the firstborn among many brethren.'[14] Renewal in the likeness of Christ is crucial to the whole work of redemption.

Christians thus have the most practical pattern for their sanctification that could possibly be given. In Christ they see one who lived a life of perfect holiness under the conditions of human life in a fallen world. Their pattern is one who was 'tempted in every way, just as we are – yet was without sin' (Heb. 4:15). The fact that he endured temptation without capitulating means that he knows the power of temptation to a degree that no-one does who surrenders part-way through the struggle.

By the grace of God, the holiness of Christ is to be reproduced in each of his people in their particular individual circumstances. The exhortation of 1 John 2:6 is clear and direct: 'Whoever claims to live in [God] must walk as Jesus walked.' The metaphor of life as a walk is common in the New Testament and emphasises the call of God to a sustained pursuit of holiness. On several occasions Christ is said to be an 'example' for believers. In 1 Peter 2:21 the apostle states that 'Christ suffered for you, leaving you an example, that you should follow in his steps'. The term employed by Peter (*hupogrammos*) was used for 'the faint outlines of letters which were traced over by pupils learning to write, then also of the sets of letters written at the top of a page or other piece of writing material to be copied repeatedly by the learner on the rest of the page.'[15] It illustrates in a vivid way the place Christ occupies in our sanctification. Using a different Greek word, the Lord himself speaks in these terms in the Upper Room after washing the disciples feet: 'I have set you an example that you should do as I have done for you' (John 13:15). Believers are of course not to reproduce the actions of Christ which were specific to his atoning work, but they are to imitate the holy living which was characteristic of his whole life.

Sanctification does not deal only with outward actions.

Throughout the Bible we are confronted with the principle stated in 1 Samuel 16:7: 'the LORD looks at the heart.' Sanctification therefore deals with the source of our actions, namely, the 'heart', which in biblical language denotes man's inmost being. Thought-life must be sanctified. Thus Paul exhorts, 'Have this attitude in yourselves which was also in Christ Jesus' (Phil. 2:5, NASB), as he goes on to speak of Christ's humbling of himself for his earthly ministry. Values, attitudes, ambitions, the whole life of the mind is to be conformed to Christ.

In the New Testament knowledge and love are particularly highlighted. Thus Paul's prayer for the Ephesians is that they may know God better (Eph. 1:17). Knowledge of the truth, applied to the heart by the Holy Spirit, will produce holy living. Christians are consequently to fill their minds with 'whatever is true, whatever is noble, whatever is right, whatever is pure, whatever is lovely, whatever is admirable' (Phil. 4:8). Love is also essential: 'God is love. Whoever lives in love lives in God, and God in him' (1 John 4:16). The whole of 1 John shows the central role that love for God and for others plays in the Christian life. Still the focus is on Christ, for 'love is fed by the increasing apprehension of the glory of him who is love, and of him in whom the love of God is manifested'.[16]

Mention of love serves as a reminder that sanctification is not a solitary pursuit. Believers grow in holiness in the context of the Church, the covenant community that is the fruit of divine grace. Scripture always thinks of the children of God as part of a body of believers. Their saving union with Christ is to be expressed in a visible union with one another. To grow in holiness they need the instruction, love, encouragement and rebukes of other believers. A solitary Christian is a weak and vulnerable Christian. Furthermore, as John Murray points out, 'sanctification itself is a process that moves to a consummation which will not be realized for the individual until the whole body of Christ is complete and presented in its totality faultless and without blemish.'[17] More will be said in the next chapter about the covenant community of the Church, but it is important to emphasise that sanctification must be understood in a community context, especially in view of the extreme individualism of much of western culture which has influenced many Christians. Sanctification is not a call for rugged individualists who believe that they need help from nobody.

Not only is Christ the pattern for believers' sanctification, but he is also the source of that growth in holiness. Sanctification flows from our union with the Mediator as surely as do justification and adoption. As Robert Reymond says, 'Christians can no more sanctify themselves by their own efforts that can sinners justify themselves by their own efforts.'[18] Christ powerfully illustrates this fact in his use of the analogy of the vine and the branches in John 15, from which he concludes, 'Without me you can do nothing.' In Greek a double negative is used which reinforces the point: you can do *absolutely nothing*. Paul acknowledges the same fact in Galatians 2:20: 'I have been crucified with Christ and I no longer live, but Christ lives in me. The life I live in the body, I live by faith in the Son of God, who loved me and gave himself for me.'

Union with Christ is crucial for sanctification, progressive as well as definitive. This is how Herman Witsius expresses it:

> For [Christ] being raised from the dead, has received, not only for himself a new and a glorious life, but a fountain of a new and holy life for all his people; from which, by a continued influence, the most refreshing streams flow to all his members.[19]

New sanctifying life has its source in Christ the Mediator, crucified and risen. 'The hand is not more dependent on the head for the continuance of spiritual life in the soul,'[20] comments Charles Hodge. Again there is great encouragement for believers in this, since it gives us the assurance that the resources needed for sanctification have been provided in Christ, to whom we are inseparably united.

The role of the Holy Spirit in the sanctification of believers is also vital. He is, after all, the *Holy* Spirit – he *is* holy and he *makes* holy. Thus in Romans 1:4 he is designated 'the Spirit of holiness'. The sanctifying influences of the Mediator are conveyed to his covenant people by the Holy Spirit who was the agent of their regeneration. This is how Wilhelmus à Brakel sums up the matter: 'the Holy Spirit, having infused the spiritual life in [believers] at regeneration, maintains that life by His continual influence, stirs it up, activates it, and causes it to function in harmony with its spiritual nature.'[21] Believers are entirely dependent on the working of the Spirit who indwells them for all their growth in grace. As Puritan Thomas Watson puts it picturesquely: 'Weeds grow of themselves. Flowers are planted. Sanctification is a flower of the Spirit's planting.'[22]

There is always an element of mystery about the working of the Holy Spirit, a dimension that is beyond our grasp. It is so with reference to regeneration and it is so with reference to sanctification. Undoubtedly his activity is indicated in Philippians 2:13: 'it is God who works in you to will and to act according to his good purpose.' Evidently the Spirit so works in believers that they desire holiness, he moulds their thinking as they take into their minds the Word of God and he enables them to obey the requirements of the covenant. Progressively he transforms believers into the likeness of Christ. It would seem to be his ministry that is described in 2 Corinthians 3:18 when Paul says that believers 'are being transformed into [the Lord's] likeness with ever-increasing glory, which comes from the Lord, who is the Spirit'.[23] However this verse is to be understood, the agency of the Holy Spirit in believers' sanctification is clear throughout the New Testament.

It must not be thought that the covenant people of God are to be passive in sanctification. Far from it. The Lord's summons is '*Be* holy.' Action is called for. This is evident from the verse preceding Philippians 2:13, the latter verse having been quoted in the previous paragraph in relation to the Holy Spirit's work. The text reads, 'Therefore, my dear friends, as you have always obeyed – not only in my presence, but now much more in my absence – continue to work out your salvation with fear and trembling' (Phil. 2:12). This is not, of course, a call to earn or achieve salvation. Rather 'your own salvation' is to be understood, as Alec Motyer says, 'not as an objective yet to be reached, certainly not as a benefit to be merited, but as a possession to be explored and enjoyed ever more fully.'[24] Christians are to work out in practice the implications for conduct of their having been saved by God's grace. They must 'carry it to its conclusion, thoroughly digest it, and apply it to day-by-day living,' as William Hendriksen comments. [25]

Sanctification is a process in which God and the believer are both involved. It must not, however, be thought of as a partnership in which each party contributes a percentage to the final product. The biblical pattern is well expressed by John Murray:

> God works in us and we also work. But the relation is that because God works we work. All working out of salvation on our part is the effect of God's working in us, not the willing to the exclusion of the doing and not the doing to the exclusion of the willing, but both the willing and the doing.[26]

The word 'for' linking verses twelve and thirteen is essential for understanding this relationship.

Believers must strive diligently to be holy: 'Make every effort to live in peace with all men and to be holy; without holiness no-one will see the Lord' (Heb. 12:14). Their best effort is required. All their activity must spring from faith in Christ their covenant Head, and it is only by faith that they can receive the grace needed to pursue holiness. As Herman Bavinck says, 'It is by no means in justification only, but quite as much in sanctification, that by faith exclusively we are saved.' [27]

By that faith believers are to make use of the 'means of grace' that God provides, such as his Word, prayer, the sacraments and the fellowship of the covenant community. As the Holy Spirit blesses these means to believers, they are progressively transformed into the image of Christ. Pre-eminent among these means is the inspired Word of God. Jesus as our High Priest prays, 'Sanctify them by the truth; your word is truth' (John

17:17), and Paul speaks of Christ's giving himself for his Church 'to make her holy, cleansing her by the washing with water through the word' (Eph. 5:26). Diligent study of and obedience to the Word of God is vital to sanctification, a fact which underlines the folly of contemporary Christians' relative neglect of serious Bible study. The following words from Wilhelmus à Brakel indicate something of the scope of the Word's ministry to believers:

> It is there that sins are held forth in their abominable nature and spiritual life is revealed in its desirability. Scripture convicts, rebukes, threatens, and judges. It contains exhortations and various inducements, Christ is presented as the Fountain of sanctification, and it contains the promises.[28]

All the needed resources for sanctification have been provided, yet as the believer uses them he finds himself frequently in a real spiritual battle. The remnants of the 'old man' in him resist the advance of holiness and he finds a vicious conflict within himself. Such a battle is described by Paul in Galatians 5:17 in these terms: 'For the flesh sets its desire against the Spirit, and the Spirit against the flesh; for these are in opposition to one another' (NASB). The path of sanctification is never easy.

This battle is described at length by Paul in Romans 7:14-25. This passage has caused great differences of opinion among commentators equally committed to the authority of Scripture, covenant theologians among them. The key issue is whether Paul in these verses is speaking as a Christian or not. The earlier part of the chapter clearly describes Paul the Pharisee before his conversion. Some argue that his statement in verse 14, 'For we know that the Law is spiritual, but I am of flesh, sold into bondage to sin' (NASB), could not possibly be true of a believer. Thus Robert Reymond argues, 'It is Paul's description of himself as the *unconverted* Saul of Tarsus, now aroused from his spiritual torpor and convicted by the reality of his sinfulness, struggling even more than before to please God through his efforts at law-

keeping.'[29] New Testament scholar Herman Ridderbos agrees
that the person in view is unconverted, but does not see the
description as autobiographical of Paul. In his opinion it depicts
the corruption of sin that extends even to those who have the
law and look to it (mistakenly) for their moral strength.[30]

The view that is more common among covenant theologians,
however, is that Paul is speaking in these verses as a believer
and that he describes the spiritual battle on the part of the
regenerate with the sin that remains in him. On this view,
progressive sanctification involves a significant element of
struggle. Theologically, they are very doubtful about regarding
Paul as in some sense 'awakened' yet not truly regenerate. Thus
Francis Turretin, in acknowledging that 'some of our
theologians' agree with Arminius and other non-Reformed
theologians in regarding Paul as being in a kind of intermediate
spiritual position, states their error thus: 'they invent a certain
new and third state between the state of nature (in which man is
as yet unrenewed) and the state of grace (in which he is now
renewed) – viz., a state under the law and the spirit of bondage
in which the man is not as yet renewed, but neither wholly
unregenerated.'[31]

Exegetically, much stress is laid by those who argue that
Paul speaks as a believer on verse 22: 'For I joyfully concur
with the law of God in the inner man' (NASB). Such a sentiment,
it is argued, could not be expressed sincerely by an unregenerate
person. It is rather a mark of grace and regeneration. Thus the
Scottish theologian James Fraser of Alness argues that 'if a
natural man, destitute of the Holy Spirit, can sincerely will,
love, delight, and hate, as is here said, I would wish to know,
what is left for Divine grace to do in regeneration'.[32]

The remaining power of sin is great – at times, as Paul's
language indicates, it is almost overwhelming. Nevertheless
those who hold the view that Paul speaks here as a Christian
are convinced that his language can be applied to the regenerate.
On balance, it appears to us that this interpretation is more
convincing than any other. The exegesis of the passage cannot

be given here, but writers such as John Murray and, from an earlier day, Charles Hodge and James Fraser, provide careful studies of Paul's words.[33] The covenant people of God find themselves in a daily battle with sin. As R C Sproul says, 'The peripheral power of sin is still raging and is very potent, but in the core of the regenerate man dwells a self that has been made over in the image of God.'[34] The battle is that described in Galatians 5:17 (NASB): 'For the flesh sets its desire against the Spirit, and the Spirit against the flesh; for these are in opposition to one another, so that you may not do the things that you please.'

The presence of the Lord by the Spirit who is his covenant gift must, however, never be lost from sight. Sanctification is possible because of him. Thus Paul follows his agonized question in Romans 7:24 ('Wretched man that I am! Who will set me free from the body of this death?' NASB) with the triumphant cry, 'Thanks be to God through Jesus Christ our Lord!' (verse 25). He is the secret of victory. Francis Schaeffer sums up Paul's argument in this way:

> The picture he paints is certainly not one of the possibility of sinless perfection, but neither is it one of hopeless defeat. For we, like Paul, can 'thank God through Jesus Christ our Lord' – once for all for our justification, but then also as a moment by moment thing as we pursue sanctification.[35]

The work of sanctification flows inevitably from justification. The idea that someone can be justified yet not be making progress in sanctification (as in 'carnal Christian' theories[36]) is preposterous and thoroughly unbiblical. Union with Christ our Mediator results in justification *and* sanctification. The latter is a comprehensive work which, as Peter De Jong says, 'embraces the whole man. Not only the soul but also the body is to experience the liberating power of belonging to Christ. Man's inner life cannot be radically changed without a corresponding transformation in outward conduct.'[37] The believer will therefore produce a life of good works, performed not in order to be saved, but because he has been saved. We are 'created in Christ Jesus

to do good works' (Eph. 2:10). Such good fruit is the evidence
that the tree is good, as Jesus states in Matthew 7:17.
Sanctification produces a life in which every part is submitted
to the lordship of Christ and conformed to his image. For the
Christian, therefore, no aspect of life is 'secular'. As Witsius
says, 'there is nothing in the sanctified person, no part, no
faculty, that remains untouched, or neglected, by the sanctifying
Spirit, and unadorned with new habits.'[38] The God-given guide
for this new life must now occupy our attention.

God's Law and the Christian

God, as we have noted, is a holy God, free from all imperfection
and sin. His rational creatures, angels and human beings, are
required to be holy. How are we to know what holiness actually
means? The answer is that God expresses it for us in practical
terms in his law, in his commandments. The law of God can be
thought of as a transcript of his holiness, a revelation of his
holiness in terms of human life in this world.

This truth is well expressed by Alec Motyer in his comments
on the expression 'the perfect law of liberty' in James 1:25:

> The law of God is perfect, first, because it perfectly expresses his
> nature and, secondly, because it perfectly matches ours. These two
> sides of the law belong together. In his commandments, the Lord
> has taken what is true about himself and has expressed that truth in a
> rule for us to obey . . . . The law which is the *perfect* expression of
> the divine nature is also the *perfect* vehicle of expression for human
> nature.[39]

The Bible indicates that all men, as image-bearers of God,
have an awareness of God's righteous requirements apart from
his written law. Thus Paul, referring to the immoral Gentiles
who lacked the written law possessed by the Jews, says of them
in Romans 1:32: 'they know God's righteous decree that those
who do such things deserve death.' That law is imprinted on
their 'hearts', their inner being. Paul can therefore speak in these
terms in Romans 2:14-15:

Indeed, when Gentiles, who do not have the law, do by nature things required by the law, they are a law for themselves, even though they do not have the law, since they show that the requirements of the law are written on their hearts, their consciences also bearing witness.

Their conduct, however, shows that sin has twisted their perception of the law and, above all, robbed them of their ability to obey God's law sufficiently. Nevertheless we have here a faint reflection of the way in which God's requirements were written on the heart of Adam in Eden before the Fall, in the Covenant of Works.

Even in Eden, however, Adam required a further, verbal, revelation of God's holy will regarding the tree of the knowledge of good and evil. After the Fall God graciously provided a fuller revelation of his moral law, culminating in the giving of the law to his people through Moses at Sinai. The moral requirements of the law (which dealt also with ceremonial and other issues) are, in the words of the Shorter Catechism, 'summarily comprehended in the Ten Commandments' (Q41).

It is vital to grasp that God's law is given in the context of God's covenant. The law Adam was given in Eden was an integral part of the Covenant of Works. Adam's response to the divine commandment decided whether he received continued blessing or the curse of a holy God. To be faithful to his covenant bond with the Lord, Adam had to keep the law God had revealed. Willing, loving, joyful obedience was to be Adam's appropriate covenant response.

After Eden the same principle holds true with regard to the Covenant of Grace. Faithfulness to the covenant relationship requires obedience to God's law. Thus when Abraham is told by the Lord to 'walk before me and be blameless' (Gen. 17:1), it is in the context of God's confirming his covenant with the man he has chosen. When we consider the definitive giving of the law at Sinai, covenant is again central. Iain D Campbell correctly observes that 'the law is given within the covenantal relationship sustained by God's people to Him. The remarks of Exodus 19:5, introductory to the giving of the law, set the

decalogue firmly within a federal context.'[40] Israel's covenant
faithfulness will be expressed in obedience to the law which
shows them what holiness means in the context in which they
live. The moral standards of the Ten Commandments are
applied in wide-ranging ways to the details of daily life,
demonstrating the practicality of God's requirements.

We would seriously misunderstand the nature of the law God
gives his people if we were to overlook the element of grace in
his covenant dealings with them. It is most significant that before
the commandments are given in Exodus 20, the Lord reminds
his people of how he has graciously made them his people. In
Exodus 20:2 the Lord says, 'I am the LORD your God, who
brought you out of Egypt, out of the land of slavery.' Clearly it
is a covenant of grace. There is no room for legalism – earning
salvation by obedience. Israel's obedience is to be a loving
response to God's action.

When the New Covenant is anticipated in Jeremiah 31, the
law of God still finds a place. With reference to his covenant
people, God promises, 'I will put my law in their minds and
write it on their hearts' (verse 33). Far from God's law being
forgotten, it will be engraved on his people's inmost being. The
writer to the Hebrews understands that this promise is fulfilled
as a consequence of the covenant-work of Christ the Mediator,
and quoted Jeremiah 31:33 in Hebrews 8:10 and 10:16. The
latter reference follows directly from the author's reference to
Christ's sacrificial offering: 'by one sacrifice he has made perfect
for ever those who are being made holy' (Heb. 10:14). Covenant,
definitive sanctification, progressive sanctification and God's
law are brought together in perfect harmony.

The New Testament makes it clear that God's law is still of
central concern to the life and sanctification of his covenant
people. The Westminster Confession states, 'True believers [are]
not under the law, as a covenant of works, to be thereby justified,
or condemned' (19:6). Donald Macleod comments that 'we are
no longer under the Covenant of Works as the way of life. Our
acceptance before God does not depend on our having kept the

law.'[41] As we have seen, Christ as our Surety has taken the punishment due to his people on account of their law-breaking. The law's condemnation has been lifted, with the result, as Calvin puts it, that 'we should not be borne down by an unending bondage, which would agonize our consciences with the fear of death'.[42] Such is the liberty of the children of God. But what then is the function of the law for believers?

It was John Calvin who was the first to formulate clearly the so-called 'three uses of the law' which were to become a commonplace of covenant theology. [43] He argued that the law first of all exposes the true nature of sin and, in those regenerated by the Spirit, leads sinners to Christ (the 'pedagogical' use of the law). In the second place, the law acts as a restraint on the expression of sin in society (the 'political' use). The 'third use of the law' is our concern in relation to sanctification: it is the God-given rule of life for believers. Thus Calvin says, 'Here is the best instrument for them to learn more thoroughly each day the nature of the Lord's will to which they aspire, and to confirm them in the understanding of it.'[44] Believers cannot do without such instruction. Indeed the law, according to Calvin, provides much-needed exhortation and encouragement to obedience: we are 'by frequent meditation upon it to be aroused to obedience, be strengthened in it, and be drawn back from the slippery path of transgression'.[45]

Scripture frequently shows the abiding validity that the moral law of God has for believers. Often Paul provides direction for believers' conduct which explicitly or implicitly draws on the Ten Commandments. In Ephesians 6:1-3, he quotes the fifth commandment regarding children's honouring father and mother and shows that this is the standard of conduct expected in the Church: 'Children, obey your parents in the Lord, for this is right. "Honour your father and mother" – which is the first commandment with a promise – 'that it may go well with you and that you may enjoy long life on the earth.' The commandments clearly underlie instructions such as Ephesians 4:25: 'Therefore each of you must put off falsehood and speak truthfully to his neighbour,' or Colossians 3:5: 'Put to death, therefore, whatever belongs to your earthly nature: sexual immorality, impurity, lust, evil desires and greed, which is idolatry.' The standard of conduct for God's covenant people has not changed, any more than the covenant God who gave the law has changed.

Precisely the same reinforcement of the moral law is to be found in the teaching of Jesus in the Sermon on the Mount. The pattern is clear in Matthew 5: 'You have heard that it was said to the people long ago . . . But I tell you . . . ' (for example, verses 21 and 22). Careful exegesis demonstrates that Jesus was not contradicting the Old Testament law but was in fact clearing away the centuries of man-made tradition that the Pharisees had built on top of God's law, in many cases obscuring its true significance. The requirements of the covenant which God had laid down were being re-emphasised by the Mediator, so that, for example, divorce was not to be available on the relatively easy basis that the Pharisees allowed (Matt. 5:31-32).

The moral demands of God's law are unchanging. It is significant that when Jesus speaks of 'fulfilling' the Law and the Prophets (Matt. 5:17), he makes it clear that he is not 'abolishing' them. He is the one to whom they pointed, but his coming does not reduce the ethical standard under which the covenant people live. As he says, 'Anyone who breaks one of the least of these commandments and teaches others to do the same will be called least in the kingdom of heaven, but whoever practises and teaches these commands will be called great in the kingdom of heaven. For I tell you that unless your righteousness surpasses that of the Pharisees and the teachers of the law, you will certainly not enter the kingdom of heaven' (Matt. 5:19-20). Jesus demonstrates the need for obedience to the commandments that begins in the heart, for example, avoiding lustful thoughts (v. 28), and so the resulting righteousness exceeds that of the Pharisees who concentrated on what was outwardly visible.

The need to focus on the person's inner attitudes, on his

'heart', is evident from Jesus' summary of the law, which draws on two Old Testament texts: 'Love the Lord your God with all your heart and with all your soul and with all your mind' (Matt. 22:37; cf Deut. 6:5), and 'Love your neighbour as yourself' (Matt. 22:39; cf Lev. 19:18). These two do not replace the commandments but sum them up. Love is central to obedience. In response to God's covenant love, believers love God with a love that results in obedience to his commandments and that overflows in love to others. The unbreakable bond between love and obedience is stated by John in this way: 'This is love for God: to obey his commands. And his commands are not burdensome, for everyone born of God overcomes the world' (1 John 5:3-4). Paul, too, having showed how the commandments are summed up in neighbour love, concluded, 'Therefore love is the fulfilment of the law' (Romans 13:10).

The moral law of God, summed up in the Ten Commandments, remains the divinely-given guide for God's covenant people in the process of sanctification. This has been recognised consistently by covenant theologians and many have provided expositions of the commandments. The Larger Catechism indicates that the special use of the law for the regenerate is 'to show them how much they are bound to Christ for his fulfilling it, and enduring the curse thereof in their stead, and for their good; and thereby to provoke them to more thankfulness, and to express the same in their greater care to conform themselves thereunto as the rule of their obedience' (Q97) and goes on in Q98–148 to give a painstaking analysis of the issues dealt with in each commandment.

As 1 John 5:3-4 indicates, the Christian's obedience flows from love and is not a burden. Such obedience, as Robert Candlish says, is 'not as seeking acceptance, but as already accepted; not as a servant on trial, but as a son abiding in the house evermore'.[46] It is the paradox of sanctification that when the Christian most faithfully obeys God's law then is he most free. Alec Motyer sums it up well in his comments on James 1:25 ('the law of liberty'):

True freedom is the opportunity and the ability to give expression to what we truly are. We are truly free when we live the life appropriate to those who are created in the image of God. The law of God safeguards that liberty for us. But it does even more, for obedience brings life and power (Lv 18:5; Dt 4:1a; Acts 5:32). The law of God is the law of liberty because it safeguards, expresses and enables the life of true freedom into which Christ has brought us. This is the blessing of which James speaks (25), the blessing of a full life, a true humanity. Obedience is the key factor in our enjoyment of it.[47]

The law and society

That the ceremonial aspects of the Mosaic Law have been abrogated is a commonplace among all orthodox Christians, covenant theologians included. Christ has fulfilled all that was foreshadowed in the sacrificial system of the Old Covenant, and so the rituals, regulations, temple and priesthood no longer figure in the Christian Church. Laws such as those relating to clean and unclean foods have passed away with them. Over such issues there is little controversy.

Rather more difficult is the question of the place (if any) that should be occupied by the civil laws given by God to Israel. It may be granted that the Israelites did not think of watertight divisions of the law into 'moral', 'ceremonial' and 'civil', and that these generally-accepted divisions do overlap at some points, but we are now considering the laws that regulated Israel as a political entity. Included in this category are, for example, regulations dealing with the criminal law and the sentences to be imposed by judges. What are Christians to do with such laws? Many would regard them as merely of historical interest, yet they are part of the inspired Word of God.

The approach generally adopted by covenant theologians is set out in XIX.4 of the Westminster Confession of Faith, where the divines state with reference to God's giving laws to Israel: 'To them also, as a body politic, He gave sundry judicial laws, which expired together with the State of that people; not obliging any other now, further than the general equity thereof may require.' What is of continuing value is the principle embodied in each regulation: this is to be sought out and enshrined in laws suited to each particular society in its historical setting.

It is clear that the Westminster Divines, like other covenant theologians, did not seek the application of the details of Mosaic penology to modern societies. The burden of their statement is on the passing away of such details – 'expired . . . not obligating any . . . '. Within that statement there is scope for a variety of views on how much of the penalties prescribed by the Mosaic law should be retained and on how closely modern laws should follow these Old Testament provisions. [48]

John Calvin argued strongly in his day that modern nations did not have to enforce the civil law of the Old Testament in order to be properly governed. He states that 'there are some who deny that a commonwealth is duly framed which neglects the political system of Moses, and is ruled by the common laws of nations. Let other men consider how perilous and seditious this notion is; it will be enough for me to have proved it false and foolish.'[49] Calvin identifies love as the heart of the law and contends that a law which preserves love is acceptable even though it does not reflect the Mosaic provisions. Thus he concludes that 'The form of [the Jews'] judicial laws, although it had no other interest than how best to preserve that very love which is enjoined by God's eternal law, had something distinct from that precept of love. Therefore, as ceremonial laws could be abrogated while piety remained safe and unharmed, so too, when those judicial laws were taken away, the perpetual duties and precepts of love could still remain.'[50] Every nation is therefore free to make laws that are suitable to its needs, as long as they serve the prupose of love. Consideration must be given to differences of time, place and culture, since 'the Lord through the hand of Moses did not give that law to be proclaimed among all nations and to be in force everywhere.'[51]

The view that the judicial law of Moses can and should be enforced in detail has seen a revival among some Reformed theologians, mainly in the United States, in the latter part of the twentieth century in the movement knows as Theonomy or

Christian Reconstruction. One of the founders of the movement, Rousas J Rushdoony, calls Calvin's views 'heretical nonsense'[52] and claims that his classical humanism had overcome his biblical exegesis. The movement has generated considerable controversy and a voluminous literature as critics tend to be dealt with at considerable length.

One of the key thinkers in the theonomic movement, Greg Bahnsen, argues in *Theonomy in Christian Ethics*[53] that the laws of the Old Testament are to be assumed to be fully in force unless there is specific indication in the New Testament to the contrary. With reference to the 'standing laws' (the judicial policy directions), they are a reflection of God's moral character and so are objective, universal and generally applicable. He concludes his list of ten basic elements of Theonomy by claiming, 'The civil precepts of the Old Testament (standing 'judicial' laws) are a model of perfect social justice for all cultures, even in the punishment of criminals.'[54]

A crucial text in Bahnsen's argument is Matthew 5:17-20, particularly verse 17 which reads in the NIV: 'Do not think that I have come to abolish the Law or the Prophets; I have not come to abolish them but to fulfil them.' Bahnsen's interpretation of Jesus' words is summed up in the title of chapter two of his book: 'The Abiding Validity of the Law In Exhaustive Detail.' His argument is that Jesus is referring to the ethical aspects of the Old Testament, so that only part of the content of the Prophets is in view, and that Jesus came to 'confirm' them. The verb generally translated 'fulfil' (*plērōsai*) is said by Bahnsen to mean 'confirm in exhaustive detail', and on this basis he argues for the continuing validity of the Mosaic judicial laws as the standard for modern societies.[55]

Theonomists differ considerably among themselves on a range of issues, and it does not seem that their approach to the judicial laws is quite as clear-cut as they might suggest. At times they clearly deduce principles from the laws which are then re-applied to modern questions, an approach which yields results little different from the standard Reformed handling of the

Mosaic civil law. Space does not permit a detailed consideration of the subject, but we may touch on one issue which relates to the function of Christ, the Mediator of the New Covenant: what does Christ state his role to be in Matthew 5:17?

Bahnsen's claim that *plērōsai* means 'confirm' rather than 'fulfil' has been decisively refuted by the detailed study carried out by Vern Poythress.[57] After examining all the relevant textual material, he concludes that 'it is safe to say that *plērōsai* does not have the sense "confirm" in Greek.'[58] What then does the statement of Jesus mean? It is important to note that Bahnsen has no exegetical justification for confining 'the Prophets' to the ethical content of these books. Jesus fulfils 'the Law and the Prophets' in their entirety:

> To fulfil has been understood in three main ways: (1) It may mean that he would do the things laid down in Scripture. (2) It may mean that he would bring out the full meaning of Scripture. (3) It may mean that in his life and teaching he would bring Scripture to its completion. Each points to an aspect of the truth, and Jesus may well have meant that he would fulfil Scripture in more ways than one.[59]

Christ is the focus of the whole of the Old Testament. As we are told in relation to his meeting with the disciples on the Emmaus road, 'beginning with Moses and all the Prophets, he explained to them what was said in all the Scriptures concerning himself' (Luke 24:27). The focus of his fulfilling the Old Testament is indicated in the previous verse as being his redemptive, mediatorial work: 'Did not the Christ have to suffer these things and then enter his glory?' (verse 26). This indicates how Matthew 5:17 is to be approached.

Whilst recognising the Theonomists' zeal for the authority of Scripture, it does not appear that their position is scriptural. It seems safer to follow the approach of the Westminster Confession of Faith regarding the 'general equity'[60] of the laws, seeking the principles enshrined in them and applying them to modern situations. The precise context in which Old Testament Israel found itself as a nation cannot be replicated.

Notes

1. Samuel Rutherford, *The Trial and Triumph of Faith*, 1645 edition (Glasgow, 1845), p. 195.
2. Johannes Wollebius, *Compendium of Christian Theology* (1626) in *Reformed Dogmatics*, translated and edited by John W Beardslee III (Grand Rapids, 1977), p. 173.
3. Thomas E McComiskey writing in *Theological Wordbook of the Old Testament*, edited by R Laird Harris et. al. (Chicago, 1980), vol 2, p. 787.
4. ibid.
5. Horst Seebass writing in *New International Dictionary of New Testament Theology*, edited by Colin Brown (Carlisle/Grand Rapids, 1986), vol 2, p. 228.
6. Herman Bavinck, *Our Reasonable Faith*, translated by Henry Zylstra (Grand Rapids, 1956), p. 469.
7. Johannes Wollebius, op. cit. , p. 171.
8. Francis Turretin, *Institutes of Elenctic Theology*, translated by G M Giger (Phillipsburg, 1992), Locus 17, Q1, para 4 (2. 690).
9. A Noordtzij, *Leviticus*, translated by Raymond Togtman (Grand Rapids, 1982), ad. loc.
10. P A Lillback, 'Covenant' in *New Dictionary of Theology*, edited by Sinclair B Ferguson and David F Wright (Leicester/Downers Grove, 1988), p. 174.
11. John Murray, 'The Agency in Definitive Sanctification', in *Collected Writings* (Edinburgh, 1977), 2. 289.
12. Wilhelmus à Brakel, *The Christian's Reasonable Service*, 1700 edition, translated by Bartel Elshout (Ligonier, 1992), vol 3, cpt 44, pp. 6ff. The same difficulty arises with the statement regarding progressive sanctification in the Westminster Confession of Faith 13. 3, namely that 'the regenerate part doth overcome'. John Murray is correct to say that 'this is not a satisfactory way of representing the relation of regeneration to the sanctifying process, nor is it in line with earlier statements in the chapter concerned. ' ('The Theology of the Westminster Confession of Faith' in *Collected Writings* [Edinburgh, 1982] 4. 262.)
13. Simon Kistemaker, *James and I-III John* (Welwyn, 1987), on 1 John 3:6.
14. John Murray, 'Progressive Sanctification' in *Collected Writings*, 2. 297. Murray is alluding to Romans 8:29.
15. F F Bruce writing in *NIDNTT*, Vol 2, p. 291.
16. John Murray, 'Progressive Sanctification' in *Collected Writings*, 2. 299.
17. ibid.
18. Robert L Reymond, *A New Systematic Theology of the Christian Faith* (Nashville, 1998), p. 778.
19. Herman Witsius, *The Economy of the Covenants Between God and Man,*

1677 edition. Translated by William Crookshank (Escondido, 1990), III. 12. 50.
20. Charles Hodge, *Systematic Theology*, 1871-73 edition (Grand Rapids, 1977), 3. 218.
21. Wilhelmus à Brakel, op. cit. , vol 3, cpt 44, p5.
22. Thomas Watson, *A Body of Divinity*, 1692 edition (Edinburgh, 1965), p. 241.
23. Interpretations of this verse, and even the translations suggested, vary considerably. Many take the final clause as a reference to Christ. For a survey of views see Charles Hodge, *A Commentary on I and II Corinthians* (Edinburgh, 1974), and Philip E Hughes, *The Second Epistle to the Corinthians* (Grand Rapids, 1962), ad. loc.
24. Alec Motyer, *The Message of Philippians* (Leicester/Downers Grove, 1984), p. 127, n3.
25. William Hendriksen, *Philippians* (Edinburgh, 1962), ad. loc.
26. John Murray, *Redemption Accomplished and Applied* (Grand Rapids, 1955), p. 149.
27. Herman Bavinck, op. cit. , p. 480.
28. Wilhelmus à Brakel, op. cit. , vol 3, cpt 44, p. 5.
29. Robert L Reymond, op. cit. , p. 781. He discusses the passage at length in Appendix F, pp. 1127-32.
30. Herman Ridderbos, *Paul: An Outline of his Theology*, translated by John R DeWitt (London, 1977), pp. 126-30.
31. Francis Turretin, op. cit. , Locus 17, Q2, para 11 (2. 697).
32. James Fraser, *A Treatise on Sanctification*, 1897 edition (Audubon, 1992), p. 289. Opponents of this view argue that Paul's statement means rather less than a spiritual love for the law of God.
33. John Murray, *The Epistle to the Romans* (London, 1967), vol 1, pp. 259ff; Charles Hodge, *Commentary on the Epistle to the Romans*, 1886 edition (Grand Rapids, 1947), pp. 227ff; James Fraser, op. cit. , pp. 254ff.
34. R C Sproul, *The Gospel of God* (Fearn, 1999), p. 127.
35. Francis Schaeffer, *The Finished Work of Christ* (Leicester, 1998), p. 186.
36. Such views are explained and effectively answered by Ernest C Reisinger in *Lord and Christ* (Phillipsburg, 1994), chapters 9 and 10.
37. P Y De Jong, *The Church's Witness to the World* (St Catharines, 1980), vol 2, p. 173.
38. Herman Witsius, op. cit. , III. 12. 31.
39. Alec Motyer, *The Message of James* (Leicester, 1985), pp. 70-71.
40. Iain D Campbell, *The Doctrine of Sin* (Fearn, 1999), p. 29. Much valuable material on the Puritans' understanding of covenant and law is to be found in Ernest F Kevan's study *The Grace of Law* (Grand Rapids, 1976).
41. Donald Macleod, *A Faith to Live By* (Fearn, 1998), p. 188.

42. John Calvin, *Institutes of the Christian Religion*, 1559 edition, translated by Ford Lewis Battles (Philadelphia, 1960), II. vii. 15.

43. John Calvin, *Institutes*, II. vii. 6-12.

44. John Calvin, *Institutes*, II. vii. 12.

45. ibid.

46. Robert S Candlish, *A Commentary on I John*, 1870 edition (Edinburgh, 1993), p. 346.

47. Alex Motyer, *The Message of James*, p. 71.

48. Thus George Gillespie, a Scottish commissioner to the Westminster Assembly, could write in 1646, 'I know some divines hold that the judicial law of Moses, so far as concerneth the punishments of sins against the moral law, idolatry, blasphemy, Sabbath-breaking, adultery, theft, etc. , ought to be a rule to the Christian magistrate, and for my part, I wish more respect were had to it, and that it were more consulted with. ' (*Aaron's Rod Blossoming*, Harrisonburg, 1985, p. 2). A tract entitled *Wholesome Severity reconciled with Christian Liberty* which argues for the enforcement of the Mosaic penalties in full is often attributed to Gillespie, but in the opinion of the present writer, it is not one of his works.

49. John Calvin, *Institutes*, IV. xx. 14.

50. John Calvin, *Institutes*, IV. xx. 15.

51. John Calvin, *Institutes*, IV. xx. 16.

52. Rousas J Rushdoony, *The Institutes of Biblical Law* (Nutley, 1973), p.9.

53. Greg L Bahnsen, *Theonomy in Christian Ethics* (Phillipsburg, 1984).

54. Greg L Bahnsen, op. cit., p. xvii. The ten-point list is repeated in Bahnsen's subsequent book *By This Standard* (Tyler, 1985), pp. 345-7.

55. See Bahnsen, *Theonomy*, pp. 39-86 for the details of Bahnsen's exegesis.

56. A book-length examination by faculty members at Westminster Theological Seminary is *Theonomy. A Reformed Critique*, edited by William S Barker and W Robert Godfrey (Grand Rapids, 1990). Note also 'Excursus: Another Look at Theonomy' in *Christ Triumphant* by Raymond O Zorn (Edinburgh, 1997) , pp. 180-201. Extensive responses by Theonomists have also been produced.

57. Vern S Poythress, *The Shadow of Christ in the Law of Moses* (Phillipsburg, 1981), Appendix C, pp. 363-77.

58. Vern S Poythress, op. cit., p. 377.

59. Leon Morris, *The Gospel According to Matthew* (Grand Rapids/Leicester, 1992), ad. loc.

60. Theonomists who appeal to the Confession tend to interpret 'general equity' in such a way (i. e. embracing the detail of the laws) that they in effect reverse the Confession's statements about the laws having 'expired' and their 'not obligating any'.

9

The Covenant Community

Various weaknesses may be identified in contemporary Evangelicalism, weaknesses which help to explain its fragmented state and its almost total marginalisation in many western societies. One of the greatest of those weaknesses is undoubtedly the absence among most·Evangelicals of a clearly articulated doctrine of the Church, built on biblical foundations. Without such a doctrine, the Church is left wondering what it is and what it should be doing. It comes as no surprise that in such a situation the Church is shaped more by the views and pressures of the surrounding culture than by the will of the God whom it professes to serve. Many Christians consequently have a low view of the Church, regarding it as one among several outlets for their spiritual energies and changing from one denomination to another with apparent ease.

Covenant theologians, on the other hand, have always had a high view of the Church because of their understanding of its God-given nature and functions. A grasp of their doctrine of the Church in all its richness provides a healthy corrective to the anaemic ecclesiologies that are now so popular.

What is the Church?
A definition of the Church which links it firmly to God's covenant work is provided by Herman Witsius in his 1681 commentary on the Apostles' Creed. He describes the Church as 'A Society of believing and holy men, called by God out of the world of mankind by the word of the Gospel, to a participation of the blessings of the covenant of grace which stands fast in Christ.'[1]

A more recent writer, John Murray, provides the following definition:

> The church is the assembly of the covenant people of God, the congregation of believers, the household of God, the fellowship of

the Holy Spirit, the body of Christ. It consists of men and women
called by God the Father into the fellowship of his Son, sanctified in
Christ Jesus, regenerated by his Spirit, and united in the faith and
confession of Christ Jesus as Lord and Saviour.[2]

It is entirely appropriate that covenant language should be used
in defining the Church. We have already considered in some detail
the blessings which Christ bestows on His people by virtue of the
Covenant of Grace. Believers do not receive those blessings as so
many isolated individuals but as part of a redeemed community.
Indeed sanctification requires a community setting, and biblical
exhortations to holiness often arise out of a community context.
For example, when Hebrews 10:24 encourages believers in these
terms – 'let us consider how we may spur one another on towards
love and good deeds' – not only is community life assumed, but
the next verse makes this explicit – 'Let us not give up meeting
together ... but let us encourage one another.' The outworking of
the Covenant of Grace requires the gathering of the Church, and
the bringing of believers into this body should be seen as a further
blessing of the covenant. Scripture never thinks of the people of
God as a collection of individuals but as a community, a covenant
community.

Covenant Theology has always sought to maintain the biblical
perspective on the continuity of the Church – namely, that there
has always been one Church of God throughout both Old and
New Testaments. More will be said on this issue in our
consideration of Dispensationalism in the appendix, but a few
comments can be made at this point.

It is significant that the Greek word for 'church' in the New
Testament (*ekklēsia*) was used in the Septuagint (Greek)
translation of the Old Testament for the Hebrew term *qahal*. This
term indicated the assembly of the covenant people of God, the
'congregation' of Israel. It is used, for example, for the gathering
of the people for the making of the covenant at Sinai in
Deuteronomy 9:10 and 10:4 ('the day of the *assembly*').[3] Stephen
in his defence in Acts 7 can therefore speak of 'the church
(*ekklēsia*) in the wilderness' (v. 38, AV).

The New Testament Church, made up of Jews and Gentiles,

clearly thought of itself as the continuation of the Old Testament people of God. The New Testament writers speak in terms of their belonging to the 'new covenant', as when Paul refers to God's having 'made us competent as ministers of a new covenant' (2 Cor. 3:6), or when Christ is described as 'the mediator of a new covenant' (Heb. 9:15). This awareness is built on Christ's words at the institution of the Lord's Supper: 'This cup is the new covenant in my blood, which is poured out for you' (Luke 22:20). The source of this 'new covenant' language is the prophecy recorded in Jeremiah 31:31-34 and applied to the New Testament Church in Hebrews 8:8-13. The covenant is made, significantly, with 'the house of Israel and the house of Judah'. This hope is understood to be fulfilled in a Church consisting of Jews and Gentiles, the increasing majority being Gentiles. As Robert Reymond correctly observes, 'when Gentiles became Christians, they entered into the fellowship of that covenant community designated by the *"new covenant" prophecy in Jeremiah 31:31 as "the house of Israel and the house of Judah"*.'[4]

The only two recorded references to the 'church' in the teaching of Jesus during his earthly ministry are also instructive. In Matthew 16:18, in response to Peter's confession of his identity as Messiah, he promises that 'on this rock I will build my church, and the gates of Hades will not overcome it'. The universal terms in which he speaks of this institution indicate that the whole body of his people is in view. As John Murray expresses it,

> When Jesus speaks of 'my church', he is thinking of those gathered and knit together after the pattern provided by the Old Testament as the people for his possession, as the community which he is to constitute, and which stands in a relation to him comparable to the congregation of the Lord in the Old Testament.[5]

The other example in Matthew 18:17, dealing with discipline, records Jesus' command 'If he refuses to listen to [two or three witnesses], tell it to the church.' It is evident that in this case 'church' refers to the local gathering of the covenant people. Both uses are evident throughout the New Testament, and we might add for the sake of completeness that 'church' can also refer to a number of congregations in a particular area, as in Acts 9:31, 'Then the church throughout Judea, Galilee and Samaria enjoyed a time of peace.'

At numerous points in the New Testament it is made clear that the body of believers in Christ stands in unbroken continuity with the covenant community of the Old Testament. Thus at the Council of Jerusalem in Acts 15, James sees God's 'taking from the Gentiles a people for himself' (v. 14) as a fulfilment of the prophetic words of Amos 9:11-12, where the Lord promises, 'After this I will return and rebuild David's fallen tent. Its ruins I will rebuild, and I will restore it, that the remnant of men may seek the Lord, and all the Gentiles who bear my name' (quoted in Acts 15:16-17).

That there is no thought of a separate community of Gentiles is clear from Paul's olive tree imagery in Romans 11. There is only one olive tree, rooted by God's grace in the soil of Israel. Whilst unbelieving Jewish branches have been broken off, (verse 17), Gentile believers do not form a separate tree. Rather, as Paul says in verse 17, 'you, though a wild olive shoot, have been grafted in among the others and now share in the nourishing sap of the olive root.' The covenant grace of God produces a single tree. As Charles Hodge says, 'The Gentiles are saved by their introduction into that church of which the patriarchs were the root.'[6]

The crucial issue is the presence or absence of saving faith. Even with regard to the Jews of Old Testament days Paul states in Romans 9:6 that 'not all who are descended from Israel are Israel', and he makes the point emphatically in Romans 2:28, 'A man is not a Jew if he is only one outwardly, nor is circumcision merely outward and physical.' The significant qualification is spelled out in verse 29, 'No, a man is a Jew if he is one inwardly; and circumcision is circumcision of the heart, by the Spirit, not by the written code.' On this account the Church, made up of Jews and Gentiles, can be termed 'the Israel of God' (Gal. 6:16), Paul having already spoken of the continuity of the covenant promises in Galatians 3:29, 'If you belong to Christ, then you are Abraham's seed, and heirs according to the promise.'

Richard Gaffin is thus correct to say that 'Pentecost is nothing less than the establishment of the Church as the new covenant people of God, as the body of Christ'.[7] The language used in the New Testament with reference to the Church is, as we would now expect, heavily influenced by Old Testament descriptions of Israel. To take but one example, in 1 Peter 2:9 Christians are said to be 'a chosen people, a royal priesthood, a holy nation, a people belonging to God', terms found in texts such as Exodus 19:6. As Coenen comments, 'What the author wishes to underline is the fact that the Christian community is nothing new; it is to be understood as the fulfilment of the promises and hopes given to Israel.'[8]

In the light of the continuity of the Church as the covenant community of the Lord throughout Old and New Testaments, which we have briefly examined, covenant theologians as a matter of course begin their study of the Church in the Old Testament. For example, the nineteenth century Scottish theologian Douglas Bannerman begins his treatise *The Scripture Doctrine of the Church* with 'The Church in the time of Abraham'.[9] Others such as Dutch theologian Wilhelmus à Brakel trace the origins of the Church back to the period immediately following the Fall in Eden.[10] The Church is thus thought of as beginning with the Covenant of Grace. It does not seem unreasonable, however, to say that the Church began with the Covenant of Works: Adam and Eve constituted the covenant community before the Fall.

Election and the Church
The Church has its origin not in the will of man but in the will of God. We have seen in chapter 3 how the salvation of sinners is rooted in their having been chosen in Christ before the creation of the world (Eph. 1:4). The goal of that election is also made clear: 'to be holy and blameless in his sight'. The same themes occur in several of Paul's greetings to the churches who were recipients of his letters. In Romans 1:7 we read, 'To all in Rome who are loved by God and called to be saints', while in 1 Corinthians 1:2 Paul sends greetings to 'the church of God in Corinth, to those sanctified in Christ Jesus and called to be holy'. The calling in view would appear to be the effectual calling which results in salvation and which is rooted in the electing love of God. In view are those given to Christ in the Covenant of Redemption and purchased by

him through the shedding of his blood.

This calling into the fellowship and benefits of the Covenant of Grace comes to the elect not merely as isolated individuals, but as the verses quoted indicate, as a body of people. As R. B. Kuiper comments, 'In the counsel of God the church existed even before the creation of man.'[11] In Scripture, the people of God are always thought of as a community. Isolationism or total independence are inconceivable. When the Christian life is traced back to its eternal origin in the sovereign decree of God, clearly it is fundamentally corporate in nature.

The fountain-head of the Church is the electing love of the triune God and, as Johannes Wollebius points out, 'properly speaking, the members of the church are the elect only.'[12] The true Church of God, the Body of Christ, is not a human invention: it is part of the eternal covenant purpose of God, and so its nature and functions cannot be a matter of relative indifference on the part of Christians. Indeed, it can be said that it is within the life of the Church, within the covenant community, that a believer comes to assurance of his election and deeper understanding of its blessings and responsibilities. A Christian ploughing a solitary furrow is in all kinds of spiritual danger.

The Trinity and the Church

As we have noted already a number of times, the covenant work of God is the activity of a God who is a Trinity. Father, Son and Holy Spirit are involved in each stage of redemption, from the election of sinners in the Covenant of Redemption through to their entrance into the full enjoyment of their inheritance promised in the Covenant of Grace. The Church as the covenant community can be thought of in trinitarian terms.

Throughout Scripture the Church is described as God's assembly and God's dwelling place. Israel was an assembly because the people gathered before the Lord, appearing in his presence, as Deuteronomy 4:10 says with regard to the covenant-making at Sinai. God's dwelling among his people is a fundamental element of the covenant promise, 'I will walk among you and be your God' (Lev. 26:12). That dwelling was symbolized for Israel in the tabernacle and, subsequently, in the temple. The radiance manifested, for example, at the dedication of the temple by Solomon (2 Chron. 7:1), demonstrated the presence of the Lord among His people.

It is in Christ pre-eminently that God came to dwell among His people. In Him the glory of God shines forth: 'We have seen his glory' (John 1:14). The incarnate Son fulfils all that was symbolized by the tabernacle and the temple, so that both have served their purpose in the unfolding of redemption. Thus Jesus can refer to his own body in these terms – 'Destroy this temple and I will raise it again in three days' (John 2:19).

By the shedding of His blood as Mediator of the covenant, Christ has purchased His people. This truth is expressed in Paul's striking reference in Acts 20:28 to 'the church of God [or 'of the Lord'] which he bought with his own blood'. The purchased covenant people themselves constitute a dwelling place for God. Thus in Ephesians 2 Paul describes the bringing together of Jews and Gentiles in the one church of Christ in these terms: 'In him the whole building is joined together and rises to become a holy temple in the Lord. And in him you too are being built together to become a dwelling in which God lives by his Spirit' (vv. 21-2). Edmund Clowney correctly observes,

> God's presence makes us his people; the presence of Jesus constitutes the church as his temple, built of living stones, joined to him as God's elect Stone (1 Pet. 2:4-6). The church itself is a temple, the house of God, sanctified by the presence of the Spirit (1 Cor. 3:16).[13]

As the Holy Spirit gives spiritual life to dead sinners, so he gives birth to the Church. As he indwells individual believers, so he indwells the Church. Just as Paul can ask of the individual believers, 'Do you not know that your body is a temple of the Holy Spirit?' (1 Cor. 6:19), so he can ask of the whole body of believers, 'Don't you know that you yourselves are God's temple and that God's Spirit lives in you?' (1 Cor. 3:16). The indwelling, empowering, sanctifying ministry of the Spirit has a corporate as well as an individual dimension. Speaking of the baptism of the Holy Spirit in 1 Corinthians 12:13, Paul states that 'we were all baptised by one Spirit into one body – whether Jews or Greeks, slave or free – and we were all given the one Spirit to drink.' As Clowney concludes, 'The Spirit joins us to Christ, and therefore to those who are Christ's.'

The Church is the fruit of the saving work of the triune God of the covenants. The Church without the involvement of any Person of the Trinity is inconceivable.

Visible or invisible?
The descriptions of those who make up the covenant community that we have considered so far apply only to those who have actually experienced the saving grace of God. Anyone who has any experience of the Church as it exists on earth, however, knows that there are those in the membership of the Church who show no evidence of true saving faith. In contrast to the biblical descriptions, it seems that the actual Church we have to deal with is a mixture of saved and unsaved, with the proportions of each varying from one congregation to another. Is the Bible presenting merely an unrealizable ideal which does not actually exist in practice?

Covenant theologians, as well as others, have often approached this problem by appealing to some form of distinction between the 'invisible Church' and the 'visible Church'. Thus we read in the Westminster Confession: 'The catholic or universal Church, which is invisible, consists of the whole number of the elect, that have been, are, or shall be gathered into one, under Christ the Head thereof ... The visible Church, which is also catholic or universal under the Gospel ... consists of all those throughout the world that profess the true religion; and of their children' (XXV.1-2).

How the distinction between 'visible' and 'invisible' is to be understood, however, has been the subject of much discussion and disagreement, particularly in explaining the position of non-elect unsaved members of particular congregations. In general, it is agreed that there are not distinct churches, but that the one true Church of Christ has visible and invisible aspects. This is simply stated by Wollebius: 'Therefore, although the church is visible at the point of its external administration, it is nevertheless invisible as to the identification of the elect, and their union with Christ.'[14] Few, if any, covenant theologians would disagree. No one would claim to be able to read the hearts of church members so as to discern which are truly elect.

The difficulties really arise, however, with the 'visible church'. The Westminster Confession of Faith defines it in terms of the outward profession of faith that church members make. This reflects the view of Calvin, for example: 'Often ... the name "church" designates the whole multitude of men spread over the earth who profess to worship one God and Christ ... In this church are mingled many hypocrites who have nothing of Christ but the name and outward appearance.'[15] All would agree that these statements describe the congregations with which we must work. A profession of faith that is not contradicted by a person's life has to be accepted as genuine: only God knows the truth of the matter. The question has to be asked, however, as to whether those hypocrites who make a false profession of faith are to be regarded as truly members of the Church and actually (in some sense) in covenant with God.

Some covenant theologians, particularly in the Scottish Presbyterian tradition, whilst emphasizing that Christ has established one true Church, speak of considerable differences between the invisible Church and the visible Church. They stress that the visible Church is based on what is outwardly visible, and so membership cannot depend on the possession of invisible grace but on the making of a visible profession. *All* members of the visible Church have entered into a real, albeit outward, relationship with Christ. This is how one of the great Scottish Presbyterians, James Bannerman, expresses it:

> The members of the Church invisible are joined in an inward relationship to Christ, in consequence of having listened to His inward call by the Spirit, and being vitally united to Him through faith. The members of the Church visible are joined in an outward connection with Christ, in consequence of having obeyed His outward call by the Word, and being now made partakers by Him in the external privileges and ordinances of a Church state.[16]

This relationship to Christ enjoyed by all in the visible Church may, according to Bannerman, be designated 'an external covenant or federal relationship'.[17]

On this view, non-elect unregenerate church members are in a real, albeit external, covenant relationship with Christ and are rightly considered members of the (visible) Church. From this principle a theologian of the eminence of Samuel Rutherford drew the conclusion that a true congregation of the visible Church could exist even when none of its members was actually regenerate, as long as the members professed faith in the true gospel, and also that Christ is not Head of the visible Church but only of those in it who are members of the invisible Church.[18] The understanding of a covenant relationship required by this view, however, is, to say the least, difficult to fit into the covenant theology which we have already considered, and we may well baulk at a definition of the (visible) Church which allows unregenerate hypocrites to be legitimate members of it.

A rather different approach to these issues has been taken by other covenant theologians, particularly in the 'Continental' Reformed tradition, pre-eminently in the Netherlands. This tradition calls into question the visible/invisible distinction with regard to the Church. In such confessional documents as the Belgic Confession of Faith (1561) and the Heidelberg Catechism (1563), comprising two of the Three Forms of Unity of the Dutch churches, no mention is made of such a distinction.[19] The eminent Dutch writer Wilhelmus à Brakel notes that, whilst the Church has visible and invisible aspects, one 'may also not divide the church into a visible and invisible church as far as the members themselves are concerned, as if the one had different members from the other'.[20] In his view the visible Church is not to be thought of as a mixture of regenerate and unregenerate people. This, in his opinion, 'is an erroneous view, generating many confusing thoughts and expressions concerning the church'.[21]

To support his position à Brakel presents several lines of argument. He says, for example, that there is no support in Scripture for such a distinction, and that it is founded on a false supposition, namely that the unconverted may truly be members of the Church with equal rights in its visible gathering, including a right to the sacraments. In addition, the distinction implies that there are two churches, since one legitimately made up of regenerate and unregenerate must have an essentially different nature from one made up only of the regenerate. If any difference in membership between the two is claimed, then there must be two different churches, a view à Brakel vigorously rejects. Like all covenant theologians, à Brakel accepts that the elders of a congregation receive members on the basis of a profession of faith, but he denies that unregenerate members are *true* members: 'they are no members, even though men view them as such externally.'[22] Although the Church treats such people as members, they are not in a covenant relationship with Christ and receive no spiritual benefits from him.

Among modern covenant theologians who share à Brakel's perspective are R. B. Kuiper and John Murray. Kuiper states, 'Very strictly speaking, the membership of the visible church coincides with that of the invisible church. And since the invisible church consists of the regenerate, only they rate as members of the visible church'.[23] Although a Scot, John Murray rejects the validity of the visible/invisible distinction.[24] He contends that the New Testament always speaks of the Church, universal or local, as a *visible* entity, a body made up of believers. Furthermore, in another essay, he shows that the New Testament does not support a definition of the Church which allows for the inclusion of unbelievers. 'When Paul addressed the church, he did not construe the church in such terms as would allow for the inclusion of those persons who might have borne the Christian name, and had been admitted to the privileges of the church, but who were not sanctified in Christ Jesus and called to be saints', writes Murray,[25] referring to Paul's greeting to the congregation in Corinth (1 Cor. 1:1-2).

It appears to us that Murray, à Brakel and those who share their view are most faithful to the biblical descriptions of the Church. No one disputes that hypocrites deceive church leaders and are accepted as members of the Church. Those who claim to know that only the regenerate are members of their congregation are making a claim that they cannot validate. Nevertheless we must not adapt the biblical definitions to legitimise in any way the position of those who have made a false profession. Murray rightly distinguishes between 'what a situation may existentially be by reason of the sin, hypocrisy, and infirmity of men, on the one hand, and the terms in which the church is to be defined, on the other'.[26] He goes on to argue that 'only if we apply the latter can we maintain the character of that to which the promises belong, indeed, maintain the primary idea in terms of which the church is to be defined, the covenant people of God'.[27]

As far as identifying a true church is concerned, the best approach is set out by G. I. Williamson in this way:

> we may say that the true Church becomes visible, not by an identification of *persons*, but by an identification of *presence*. The true Church of Christ (his body of elect persons) will manifest itself, not by a disclosure that particular persons are elect, but by a disclosure of certain things that true believers will do (even though there be hypocrites mixed in with them). They will profess the true religion and maintain fidelity to word, sacraments and discipline, which is required of a true visible Church. It is the presence of these activities of elect persons which makes the body of Christ visibly evident.[28]

One Church

The elect are given to Christ according to the one Covenant of Redemption, and they receive the fruits of his redemptive work according to the one Covenant of Grace. Consequently there is one true Church made up of the covenant people of God. That Church includes those saints who are already in glory, traditionally termed 'the Church triumphant', and those who are still on earth, termed 'the Church militant'.

It is important to stress that the Church of Christ *is* a unity. All believers are in indissoluble union with Christ, whatever organizational divisions there may be within the Church on earth. Everything that has been said about our union with Christ points to the fact of the spiritual unity of the Church which is His body. This is reflected, for example, in Paul's statement in 1 Corinthians 12:13, 'For we were all baptised by one Spirit into one body –

whether Jews or Greeks – slave or free – and we were all given the one Spirit to drink.' Equally emphatic is Ephesians 4:4-6, 'There is one body and one Spirit – just as you were called to one hope when you were called – one Lord, one faith, one baptism; one God and Father of all, who is over all and through all and in all.' Such statements are reinforced by Paul's teaching regarding the unity of Jews and Gentiles in Christ. In Romans 11 Paul envisages only one olive tree of which Jewish and Gentile believers are equally a part. We may add to this Ephesians 2:14ff., where Paul describes Christ's purpose 'to create in himself one new man out of the two, thus making peace, and in this one body to reconcile both of them to God through the cross' (vv. 15-16).

Covenant theologians have been careful to maintain this biblical emphasis on the spiritual unity of the Church, in spite of the divisions that have so often occurred in the visible organisation of the Church. R. B. Kuiper puts it in these striking terms:

> the church of God, far from being a tangled heap of wreckage, is even now God's own perfectly proportioned temple, built upon the foundation of the apostles and prophets, with Jesus Christ Himself as the chief cornerstone ... (Eph. 2:20-2). God omniscient sees it thus. So does God's child with the eye of faith.[29]

One of the great Scottish ecclesiologists, Thomas McCrie, says, 'All genuine saints are invisibly and vitally united to Christ, and to one another, be the indissoluble bond of the Spirit and of the faith.'[30] Few have had a higher regard for the unity of the Church than the Scottish covenant theologians of the seventeenth century, men such as Samuel Rutherford and George Gillespie, in spite of popular caricatures of them as divisive, narrow-minded fanatics.[31]

Various elements of this existing spiritual unity have been identified by different writers. Francis Turretin, for example, writes of 'six heads: unity (1) of body; (2) of head; (3) of spirit; (4) of faith; (5) of love; (6) of hope.'[32] A similar list is provided by Thomas McCrie: '1. This unity consists in her having one Head and Lord ... 2. The unity of the faith ... 3. "One baptism", and fellowship in the same acts of worship ... 4. Unity in respect of external government and discipline ... 5. The bond of mutual charity and peace.'[33] Essential to the unity of the Church, whatever other elements may be identified, is of course Christ the Mediator who purchased the Church with His blood.

McCrie's reference to unity in 'external government and discipline' should not be taken as an indication that covenant theologians believed in or sought the organizational unity of the universal Church in some supra-national institution. Such is the view of Rome regarding the Church's unity. The most authoritative recent statement of the Papacy's position is to be found in the *Catechism of the Catholic Church*:

> The sole Church of Christ [is that] which our Saviour, after his Resurrection, entrusted to Peter's pastoral care, commissioning him and the other apostles to extend and rule it ... This Church, constituted and organized as a society in the present world, subsists in (*subsistit in*) the Catholic Church, which is governed by the successor of Peter and by the bishops in communion with him.[34]

Covenant theologians have generally had a worldwide vision of the Church. In the seventeenth century George Gillespie expressed the hope that there might be an 'ecumenical synod' representing many national churches, to discuss general theological and pastoral issues of concern to the whole Church.[35] The Church's unity, however, was not to be sought in a single organization.

That is not to say that covenant theologians have not attached great importance to the visible unity of God's covenant community. They do not believe that Scripture permits complacency on this issue. In contrast to many contemporary evangelicals who stress the invisible spiritual unity of believers, whilst claiming that visible unity is relatively unimportant, covenant theologians generally emphasize that Christ's revealed will for His Church is visible unity. Alongside the statement of Ephesians 4:4 that there is 'one body', Paul sets the exhortation, 'Make every effort to keep the unity of the Spirit through the bond of peace' (v. 3). The unbreakable spiritual unity that exists by virtue of believers' union with Christ should be expressed visibly in the Church, and, as Paul knows, that is not always the case.

A crucial passage on this theme is Christ's 'high priestly' prayer in John 17. Viewing proleptically His imminent death on the cross, He prays for those His Father has 'given' Him (v. 9), his disciples at that time. His prayer is 'Holy Father, protect them by the power of your name – the name you gave me – so that they may be one as we are one' (v. 11). Subsequently he prays for later generations of believers too: 'that all of them may be one, Father, just as you are in me and I am in you ... May they be brought to complete unity to let the world know that you sent me and have loved them even as you have loved me' (vv. 21, 23).

There is no honest way to avoid the conclusion that Christ is praying for visible unity among his people: it is a unity that the world will be able to see. G. C. Berkouwer makes the point forcefully:

> In the light of Christ's prayer, the Church may not be viewed as a hidden, mystical, mysterious present reality full of inner richness, which the world cannot see ... To flee to the continuing sinfulness of the Church as an 'explanation' of her disunity or into the reassurance that a hidden unity can survive in the division does not take Christ's prayer seriously.[36]

The very fact that Christ makes this a matter for such fervent prayer at this point in His ministry emphasizes how difficult it will be for the covenant community to maintain unity. His people will themselves be driven to the Lord constantly in prayer for this very matter. In making 'every effort', they will be conscious of their need of grace from their covenant Lord. Scottish Covenanter George Hutcheson, writing on John 17:11 in 1657, comments,

> Whatever be the bonds tying Christians together ... and whatever prudential considerations and motives they have to induce them to obey the command of God in keeping together in unity, ... yet it is only the power of God that can keep the bond of unity inviolable; and unless he keep them near him, and free from the evils of the world, their union will break, and their being overpowered with flesh will break out in the bitter fruits of strife and division.[37]

Every epoch of church history supplies all too many examples of such failure on the part of the Church.

The Lord's intercession should stir believers to work zealously for the visible unity of God's covenant people. The disunity of the Church has been of great concern to covenant theologians. One of the greatest writers in seventeenth century Scotland, James Durham, expressed that concern in his famous work *The Dying Man's Testament to the Church of Scotland or A Treatise Concerning Scandal,* [38] in which many causes of division in the church are addressed. Our chief concern must be the dishonour done to our covenant Lord when His people are divided, but, as John 17:21-23 indicates, visible unity would provide a witness to the watching world. Conversely, disunity hinders such a witness severely. Listen again to George Hutcheson:

> The people of God walking in a united way is a special mean to convince the world of the excellency of Christ, and of the truth of the Christian religion, and so either leave them inexcusable or convert them; whereas schisms and rent among them is a ready mean to beget and cherish atheism in the world.[39]

Unity can of course only be in Christ and in his truth, but such unity is a duty laid upon His people.

Christ the Head of the Church
'There is no other head of the Church but the Lord Jesus Christ', asserts the Westminster Confession of Faith (XXV.6). At the heart of the life and death struggle of the Covenanters in Scotland was their assertion of the unique authority of Christ over His Church. This was foreshadowed in the famous encounter between James VI and the eminent Reformed theologian Andrew Melville in 1596. In response to the king's attempts to assert his authority over the Church of Scotland, Melville told him bluntly:

> 'There are two kings and two kingdoms in Scotland. There is Christ Jesus the King, and his kingdom the Kirk, whose subject King James the Sixth is, and of whose Kingdom he is not a king, nor a lord, nor a head, but a member.'[40]

In those days the question of Christ's authority over His Church was of profound importance. It must still be viewed in the same light, in days when Christians are careless regarding His will for the Church and governments seek to bring ever-increasing areas of life under their jurisdiction.

We have previously considered how Christ is the covenant Head of His people, drawing for example on Romans 5:12ff. and 1 Corinthians 15:22. By virtue of the position which He has been assigned, Christ purchased His people by the shedding of His blood and, by the power of the Holy Spirit, they are brought into living spiritual union with Him. On several occasions Paul speaks of the Church which results from Christ's atoning work as a body which has Christ as its Head. According to this metaphor, Christ is the organic Head of His body, the Church.

In a number of passages in Ephesians and Colossians Paul speaks of Christ and the Church in these terms. When believers speak the truth, 'we will in all things grow up into him who is the Head, that is, Christ' (Eph. 4:15). 'For the husband is the head of the wife as Christ is the head of the church, his body, of which he is the Saviour' (Eph. 5:23). 'And he is the head of the body, the church' (Col. 1:18). 'He has lost connection with the Head, from whom the whole body, supported and held together by its ligaments and sinews, grows as God causes it to grow' (Col. 2:19). Particularly striking is Paul's language in 1 Corinthians 10:16-17, 'And is not the bread that we break a participation in the body of Christ? Because there is one loaf, we, who are many, are one body, for we all partake of the one loaf.' Paul sets side by side references to the physical body of Christ and to the Church. As John Murray observes,

> It is because we are partakers of Christ's body that we are one body in him. It is because we are the beneficiaries of the offering of the body of Christ once for all, because he bore our sins in his own body upon the tree, that we are constituted the body of Christ. It is because representatively, and by mysterious identification with Christ in his death and resurrection, yea, even in his ascension to the heavenlies (Eph. 2:4-7), and thus identification with him in that which he accomplished in his own body, that we are one body in him.[41]

This is a most precious truth for the Church to grasp. Not only is Christ the means of the Church's unity but also of its growth and progress. The Church is entirely dependent on Christ and must look to Him for everything. As R. B. Kuiper says, 'It means that the church in all of its members lives and operates only through Christ.'[42] The Church consequently must focus on Christ and seek to carry on its work in ways that please Him and draw on His provision. Thus 'my God will meet all your needs according to his glorious riches in Christ Jesus' (Phil. 4:19). With reference to Colossians 2:19 Calvin comments, '[Paul] simply means that the Church only stands if all things are supplied to her by Christ her Head and, consequently, that her entire safety lies in Him.'[43]

Covenant theologians have also noted the fact that Christ's headship over His Church has inescapable implications of ruling authority over it. This is clear in Ephesians 5:23, where the headship of the husband in the marriage relationship parallels the headship of Christ over the Church, with the consequent call for submission to the authorities God has established, in verse 24. The headship Christ exercises is of course characterized by infinite self-giving love, but the term 'head' (*kephalē* in Greek) cannot be emptied of any implications of authority. The use of the word in Ephesians 1:22 ('God placed all things under his feet and appointed him to be head over everything for the church') is equally clear. Commenting on the latter text, James Hurley says, 'In the context, saturated with the language of authority, Paul parallels his assertion that things are subject to Christ with a declaration that Christ is appointed to be head (*kephalē*) over everything. There can be no escaping the idea of rule and authority.'[44] It recent years it has become common to find Christian feminist scholars such as Catherine Clark Kroeger arguing that *kephalē* really means 'source, origin' and has no implications of authority or rule.[45] This view has been comprehensively refuted in the painstaking studies of Wayne Grudem.[46]

The authority of Christ over His Church has wide-ranging implications. Every aspect of the Church's life and work must be conformed to His revealed will, rather than being determined by the preferences of any particular culture. Thus the beliefs and practices of any part of the Church must be shaped by Scripture, as must the form of government and pattern of worship. To allow anything other than the Lord's will to be the supreme authority in these areas results in the Church being, to some degree, *of* the world as well as *in* it.

The Church's spiritual union with Christ, its Head, leads to ongoing communion and fellowship with him. The union cannot change: the communion must be cultivated by the faithful use of such means of grace as the word, prayer and the sacraments. This in turn provides the basis for fellowship among God's people, the 'sharing' in spiritual things, which is the root meaning of 'fellowship' *(koinōnia* in Greek). Although the term 'fellowship' is much used in Christian circles, it must be stressed that apart from a living relationship with the Head of the Church, true fellowship with His people is not possible: it would be a contradiction in terms.

What is in view here is what covenant theologians, in harmony with earlier Christian thinking, term 'the communion of the saints'. Such communion embraces the whole Church, including glorified believers in heaven. This is not in any way to suggest that personal contact is possible between saints in heaven and saints on earth. Covenant theologians would not for a moment countenance such an idea. Nevertheless, on the basis of such a passage as Hebrews 12:22, which speaks of believers having now come to 'the heavenly Jerusalem ... to the church of the first-born', it is possible to argue that a universal communion of believers is a reality. Witsius puts it in these terms:

> the souls of the blessed, although they be entirely ignorant of the particular persons of believers on earth, and of their necessities, yet by their earnest prayers unite with us in soliciting, and, so to speak, accelerating, the day of the complete redemption of the Church; whilst the saints on earth are associated with those in heaven, in spirit, affection, and desire, having their conversation in heaven.[47]

Others speculate that the glorified saints may have specific information from the angels or by divine revelation, but acknowledge that Scripture is silent on the subject.[48]

The saints on earth are united to one another in Christ: as a result, they have the privilege of fellowship with one another and the duty to strengthen that bond. The congregations of the Church are to be true communities, loving all the members and seeking their welfare, both spiritual and physical. The Church as it is described in the early chapters of Acts provides an instructive pattern, with devotion to spiritual nurture and practical material help. Thus the believers 'devoted themselves to the apostles' teaching ... and had everything in common. Selling their possessions and goods, they gave to anyone as he had need ... They broke bread in their homes and ate together with glad and sincere hearts' (Acts 2:42-5). In a world hungry for love and true community, the Church alone, as Christ's covenant community, is in a position to offer all that is required, beginning with the redemptive love of Christ. Above all, God Himself is honoured and delighted by the fellowship enjoyed by His people. It is recounted in Malachi 3, in days of great spiritual declension, that 'those who feared the Lord talked with each other, and the Lord listened and heard. A scroll of remembrance was written in his presence concerning those who feared the Lord and honoured his name' (v. 16). As Jerry Bridges comments:

> The infinite, eternal mind of God obviously does not need a scroll of remembrance to remind Him of the gracious acts of His people. The allusion to such a scroll is for our benefit, that we might see the importance God places on true spiritual fellowship among His people and the delight it brings to His heart.[49]

Three attributes of the Church

Drawing on the statement in the Niceno-Constantinopolitan Creed of 381, it has become standard practice, among covenant theologians as among others, to identify four 'attributes' of the Church: it is 'one, holy, catholic and apostolic'. We have looked in some detail at the unity of the Church. Now the other three attributes will occupy our attention briefly.

(i) holiness

The Church belongs to a holy covenant Lord who 'loved the church and gave himself up for her to make her holy, cleansing her by the washing with water through the word' (Eph. 5:25-6). In many respects the Church is the individual writ large, and with regard to holiness this is certainly the case. We may speak of both definitive and progressive sanctification when considering the holiness of Christ's Church or, as R. B. Kuiper puts it, holiness is both 'fact' and 'duty'.[50]

By virtue of its union with Christ, the Church *is* holy. The radical, decisive break with sin has been made. The members of the Church are rightly addressed as 'saints' ('holy ones'). Thus Peter can say, 'You are a chosen people, a royal priesthood, a *holy nation*' (1 Pet. 2:9). In similar vein, Paul warns, 'If anyone destroys God's temple, God will destroy him; for God's temple is sacred [or 'holy'], and you are that temple' (1 Cor. 3:17). The Church, set apart for its covenant Lord, shares in his holiness and is indwelt by His Spirit. Thus Kuiper can say of the Church, 'its holiness is its very essence. Holiness constitutes it the church. The church is synonymous with holiness.'[51]

On the other hand, the Church, like its members, is to *become* holy. Peter addresses the 'holy nation' in these terms: 'But just as he who called you is holy, so be holy in all you do' (1 Pet. 1:15). The necessity to seek purity is clear in Paul's exhortation in 2 Corinthians 6:16-7:1:

> What agreement is there between the temple of God and idols? For we are the temple of the living God. As God has said, 'I will live with them and walk among them, and I will be their God, and they will be my people'. 'Therefore come out from them and be separate,' says the Lord. 'Touch no unclean thing, and I will receive you.' 'I will be a Father to you, and you will be my sons and daughters, says the Lord Almighty.' Since we have these promises, dear friends, let us purify ourselves from everything that contaminates body and spirit, perfecting holiness out of reverence for God.

According to His covenant promise the Lord walks in His Church, and so it must be holy.

As the Lord uses the means of sanctification He has provided
for His people He is sanctifying his Church. As Calvin, alluding
to Ephesians 5, comments, 'the Lord is daily at work in smoothing
out wrinkles and cleansing spots. From this it follows that the
church's holiness is not yet complete. The church is holy, then in
the sense that it is daily advancing and is not yet perfect.'[52] In this
process the faithful exercise of discipline by the Church plays a
vital part. If the public sins of members are not addressed, the
Church's witness to the world is crippled and the Head of the
Church is dishonoured. This pursuit of holiness, although never
complete before the last day, will be complete when Christ presents
the Church to Himself 'as a radiant church, without stain or wrinkle
or any other blemish, but holy and blameless' (Eph. 5:27). Until
then, the covenant people dare not be careless about the holiness
of the church any more than they may be careless about their own
sanctification.

(ii) catholicity
'Catholic' means universal, and the attribute of catholicity, applied
to the true Church of Christ, indicates its extension throughout
the world. The Church is a single body extending to the farthest
reaches of the world. Johannes Wollebius defines it thus: 'It is
called catholic by reason of time, place and persons'.[53] With respect
to time, he points out that the Church has never entirely disappeared
from the world: a true Church is always to be found somewhere
on earth. As far as place and persons are concerned, the Church
does not exclude any true believer on account of his national or
racial or social background. Peter, as a result of his encounter
with Cornelius, came to this awareness: 'I now realise how true it
is that God does not show favouritism but accepts men from every
nation who fear him and do what is right' (Acts 10:34-5). No
qualifications for membership in the Church can be laid down
which go beyond the Lord's requirements.

The catholicity of the Church, with its bringing together of
diverse races and cultures, is a glorious testimony to the richness
of God's covenant grace. As Ephesians 2 demonstrates, the work
of Christ brought together into one body the most unlikely partners,

Jews and Gentiles, and in Christ such barriers have continued to be overcome. Nothing must be allowed to obscure the true catholicity of the Church, whether it be some form of apartheid, however enforced, or a missionary methodology that seeks to focus on separate social or racial groups. At the local level, every believer must be welcome among the Lord's people. James is one New Testament writer who highlights the sinfulness of bias on social grounds (Jas. 2:1ff.).

In contrast to the biblical catholicity of which covenant theologians speak, there is the false catholicity of Rome, which claims for itself the exclusive right to the term 'catholic'. Believing that as an institution it has 'correct and complete confession of faith, full sacramental life, and ordained ministry in apostolic succession'[54] it concludes that it is *the* Catholic Church. A 'Particular Church' can be considered catholic only if it is in communion with the Church of Rome, since 'with this church, by reason of its pre-eminence, the whole Church, that is the faithful everywhere, must necessarily be in accord'.[55] Organisational connection with an institution full of error has been substituted for true biblical catholicity.

(iii) apostolicity

Robert Reymond rightly observes that 'apostolicity must be primarily concerned with faithful adherence to the doctrine of the apostles, which was communicated to them by supernatural revelation and inscripturated by supernatural inspiration'.[56] Covenant theologians view the apostolicity of the Church as a matter of doctrine, not of organization. They rightly point out that organizational continuity does not necessarily indicate continued adherence to the truth. It is in this sense that they understand Ephesians 2:20, which speaks of the Church 'built on the foundation of the apostles and prophets, with Christ Jesus himself as the chief cornerstone'. Thus Calvin comments, '*Foundation* unquestionably here refers to doctrine; for he does not mention patriarchs or godly kings, but only those who held a teaching office, and whom God had appointed to build His Church.'[57] Since the centre of apostolic teaching was Christ Himself, there is no conflict between this text and 1 Corinthians 3:11, 'For no-one can lay any foundation other than the one already laid, which is Jesus Christ.'

Rome's view of apostolicity, however, is built on (alleged) unbroken organizational continuity with the apostles, above all the 'supreme pastor', Peter. Ludwig Ott provides a comprehensive view of Rome's position on apostolicity:

> In its origin the Church goes back to the Apostles. She has always adhered to the teaching which she received from the Apostles. The Pastors of the Church, the Pope and the Bishops are connected with the Apostles by the succession of office. The apostolicity of the succession guarantees the unfalsified transmission of doctrine and makes manifest the organic connection between the Church of the present day and the Church of the Apostles.[58]

A crucial text in the polemical exchanges between Reformed and Roman Catholic theologians has been Matthew 16:18, where Jesus, in response to Peter's confession of his Messiahship states, 'And I tell you that you are Peter, and on this rock I will build my church.' The view that became the accepted position of Rome is that the Church is built especially on Peter (whose name means Rock), who was given the crucial primacy which has been handed on to his successors in the Papacy. Reformed writers, including Calvin, have generally argued that the 'rock' is Peter's confession of faith and that no personal power was conferred on him.[59] Without in any way accepting that some unique authority was conferred on Peter, other Reformed writers hold that Jesus did indeed address Peter, but only as the representative of the whole group of apostles. R. B. Kuiper states, 'Very likely "this rock" is none other than the confessing Peter as representative of the apostles.'[60] Robert Reymond, after a long examination of the issue and defence of the possibility of the confession of Peter being the rock, also says that it is 'entirely possible' that Peter is addressed personally. It is, however, Peter 'as the confessing apostle' who is in view. He goes on to state that 'Peter is the rock only in his office as a confessing apostle speaking the Word of God'.[61] Whichever view is accepted, it is clear that the verse gives no support to Rome's claims regarding Peter as first Pope and foundation of the Church.[62]

Marks of the Church

Although covenant theologians readily acknowledge the truth of the statement in the Westminster Confession that the 'purest Churches under heaven are subject both to mixture and error' (XXV.5), they have always been concerned to identify which bodies of believers may be counted as part of Christ's covenant community.

Covenant theologians speak of the 'marks' of the true Church, namely the true preaching of the word of God, the administration of the sacraments according to Christ's institution and, in some cases, the exercise of biblical church discipline. An early example of the threefold pattern is to be found in the Scots Confession of 1560:

> The notes therefore of the trew Kirk of God we beleeve, confesse and avow to be, first the trew preaching of the Worde of God ... Secundly, the right administration of the Sacraments of Christ Jesus, quhilk man be annexed unto the word and promise of God ... Last, Ecclesiastical discipline uprightlie ministred, as Goddis Worde prescribes.[63]

In a sense the second and third marks are applications of the first, since the sacraments must be explained by the word and discipline is to be determined by the word. The preaching of God's revealed truth is crucial to the existence of the Church, not forgetting that the truth must also be heard and acted upon by the covenant community. Thus Calvin describes the first mark of a true church: 'If it has the ministry of the Word and honours it'.[64] It is interesting that Zacharias Ursinus, one of the authors of the Heidelberg Catechism, makes 'profession of obedience to this doctrine, or to the ministry' the third mark of the Church.[65] The covenant community must sit under the word of its covenant Lord, and the teachers of the Church must teach nothing additional to or contrary to His word.

The second mark, namely the administration of the sacraments according to Christ's institution, will occupy our attention in the next chapter and so need not be considered further here. Again the Church is to be willingly obedient to its Head, making use of a precious means of grace that He has provided. Their value is well stated by Calvin's successor at Geneva, Theodore Beza:

> they are established so that we may receive from His grace and liberality what is more precious than heaven and earth: the strengthening of our faith. Each day we will be thus more closely united and joined to Jesus Christ our Head, as respects our eternal life.[66]

The third mark, or, in the view of some covenant theologians, a requirement for the well-being of the Church, is the administration of biblical discipline. In Calvin's striking expression, discipline serves as the 'sinews' of the Church, 'through which the members of the body hold together, each in its own place'.[67] Scripture provided many examples of the way in which the leaders of God's people are to promote the holiness of the church by disciplinary action where sin is openly and publicly practised. In Matthew 18:15ff., for example, Jesus instructs his disciples to deal with offences in as private a way as possible, yet if the offender will not respond positively, 'tell it to the church; and if he refuses to listen even to the church, treat him as you would a pagan or a tax collector.' Similarly in regard to incest in the church at Corinth, Paul expects the congregation to take disciplinary action. The offender, according to 1 Corinthians 5:2, should have been removed from the fellowship. Such New Testament examples build on an Old Testament basis, since great care was taken, at least when the spiritual level of the people was high, to ensure that the impure did not profane the feasts in the Temple. This Old Testament background was examined in detail by writers such as George Gillespie in the seventeenth century and lessons were drawn for the contemporary Church.[68]

The threefold purpose of church discipline was well set out by Calvin in his *Institutes*, reflecting the experience of a man who struggled for many years to establish an ecclesiastical discipline in Geneva free from interference from the civil power. The three ends of discipline he describes thus:

The first is that they who lead a filthy and infamous life may not be called Christians, to the dishonour of God ... The second purpose is that the good be not corrupted by the constant company of the wicked ... The third purpose is that those overcome by shame for their baseness begin to repent.[69]

The Church must be willing to swim against the tide of a culture which despises authority and mocks the very idea of church discipline. Given the sinfulness of even the best church leaders, abuses will occur, but when attention is fixed prayerfully on these three goals – the glory of God, the protection of believers, the restoration of offenders – much will be achieved in promoting the holiness of the Church and its witness before a watching world. Formal discipline should be seen as a positive activity and as a supplement to believers' disciplining of one another within the fellowship of the Church.

The ministries of the Church
The covenant people are called to serve their Lord: they are to engage in 'ministry'. It is not only those who have come to be termed 'ministers' who have this calling. Every believer is a servant, a 'minister'. The term 'ministry', however, is nowadays applied to a vast range of activities, some of which have nothing to do with the Church's God-given tasks, and so recourse has to be had to the infallible word of the Church's Head. What are the biblical ministries of the Church? A most useful exposition of this subject has been provided by Edmund Clowney in his book *The Church*,[70] and we make no apology for drawing heavily on his work.

(i) the goals of ministry
These may be thought of in terms of three 'directions'. The Church ministers 'upwards' to God in the ministry of worship. John Murray observes that 'as the church is the assembly of God's people, the household of God, and the body of Christ, as living stones built up a spiritual house, to be a holy priesthood to offer up spiritual sacrifices, the central function is the worship of God.'[71] Above

all, the covenant people are to worship their covenant Lord.

The Church also ministers 'inwards' to its own people in the ministry of nurture. The saints are to be built up and prepared for service, as indicated in Ephesians 4:12. The phrase translated 'for the work of the ministry' in the AV is *not* an exclusive reference to the work of preachers ('ministers'), but to the service all must render. In the ministry of nurture particular attention must be given to covenant children within the Church, since, as Robert Reymond observes, 'when the church contemplates its growth, either quantitatively or qualitatively, it cannot afford to ignore its responsibility to its own children.'[72] More will be said about covenant children in the next chapter.

Finally, the Church ministers 'outwards' to the world in the ministry of witness. The Lord's mandate to His Church is 'Go and make disciples of all nations' (Matt. 28:19). Thus the elect are to be brought in, as the Holy Spirit blesses the ministry of witness, so that they then benefit from the ministries of nurture and worship. The mission of the covenant community is considered in more detail below.

(ii) the means of ministry

Again these may be thought of as three in number. Fundamental is the ministry of the word. It is the word 'that calls to worship, addresses us in worship, teaches us how to worship and enables us to praise God and to encourage one another'.[73] The word is also essential for the nurture of believers: no other writings can take its central place in instruction since it is God's inspired covenant word. Similarly in mission, the Church is to proclaim the biblical gospel in a biblical way. There is no other way to accomplish genuine church growth. The wording of Acts 6:7 is profoundly significant: 'So the word of God spread. The number of disciples in Jerusalem increased rapidly.'

The second means of achieving the Church's goals is the ministry of order, i.e. government and discipline. Although many believers reflect their western culture in having little concern for such issues, the ministry of order is necessary and biblical. The Church that is described as an organism (a body, an olive tree) is also an organization (a building, a temple). As Clowney shows, the three goals of ministry are to be carried out in the obedience of love, and on this he comments, 'Love that is real requires accountability, and accountability means order.'[74] Where love is the motivating power, such order is kept from becoming oppressive or tyrannical. Instead it enables the Church to do its work well and to the Lord's glory.

The third means is the ministry of mercy, the performing of acts of loving service. This has a place in connection with worship, in the giving of gifts for the poor. Paul, significantly, speaks of gifts sent to him by the Philippians as 'a fragrant offering, an acceptable sacrifice, pleasing to God' (Phil. 4:18). Nurture of believers requires willingness to give practical help, as James 2:15-16 illustrates, and the mission of the Church must combine proclamation of God's love with practical demonstrations of love. The pattern is set in Galatians 6:10, 'Therefore, as we have opportunity, let us do good to all people, especially to those who belong to the family of believers.' Donald Macleod goes so far as to argue, 'Just, then, as a church is not a church if it does not evangelise, so a church is not a church if it has no concern for the poor.'[75]

(iii) the forms of ministry

Every member of the covenant community is called to minister, and one of the great rediscoveries of the Reformation was the priesthood of all believers. As Paul's development of the body metaphor in 1 Corinthians 12 demonstrates, the Spirit gives gifts to all of God's people. Referring to spiritual gifts, Paul says, 'All these are the work of one and the same Spirit, and he gives them to each one, just as he determines' (verse 11). To share in the blessings of the Covenant of Grace brings responsibilities to use the gifts God has provided. In this way believers minister to God as they engage in worship; they minister to each other as they share God's word, bring encouragement and loving rebuke to one another, and provide practical help as needed; they minister to the world as they proclaim Christ by word and deed. The ministry that every member can provide is vital to the welfare of the Church, and none should try to bury the talent God has entrusted (cf. Matt. 25:18, 24-25).

Nevertheless, the Lord also calls particular men to occupy distinct 'offices' in the Church, with an official responsibility for fulfilling the ministries of the Church. The ministries of worship and nurture are particularly in the hands of those designated 'elders' in the New Testament. Drawing on the tradition of the elders who had oversight of the community of Israel, the New Testament Church was under the oversight of elders who exercised authority under and in the name of Christ, the Head of the Church. As congregations were established by the apostles' missionary endeavours, elders were provided to lead the community. Thus in Acts 14:23 Paul and Barnabas 'appointed elders for them in each church'. These elders or 'presbyters' are the same as those designated 'bishops' (*episkopoi* in Greek).

The elders are to rule in love over the people of God. Thus in 1 Timothy 5:17 we read 'The elders who rule well are to be considered worthy of double honour' (NASB). They are to be shepherds, feeding God's people, leading and protecting them, disciplining them as required. Note Paul's exhortation to the Ephesian elders: 'Keep watch over yourselves and all the flock of which the Holy Spirit has made you overseers. Be shepherds of the church of God, which he bought with his own blood' (Acts 20:28). All elders are to be 'able to teach' (1 Tim. 3:2), but it seems clear that some were devoted especially to the ministry of the word. Thus 1 Timothy 5:17 speaks of 'those who work hard at preaching and teaching' (NASB). These are the 'pastors and teachers' of Ephesians 4:11, known today as 'pastors', 'teaching elders' or 'ministers'. They are elders like the 'ruling elders' and the Church must be careful that this equality is observed in practice.

Some covenant theologians have argued that 'elders' as the Presbyterian tradition knows them are in fact not the 'presbyters' of the New Testament, and that only ministers are presbyters. This issue was vigorously debated, especially in American Presbyterianism in the nineteenth century, but it seems to us that the biblical view is that defended by, among others, J. H. Thornwell, namely that *all* elders are presbyters.[76]

Covenant theologians have generally recognized that the elders of the New Testament Church exercised an oversight that extended beyond their local congregation. Such wider oversight reflects the fact that the covenant community forms one body in Christ. Thus gatherings of elders representing particular geographical areas, with a measure of authority over several congregations, are held to be biblical, with appeal being made to such examples as the Council of Jerusalem in Acts 15. The practical outworking of this principle has varied considerably within the Reformed tradition. Churches which look to the standards of the Westminster Assembly, particularly the Scottish Presbyterians, have an outlook that differs significantly from their 'Continental' Reformed brothers. Even within Presbyterianism some have viewed authority as coming from the 'top' down to local congregations whilst others have viewed it as beginning as the local level and being delegated upwards (a view closer to the Continental outlook).[77]

The office which deals particularly with the ministry of mercy is that of deacon, which some trace back to the appointment of men to ensure fair distribution of aid to widows, recorded in Acts 6. The biblical qualifications for deacons are set out in 1 Timothy 3:8ff. and indicate that spiritual maturity is the key factor in evaluating candidates. In many Reformed churches deacons, if they have not been replaced by boards or committees, have come to deal mostly with the finances and fabric of churches. The biblical focus of their work, however, is clearly to show practical love in the name of Christ's Church to those in need. An almost endless list of possible avenues of service could be drawn up, including giving financial advice or help, visiting the sick, none of these tasks being limited to helping those within the Church, since the ministry of mercy is part of the Church's missionary task. The deacons' qualifications indicate that spiritual counsel could well be part of the assistance they give. As Leonard Coppes says, 'In a world swamped in misery and suffering one does not need to look far for someone oppressed by physical and material needs. Indeed, how can there be a clean separation between the spiritual and the non-spiritual?'[78]

For most of the history of the Church there has been no debate

among the orthodox concerning the occupation of church offices
by men only. Many covenant theologians have felt no need to
address the issue at length, if at all. The development of the feminist
movement in the late twentieth century has exercised considerable
influence on Christians, however, with the result that there have
been many calls for the opening of all offices in the Church to
suitably qualified women. The issue is often stated in terms of
equal rights. Thus evangelical feminist Gretchen Gaebelein Hull
says:

> Therefore biblical feminists lovingly ask the Christian community
> to abandon artificial role playing and to be sex blind in assessing
> each individual's qualifications for ministry and in matching each
> individual's gifts with service opportunities. We reverently affirm
> that our great God is an Equal Opportunity Employer. Can His church
> be less?[79]

Covenant theologians have replied that in regard to the
eldership, since it requires the exercise of authority, it cannot be
carried out by women, appealing to Paul's statement in 1 Timothy
2:12, 'I do not permit a woman to teach or to have authority over
a man.' By definition, women cannot be qualified for eldership.
The complex debates over this issue cannot be examined here,
but have received comprehensive treatment in a number of recent
works.[80] The situation is not quite as clear-cut regarding deacons,
since some consider that no exercise of authority is involved in
their work. Thus covenant theologians are divided as to whether
women may be ordained, with most arguing that they may not,
whilst others, like Edmund Clowney, argue that they may.[81]

The covenant community at worship

A fundamental mark of having truly received the grace of God is
that we worship the Lord. That is the believer's immediate response
to the God who has saved him. When the covenant community
gathers, its chief activity, its supreme delight, will be to worship
the Lord. We were made to worship God, and as those who have
been brought into the Covenant of Grace we now *can* worship
Him, with His gracious assistance. As Clowney says, 'God's

assembly stands in his presence; to be the assembly, i.e. to be the church, is to worship God together.'[82]

There are those who argue that 'all of life is worship', but the Bible, in both Old and New Testaments, shows that the people of God are to gather in His presence for particular activities that may be designated 'worship', such as singing praise, praying corporately, hearing the word of God read and expounded, and partaking of the sacraments. All of life is to be lived to God's glory, but God is present among His people in a special sense when they gather for worship.[83] Worship is a separate and special activity of the covenant people.

God must be the centre of true worship, God as He has revealed Himself in nature, providence and, supremely, in His word. Worship is the only fitting response by those who have seen God's glory, and of believers it can be said that God 'made his light shine in our hearts to give us the light of the knowledge of the glory of God in the face of Christ' (2 Cor. 4:6). In love and joy and reverence they worship their covenant God. R. B. Kuiper observes,

> How lofty a conception of corporate worship Scripture presents! When God's people assemble for worship they enter into the place where God dwells. God meets them, and they meet God. They find themselves face to face with none other than God Himself. Their worship is an intimate transaction between them and their God.[84]

Such worship must be offered through Christ, the only Mediator, and in the power of the Holy Spirit.

Those who belong to the Covenant of Grace love the Lord, and that love issues in obedience to His will, as texts such as John 14:15 and 1 John 5:3 indicate. The activities of worship cannot be excluded from that obedience. The Church willingly must submit to God's will regarding worship. Throughout the Old Testament God showed Himself to be most concerned about the way in which He is worshipped, and additions made without divine sanction brought dramatic retribution, as in the case of Nadab and Abihu offering 'unauthorised fire before the Lord' (Lev. 10:1). The Lord has not changed when we come to the New Testament. The

230 of 352 (document id

multitude of ceremonial regulations may have gone, but New Covenant worship is still to be directed by God's will.

This view of worship, which covenant theologians have expounded, often in great detail, is termed 'the regulative principle of worship'. It is stated thus by John Calvin: 'whatever is not commanded, we are not free to choose.'[85] The classic statement of the principle is to be found in the Westminster Confession:

> the acceptable way of worshipping the true God is instituted by Himself, and so limited by His own revealed will, that He may not be worshipped according to the imaginations and devices of man, or the suggestions of Satan, under any visible representation, or any other way not prescribed in the holy Scripture. (XXI.1).

It guided the worship of the English Puritans and the Scottish Covenanters, and has been defended in detail by modern writers such as Michael Bushell[86] and Hector Cameron.[87] All recognize that some 'circumstances' of worship, such as the times of services, are left to the discretion of elders, within the general guidance of the word, but as far as the elements of worship are concerned, 'what is not commanded is forbidden'.

Many Christians, if they have heard of the regulative principle, reject it without serious consideration of its biblical basis. There have, however, been rather more sophisticated attacks on it from within the Reformed tradition. In recent years John Frame has formulated a new understanding of the principle which has proved to be influential, professing as it does to retain the principle yet allowing for, among other things, dance and drama in worship. Frame argues in *Worship in Spirit and in Truth*[88] that the intent of the regulative principle was to safeguard the Church from introducing anything into worship that displeases God, and that in a profound sense worship is no different from any other part of the Christian life. Everything we do is to be guided by God's commands and we are not free to go beyond them. He says that

> the regulative principle for worship is no different from the principles by which God regulates all of our life. That is to be expected, because ... worship *is*, in an important sense, all of life. In both cases, 'whatever

is not commanded is forbidden' – everything we do must be done in obedience to God's commands.[89]

The difference between worship and the rest of life, however, is that God does not *command* many things Christians may legitimately do, for example to join a golf club or holiday in Barbados, whereas He does lay down specific rules to guide the worship of the whole Church. For individual decisions about holidays or leisure pursuits, Christians must apply the general principles of the Bible, for example regarding stewardship of money, but the regulative principle of worship, as traditionally understood, removes the need for individual decisions regarding the elements of worship. Frame, however, makes *application* the key procedure in worship too, and all of worship (there are no circumstances that are 'indifferent') must be determined in this way. The end result of Frame's method is in fact a version of the principle 'what is not forbidden is allowed', characteristic of Lutheranism, Anglicanism and most Evangelicalism. He concludes:

> My own formulation does not contradict the confession, but goes beyond it. In my view, we are free from anything 'beside' the word, not only in 'matters of faith, or worship', but in all other areas of life as well. In all areas of life, we are subject to biblical commands ... Human wisdom may never presume to *add* to its commands. The only job of human wisdom is to *apply* those commands to specific situations.[90]

In contrast to Frame's redefining away of the regulative principle, many covenant theologians have concluded that a thoroughly biblical understanding of the principle requires the Church to follow the New Testament pattern of singing psalms without instrumental accompaniment. Such was the pattern among the Puritans and Covenanters, and, although a minority position in the contemporary Church, it has been vigorously defended by writers such as Michael Bushell and in a number of symposia on worship.[91] It is interesting that in 1947, when the Committee on Song in the Public Worship of God presented its report to the

General Assembly of the Orthodox Presbyterian Church in America, a Minority Report defending exclusive Psalmody was also presented by John Murray and William Young.[92] In recent years disenchantment with modern worship practices has led some to consider more seriously the place of psalms in worship.[93]

In closing our consideration of worship according to Covenant Theology we must note that the day of worship set aside by the Lord for His people has covenantal significance. In Eden, the Sabbath arose out of the Lord's 'resting' on the seventh day: 'God blessed the seventh day and made it holy, because on it he rested from all the work of creating that he had done' (Gen. 2:3). Francis Nigel Lee comments on the situation in Eden under the Covenant of Works:

> The punishment for disobedience to the covenant was (*restless*) death, but the reward for obedience was eternal life, i.e. eternal rest, which rest was portrayed to him each week by the day of rest or the weekly Sabbath.'[94]

After the Fall God promised salvation through the Mediator of the Covenant of Grace, and so the Sabbath became a weekly reminder that God would provide eternal rest in due time by the promised Redeemer. It is significant that the Sabbath was included among the Ten Commandments: its intent is clearly moral, whatever ceremonial elements may have been attached to it. Joseph Pipa correctly observes,

> For the Israelites the Sabbath sign pointed in two directions: backwards, reminding them of God as Creator who after the Fall had promised salvation through a Redeemer, and forwards, reminding them that they were to wait in faith for the promised Saviour.[95]

With the death and resurrection of Christ, the New Covenant has been sealed: the Christian Church lives in the age of fulfilment. The Sabbath commandment, however, continues as a moral obligation, with believers observing the first day of the week as their Sabbath, following the example of the New Testament Church, designating it the Lord's Day. Theologians and biblical scholars are divided over whether the Lord's Day is a Sabbath.[96] We cannot rehearse the arguments here, but agree with most covenant theologians, and many others, that it is. The Sabbath therefore still has covenantal significance. As Hebrews 4:9 says, 'There remains, then a Sabbath-rest for the people of God', a rest we will receive through a crucified and risen Mediator. Thus Pipa argues:

> We who live in the full reality of accomplished redemption have our Sabbath on the first day of the week to signify that God has completed the objective work of redemption and that we have begun to participate in that redemption. Like Israel's Sabbath, ours also points backwards and forwards. It points back to the resurrection of Christ and reminds us that as we rest in Him, all our sins are forgiven. It also points forwards, reminding us that Christ will return and we shall live with Him in perfect bliss for evermore.[97]

It is vital, of course, that Christians observe the Lord's Day in a reverent and joyful spirit that is a witness to the surrounding world. Joyless Sabbath-keeping is an affront to the Lord. It is a day that gives great opportunities for worship, fellowship and loving care for others. It is a day to be used: hence the Larger Catechism's reference to 'profaning the day by idleness' (Q119). The Catechism also stresses preparation of heart and forward planning to allow the Sabbath to be a day of rest. Jonathan Edwards, the greatest American Puritan, left behind three sermons on 'The Perpetuity and Change of the Sabbath'.[98] Near the end of the third sermon, he manifests the true Puritan spirit:

> We should on this day contemplate the wonderful love of God and of Christ, as expressed in the work of redemption; and our remembrance of these things should be accompanied with suitable exercises of soul with respect to them. When we call to mind the love of Christ, it should be with a return of love on our part. When we commemorate this work, it should be with faith in the Saviour. And we should praise God and the Lamb for this work, for the divine glory and love manifested in it, in our private and public prayers, in talking of the wonderful works of God, and in singing divine songs.[99]

Covenantal mission

The covenant community as it is depicted in Scripture is a multiracial, multicultural, multinational body. 'After this I looked and there before me was a great multitude that no-one could count, from every nation, tribe, people and language, standing before the throne and in front of the Lamb' (Rev. 7:9). The source of this body is traced to the redemptive work of the Lamb: 'You are worthy to take the scroll and to open the seals, because you were slain and with your blood you purchased men for God from every tribe and language and people and nation' (Rev. 5:9). The elect given to the Mediator in the Covenant of Redemption break all barriers of colour, language or culture, a truth reflected in the 'catholicity' of the Church.

In order that this great assembly may be gathered, the Church is called to take the gospel message throughout the world. The mandate of the risen Christ makes this clear: 'Therefore go and make disciples of all nations' (Matt. 28:19). The Lord's covenant community is to be a missionary community, fulfilling its calling faithfully so that all of the elect are brought into the blessings of the Covenant of Grace. Indeed, Thomas Goodwin argues that, as a result of the regenerating work of the Holy Spirit, 'one eminent disposition immediately flowing from the new creature is a desire to convert and beget others to God'.[100]

It will be helpful at this point to have a definition of mission that is thoroughly biblical and consonant with Covenant Theology. Such a definition is provided by mission executive Mark Bube in a paper presented at the International Conference of Reformed Churches in South Korea in 1997. Drawing on earlier thinking, Bube defines missions thus:

> Missions is the work of the Triune God, through His Church, of sending ambassadors of Christ's covenant to all nations to proclaim His whole Word, for the salvation of lost men, the establishment of indigenous churches, and the coming of God's kingdom, all for the glory of God.[101]

This definition serves to stress that mission, wherever carried out, is to be God-centred. The message, the methods and every other aspect of the work are to be carried out according to the will of the God of the covenant. The Great Commission of Matthew 28 is based on the exaltation of Christ crucified and risen as the Mediatorial King: 'All authority in heaven and on earth has been given to me. *Therefore*, go ...'. His completed work as Surety provides the foundation for the missionary mandate. All centres on the Lord and the Church's goal is to make disciples *for Him*.

In eternity, as we have seen, God chose a people to be His own and these people were given to Christ in the Covenant of Redemption. The elect are, according to God's purpose, to be brought in time into the Covenant of Grace. He has promised, 'I will be your God and you will be my people'. In order that this purpose may be fulfilled, God has also provided the necessary means, namely the preaching of the gospel, with the blessing of the Holy Spirit. As R. B. Kuiper says, 'It is apparent, then, that the preaching of the gospel is an important link in the chain of events that constitute the realization of election. And not only is it an important link; it is a necessary one.'[102] Election demands evangelism. The Covenant of Grace will benefit no one unless the gospel is preached, and so Kuiper concludes, 'Evangelism is inherent in the covenant of grace.'[103]

God's people should undoubtedly be moved by the plight of the unsaved: if they really believe in eternal punishment, it cannot be otherwise. The Puritan writer Richard Baxter puts it vividly:

> Oh, if you have the hearts of Christians or of men in you, let them yearn towards your poor, ignorant, ungodly neighbours. Alas! there is but a step betwixt them and death and hell ... Hath God had such mercy on you, and will you have no mercy on your poor neighbours?[104]

Nevertheless, the deepest missionary motivation must come from love for God, from which true love for neighbours springs. The more we love the Lord, the more eagerly we obey all His commandments, including the command to evangelize. Kuiper puts it well:

Love for God and his Christ guarantees on the part of the believer loving, hence genuine and devoted, in distinction from external and legalistic, obedience to the divine command to evangelise the nations.[105]

To have a 'vision' for mission means above all to have a vision of God. That is the central thrust of Tom Wells' book *A Vision for Missions*. As he says, 'those who know the most about God are the most responsible and the best equipped to tell of Him.'[106] We must therefore strive to know God better, never forgetting the responsibility that knowledge brings.

It is clear from Scripture that the Church, the covenant community, is the God-ordained agent of evangelism. Every believer has a responsibility to be a witness and those set aside by the Church for preaching and teaching have a particular responsibility, but this is only to say that the Church must evangelize. Whatever individuals do to 'gossip the gospel' (Acts 8:4, paraphrased), it is the Church that commissions and oversees missionaries and evangelists. The book of Acts, to go no further, provides ample evidence of that fact. Parachurch agencies have often grown up because the Church has failed in its task, but that must not be allowed to obscure the biblical pattern. Through the apostles the Great Commission was given to the Church. 'Whoever else may properly engage in evangelism, the organized church is the supreme Scriptural agency for evangelism.'[107]

Covenant theologians have often asserted that in mission priority must be given to the Jewish people. In part this reflects the statements of texts such as Romans 1:16 that the gospel is 'the power of God for the salvation of everyone who believes: first for the Jew, then for the Gentile', and in part it flows from the hope of a great turning of the Jews to Christ which many have drawn from Romans 11, (a hope discussed in chapter 10). This view has been common, although rejected by prominent Reformed missiologist J. H. Bavinck.[108] The priority to be accorded to the Jews is reflected in the inclusion of prayer for their conversion in the Westminster Assembly's Directory for the Publick Worship of God ('Of Publick Prayer before the Sermon') and the frequent efforts of Reformed churches to provide for Jewish evangelism.[109]

The motive for such mission is clearly love for the Jewish people, not, as is often claimed today, antisemitism and a desire to obliterate the Jews. Thus Richard de Ridder is correct to conclude, 'For today this means that salvation, ministry, life are not to be organised and adapted according to what looks most urgent or efficient without reference to Israel.'[110]

The biblical truths regarding election and the covenants are the source of the Church's hope of success in mission. These are the guarantees that sinners will be saved: on any other premises, the outcome is uncertain. Far from hindering evangelism, as some claim, these truths empower evangelism. Paul was encouraged by the Lord when evangelizing in Corinth with the assurance, 'I have many people in this city' (Acts 18:10). Many of the greatest missionaries have believed these truths. The God of the covenants is a sovereign God. Of this truth J. I. Packer says:

> Not only does it undergird evangelism, and uphold the evangelist, by creating a hope of success that could not otherwise be entertained; it also teaches us to bind together preaching and prayer; and as it makes us bold and confident before men, so it makes us humble and importunate before God.[111]

As the covenants are indestructible, so the Church which they produce is indestructible. The Lord has promised, 'I will build my church, and the gates of Hades will not overcome it' (Matt. 16:18). In that confidence the Church proclaims the gospel.

Notes

1. Herman Witsius, *Sacred Dissertations on the Apostles' Creed*, translated by Donald Fraser, 1823 edition, 2 volumes. (Escondido, 1993), 2.350.

2. John Murray, 'The Church: Its Identity, Functions and Resources' in *Collected Writings of John Murray* (Edinburgh, 1976), 1.237-8.

3. L. Coenen, 'Church' in *New International Dictionary of New Testament Theology*, edited by Colin Brown (Carlisle/Grand Rapids, 1986), vol. 1, p. 305.

4. Robert L. Reymond, *A New Systematic Theology of the Christian Faith* (Nashville, 1998), p. 525.

5. John Murray, 'The Nature and Unity of the Church' in *Collected Writings of John Murray*, 2.323.

6. Charles Hodge, *Commentary on the Epistle to the Romans*, 1886 edition (Grand Rapids, 1947), ad. loc.

7. Richard B. Gaffin, *Perspectives on Pentecost* (Phillipsburg, 1979), p. 21.

8. L. Coenen, art. cit., p. 305.

9. D. Douglas Bannerman, *The Scripture Doctrine of the Church*, 1887 edition (Grand Rapids, 1976).

10. Wilhelmus à Brakel, *The Christian's Reasonable Service*, 1700 edition, translated by Bartel Elshout, vol. 4, Appendix, pp. 373ff.

11. R. B. Kuiper, *The Glorious Body of Christ* (London, 1967), p. 37.

12. Johannes Wollebius, *Compendium of Christian Theology* (1626), in *Reformed Dogmatics*, translated and edited by John W. Beardslee III (Grand Rapids, 1977), p. 137.

13. Edmund P. Clowney, *The Church* (Leicester, 1995), p. 46. Clowney deals helpfully with a number of trinitarian prespectives on the Church in chapters 2-4 of this book. See also his essay 'The Biblical Theology of the Church' in *The Church in the Bible and the World*, edited by D. A. Carson (Exeter/Grand Rapids, 1987), pp. 13-87.

14. Johannes Wollebius, op. cit., p. 137.

15. John Calvin, *Institutes of the Christian Religion*, 1559 edition, translated by Ford Lewis Battles (Philadelphia, 1960), IV.i.7.

16. James Bannerman, *The Church of Christ*, 1869 edition (London, 1960), 1.31.

17. ibid.

18. See the comments of John Macpherson in *The Doctrine of the Church in Scottish Theology* (Edinburgh, 1903), pp. 64-5. The whole of Lecture 2 is relevant to the present discussion.

19. These may be found in *The Creeds of Christendom* edited by Philip Schaff, 6th edition (Grand Rapids, 1983), vol. 3.

20. Wilhelmus à Brakel, op. cit., vol. 2, p. 6.

21. ibid.

22. Wilhelmus à Brakel, op. cit., vol. 2, p. 13.

23. R. B. Kuiper, op. cit., p. 26.

24. John Murray, 'The Church: Its Definition in Terms of "Visible" and "Invisible" Invalid' in *Collected Writings of John Murray*, 1.231ff.

25. John Murray, 'The Nature and Unity of the Church' in *Collected Writings of John Murray*, 2.327.

26. ibid.

27. ibid.

28. G. I. Williamson, *The Westminster Confession of Faith for Study Classes* (Philadelphia, 1964), p. 189.

29. R. B. Kuiper, op. cit., p. 43.

30. Thomas McCrie, *The Unity of the Church*, 1989 revision of 1821 edition (Dallas, 1989), p. 15.

31. This is convincingly demonstrated by John Macpherson, op. cit., Lecture 3.

32. Francis Turretin, *Institutes of Elenctic Theology*, translated by G. M. Giger (Phillipsburg, 1997), Locus 18, Q5, para. 3 (3.27).

33. Thomas McCrie, op. cit., pp. 21-5.

34. *Catechism of the Catholic Church* (Dublin, 1994), para. 816. The statement is taken directly from the decree 'Lumen Gentium' of the Second Vatican Council.

35. George Gillespie, *One Hundred and Eleven Propositions concerning the Ministry and Government of the Church* (1647) in *The Presbyterian's Armoury* (Edinburgh, 1846), volume 2, Proposition 36. For a study of Gillespie's ecclesiology, see *An Ecclesiastical Republic* by W. D. J. McKay (Carlisle, 1997).

36. G. C. Berkouwer, *The Church* (Grand Rapids, 1976), p. 45.

37. George Hutcheson, *The Gospel of John*, 1841 edition (London, 1972), ad. loc.

38. James Durham, *The Dying Man's Testament to the Church of Scotland or A Treatise Concerning Scandal*, 1990 revision of 1680 edition (Dallas, 1990).

39. George Hutcheson, op. cit., on John 17:20-1.

40. James Melville, *Autobiography and Diary*, 1556-1610, edited by R. Pitcairn (1842), quoted by J. D. Douglas, *Light in the North* (Grand Rapids, 1964), p. 19.

41. John Murray, 'The Nature and Unity of the Church' in *Collected Writings of John Murray*, 2.328.

42. R. B. Kuiper, op. cit., p. 94.

43. John Calvin, *The Epistles of Paul the Apostle to the Galatians, Ephesians, Philippians and Colossians*, translated by T. H. L. Parker (Edinburgh, 1965), on Colossians 2:19.

44. James B. Hurley, *Man and Woman in Biblical Perspective* (Grand Rapids, 1981), p. 146.

45. Catherine Clark Kroeger, 'The Classical Concept of Head as "Source"', Appendix III in *Equal to Serve*, by Gretchen Gaebelein Hull (London, 1989).

46. Wayne Grudem, 'Does *Kephalē* ("Head") Mean "Source" or "Authority Over" in Greek Literature? A Survey of 2,336 Examples', *Trinity Journal* 6NS (1985), pp. 38-59, and 'The Meaning of *Kephalē* ("Head"): A Response to Recent Studies', Appendix 1 in *Recovering Biblical Manhood and Womanhood*, edited by John Piper and Wayne Grudem (Wheaton, 1991).

47. Herman Witsius, op. cit., 2.380.

48. See e.g. Wilhelmus à Brakel, op. cit., vol. 2, ch. 26, p. 99.

49. Jerry Bridges, *True Fellowship* (New Malden, 1986), p. 93.

50. R. B. Kuiper, op. cit., pp. 56ff.

51. R. B. Kuiper, op. cit., p. 58.

52. John Calvin, *Institutes*, IV.i.17.

53. Johannes Wollebius, op. cit., p. 137.

54. *Catechism of the Catholic Church*, para. 830. A fuller treatment of Rome's traditional position is provided by Ludwig Ott, *Fundamentals of Catholic Dogma* (Rockford, 1974), pp. 306-8.

55. *Catechism*, para. 834.

56. Robert L. Reymond, op. cit., p. 844.

57. John Calvin, *The Epistles of Paul the Apostle*, on Ephesians 2:20.

58. Ludwig Ott, op. cit., p. 308.

59. John Calvin, *A Harmony of the Gospels of Matthew, Mark and Luke*, translated by T. H. L. Parker (Edinburgh, 1972), 2.186, on Matthew 16:16. See also *Institutes* IV.vi.3,5,7.

60. R. B. Kuiper, op. cit., p. 68.

61. Robert L Reymond, op. cit., p. 822.

62. It is interesting to note Thomas Aquinas' view that the rock is Peter's confession. See *Summa Theologica*, translated by the Fathers of the English Dominican Province (New York, 1948), 2-2, Q174, art. 6.

63. *Scots Confession, 1560, and Negative Confession, 1581*, with Introduction by G. D. Henderson (Edinburgh, 1937), Article XVIII, p. 75.

64. John Calvin, *Institutes*, IV,i.9.

65. Zacharias Ursinus, *Commentary on the Heidelberg Catechism*, translated by G. W. Williard, 1852 edition (Phillipsburg, n.d.), p. 288.

66. Theodore Beza, *The Christian Faith*, 1558 edition, translated by James Clark (Lewes, 1992), 4.51.

67. John Calvin, *Institutes*, IV.xii.1.

68. George Gillespie, *Aaron's Rod Blossoming*, 1846 edition (Harrisonburg, 1985), Book 1.

69. John Calvin, *Institutes*, IV.xii.5.

70. Edmund P Clowney, op. cit., ch. 14.

71. John Murray, 'The Church and Mission' in *Collected Writings of John Murray*, 1.247.

72. Robert L. Reymond, op. cit., p. 881.

73. Edmund P. Clowney, op. cit., p. 199.

74. Edmund P. Clowney, op. cit., p. 200.

75. Donald Macleod, *A Faith to Live By* (Fearn, 1998), p. 228.

76. James Henley Thornwell, *Collected Writings*, 1875 edition (Edinburgh, 1974), 4.43ff. The present author has considered this debate against the background of seventeenth century Scottish Presbyterianism in *An Ecclesiastical Republic*, ch. 5. The nature of 'ruling elders' has continued to be a matter of debate in Reformed circles.

77. The distinctions within Presbyterianism are helpfully outlined by Robert Reymond, op. cit., pp. 900-4. An accessible presentation of the traditional Scottish view is to be found in George Gillespie's 1641 treatise *An Assertion of the Government of the Church of Scotland* in *The Presbyterian's Armoury* (Edinburgh, 1846), vol. 2.

78. Leonard J. Coppes, *Who Will Lead Us* (Phillipsburg, 1977), pp. 148-9. This book has some very useful material on the diaconate.

79. Gretchen Gaebelein Hull, op. cit., p. 128.

80. For example, *Men, Women and Authority*, edited by Brian Edwards (London, 1996), especially the chapters by Edward Donnelly, and *Recovering Biblical Manhood and Womanhood*, edited by John Piper and Wayne Grudem (Wheaton, 1991).

81. Edmund P. Clowney, op. cit., pp. 231-5. The opposing view is put by Leonard J. Coppes, op. cit., pp. 135-7.

82. Edmund P. Clowney, op. cit., p. 118.

83. The 'special presence' of God is made an integral part of the definition of worship by Frank J. Smith in his essay 'What is Worship?' in *Worship in the Presence of God*, edited by Frank J. Smith and David C. Lachman (Greenville, 1992), pp. 11ff.

84. R. B. Kuiper, op. cit., p. 347.

85. John Calvin, *Selected Works of John Calvin. Tracts and Letters*, edited and translated by Henry Beveridge, 1849 edition (Grand Rapids, 1983), 2.118.

86. Michael Bushell, *The Songs of Zion* (Pittsburgh, 1980).

87. Hector Cameron, 'Purity of Worship', in *Hold Fast Your Confession*, edited by Donald Macleod (Edinburgh, 1978), pp. 93ff.

88. John Frame, *Worship in Spirit and in Truth* (Phillipsburg, 1996).

89. John Frame, op. cit., p. 42.

90. John Frame, op. cit., p. 43.

91. Michael Bushell, *The Songs of Zion*; Smith and Lachman (eds), *Worship in the Presence of God*; Reformed Presbyterian Church of North America, *The Biblical Doctrine of Worship* (Pittsburgh, 1974).

92. This is available, under Murray's name, in *Worship in the Presence of God*, pp. 179-92.

93. The classic defence of the refusal to use instrumental music is by John L. Girardeau, *Instrumental Music in the Public Worship of the Church*, 1888 edition (Haverton, 1983).

94. Francis Nigel Lee, *The Covenantal Sabbath* (London, n.d.). Lee's book, which was his doctoral thesis, is an exhaustive study of the subject.

95. Joseph A. Pipa, *The Lord's Day* (Fearn, 1997), p. 61.

96. For arguments that it is the Sabbath, see *This is the Day*, by Roger T. Beckwith and Wilfred Stott (London, 1978). For opposing arguments, see *From Sabbath to Lord's Day*, edited by D. A. Carson (Grand Rapids, 1982).

97. Joseph A. Pipa, op. cit., p. 64.

98. Jonathan Edwards, *The Works of Jonathan Edwards*, 1834 edition (Edinburgh, 1974), vol. 2, pp. 93-103.

99. Jonathan Edwards, op. cit., vol. 2, p. 103.

100. Thomas Goodwin, *The Work of the Holy Spirit in our Salvation* (Edinburgh, 1979), p. 509.

101. Mark T. Bube, 'The Principles of Reformed Missions', in *Proceedings of the International Conference of Reformed Churches*, October 15-23, 1997, Seoul, South Korea (Neerlandia/Pella, 1997), p. 111.

102. R. B. Kuiper, *God-Centred Evangelism* (Grand Rapids, 1961), pp. 45-6.

103. R. B. Kuiper, *Evangelism*, p. 46.

104. Richard Baxter, *The Saints' Everlasting Rest* (Fearn, 1998), p. 416.

105. R. B. Kuiper, *Evangelism*, p. 89.

106. Tom Wells, *A Vision for Missions* (Edinburgh, 1985), p. 9.

107. R. B. Kuiper, *The Glorious Body of Christ*, p. 239.

108. J. H. Bavinck, *An Introduction to the Science of Missions* (Philadelphia, 1960), pp. 69ff.

109. On Scottish and Irish Presbyterianism see *The Puritan Hope* by Iain Murray (Edinburgh, 1971), pp. 173, 175-8, 283. On views of Romans 11, see pp. 58-76.

110. Richard R. de Ridder, *Discipling the Nations* (Grand Rapids, 1975), p. 155.

111. J. I. Packer, *Evangelism and the Sovereignty of God* (London, 1961), p. 125.

10

Signs and Seals of the Covenant

Covenant Theology presents to us a God who is supremely gracious. All His dealings with His people are characterized by overflowing grace. The gift of a Saviour and the work which He willingly performed are the fruit of God's grace. It must be emphasized that salvation is by grace from start to finish. Thus the Christian life which begins by grace, as a sinner is brought into covenant with God, is to be continued by grace as the work of sanctification unfolds. In 2 Peter 1:3 believers are encouraged by this assurance: 'His divine power has given us everything we need for life and godliness through our knowledge of him who called us by his own glory and goodness.' In a similar way Paul sets out the unbreakable promise that 'my God will meet all your needs according to his glorious riches in Christ Jesus' (Phil. 4:19).

In order to fulfil His promises, the Lord has provided 'means of grace' for His covenant people. Pre-eminent among these means is the inspired word which nourishes believers and directs them in holiness. As covenant theologians have recognized, however, among the means of grace are the biblical sacraments of baptism and the Lord's Supper. As Theodore Beza says of the sacraments, 'They are established so that we may receive from His grace and liberality what is more precious than heaven and earth: the strengthening of our faith. Each day we will be thus more closely united and joined to Jesus Christ our Head, as respects our eternal life'.[1] It is to the sacraments, particularly in their covenantal significance, that we now turn our attention.

What are the sacraments?
The word 'sacrament' is not a biblical term, but was used originally to designate the oath taken by a Roman soldier. In the Latin Vulgate translation of the Bible it was used to translate the Greek word for 'mystery' (*mustērion*). Thus in Paul's discussion of marriage in

Ephesians 5, when he says that this is a great 'mystery', the Vulgate states that it is a great sacrament (v. 32), among other problems, helping to bolster Rome's view of marriage as a sacrament. By this highly dubious route 'sacrament' made its way into theological discourse. No alternative term can be invented at this stage, but it is obvious that 'sacrament' has to be given a clear, biblical definition.

So what is a sacrament? Early theological writers provided quite brief definitions: 'a sacred sign' (Augustine) or 'a visible form of an invisible grace' (Peter Lombard). The fuller definitions provided subsequently by covenant theologians, in addition to greater fullness and precision, emphasize the links that exist between sacraments and the Covenant of Grace. Thus Johannes Wollebius of Basel writes,

> A sacrament is a divinely instituted act of worship, in which the grace promised by God to the people of the covenant is sealed by visible signs, and the people of the covenant are at the same time bound to obedience to him.[2]

Most familiar to those of the Presbyterian tradition is the definition of the Shorter Catechism:

> A sacrament is an holy ordinance instituted by Christ, wherein, by sensible signs, Christ and the benefits of the New Covenant, are represented, sealed and applied to believers (Q92).

The sacraments are thus acts of worship, covenantal signs, which embody what R. A. Finlayson termed 'the sacramental principle'.[3] This he defined as 'the material expression of a spiritual reality'.[4] The sacraments indicate to us how well the Lord understands us. Although there is no obscurity in His word which reveals spiritual realities to us, nevertheless He knows our slowness to grasp such spiritual things and so He has provided additional help by means of things that we can see, touch and taste. These are the striking terms in which Calvin describes this sacramental principle:

Here our merciful Lord, according to his infinite kindness, so tempers himself to our capacity that, since we are creatures who always creep on the ground, cleave to the flesh, and do not think about or even conceive of anything spiritual, he condescends to lead us to himself even by these earthly elements, and to set before us in the flesh a mirror of spiritual blessings.[5]

The sacraments are not products of human wisdom but have been ordained by God.

The material 'elements' of the sacraments, the water, the bread and the wine, are of course not ends in themselves: they stand for spiritual realities. It is on this account that the sacraments have been termed 'signs'. A sign points away from itself to the reality of which it speaks. The sacraments point to certain vital aspects of spiritual truth. A sacrament, as Calvin says, 'represents God's promises as painted in a picture and sets them before our sight, portrayed graphically and in the manner of images'.[6]

What then is the 'matter' of the sacraments, the realities to which they point? Covenant theologians are at one in answering this question: 'Christ and all His merits' (à Brakel),[7] 'Christ and the benefits of the New Covenant' (Shorter Catechism Q92). The focus is invariably upon Christ in His role as Mediator and Redeemer. The fundamental promise of the covenant, as we have noted a number of times, is 'I will be your God and you will be my people'. In other words, believers enjoy union and communion with God in the covenant, in particular union with Christ. The sacraments are signs of this covenantal and spiritual union with Christ, and of the blessings which flow from Him to His people. As Louis Berkhof says, 'They visibly represent, and deepen our consciousness of, the spiritual blessings of the covenant, of the washing away of our sins, and of our participation of the life that is in Christ'.[8] Thus Paul, in speaking of the reality symbolized by water baptism, can state, 'We were therefore buried with him through baptism into death in order that, just as Christ was raised from the dead through the glory of the Father, we too may live a new life' (Rom. 6:4). Similarly he can ask rhetorically, 'Is not the cup of thanksgiving for which we give thanks a participation in the blood of Christ? And is not the bread that we break a participation in the body of Christ?' (1 Cor. 10:16).

More will be said on this issue when we look at each of the sacraments separately, but it is important to see that there is a profound unity in the relationship which they bear to the covenant work of Christ. Baptism relates to the beginning of covenant life in union with Him; the Lord's Supper relates to the continual nourishing of that life. The sacraments are rightly described as signs of the Covenant of Grace.

Along with the sign and the matter signified by the sign, we must also note the nature of the union between them. As the Westminster Confession states, 'There is, in every sacrament, a spiritual relation, or sacramental union, between the sign and the thing signified' (XXVII.2). There is, as we would expect, an element of mystery here, as there is in every spiritual transaction effected by the Lord, yet it is none the less real for all that. As R. A. Finlayson puts it, 'They are sacramental signs because Christ is conjoined to them in such a reality that the moment we receive the sign, faith receives Christ. This is the sacramental union.'[9]

That union is effected by the Holy Spirit, whose role must never be neglected when considering any aspect of the divine activity. Beza is doing no more than echo the consensus of covenant theologians when he states that

> the conjunction between the sign and the reality signified is made by the force and power of the Holy Spirit alone. Through Him, Jesus Christ, who, as Scripture testifies, as a man is in Heaven and nowhere else, is as truly given to us, to us who are on the earth, as the signs which are used in the Sacraments.[10]

It would appear that the children of Reformation Geneva were well instructed in this truth (as in many others). In Calvin's 1545 Catechism we read this exchange:

> *Minister*: Then you judge the power and efficacy of a sacrament not to lie in the external element, but wholly to emanate from the Spirit of God?
> *Child*: I think so: that it please God to exercise his virtue through his instruments, for to this end he destined them.[11]

The importance of this truth should not be overlooked or minimized. 'It is this spiritual union that constitutes the essence of the sacrament', says Robert Reymond, 'and it is because of this union that the sacraments confer grace when they are received in faith'.[12]

These comments also serve to show that covenant theologians consider the sacraments to be more than signs. The view that sacraments are no more than signs has historically been linked with the name of Ulrich Zwingli, the Swiss Reformer. It is, however, highly debatable whether he in fact held this view. His concern in formulating his theology of the sacraments was to avoid attributing any power to the elements themselves in communicating grace. Nevertheless he did believe in Christ's spiritual presence in the sacraments and attributed to the Holy Spirit the conferring of grace. As Zwingli scholar W. P. Stephens says, 'His concern is that glory shall be given to God and not to the sacraments.'[13] A reading of treatises such as *Of Baptism* and *On the Lord's Supper*[14] suggests that Zwingli was not far from the position now associated with Covenant Theology. Among Baptists, however, the view generally held is that the sacraments are no more than signs of spiritual realities and a profession of the believer's faith. Thus Millard Erickson states with reference to baptism that 'it is both a sign of the believer's union with Christ and, as a confession of that union, an additional act of faith that serves to cement the more firmly that relationship.'[15]

The 'more' which covenant theologians perceive in the sacraments is summed up in the term 'seals'. As seals confirm the genuineness of the document, so the sacraments confirm in a visible, tangible way the promises of grace contained in the word of God and so strengthen the faith of believers. Thus Calvin says that the sacraments 'are like seals of the good will that [God] feels toward us, which by attesting that good will to us, sustain, nourish, confirm, and increase our faith'.[16] The focus is very definitely on *God's* action in the sacraments, recalling what we have already said about the work of the Holy Spirit. The same view is stated by à Brakel: 'The sacraments do not only signify, but they above all seal to true communicants that they are partakers of the promises of the gospel, all the benefits of the covenant of grace, and of Christ and all His fullness [sic]'.[17] Although God does not need to give additional weight to His promises, that is precisely what He does in the sacraments, so great is His love for His people.

The sacraments are thus to be compared to seals attached to the word of God. The word and the sacraments are inseparable, since the word is required to explain them and the promises which the sacraments depict are none other than those proclaimed in the word. The word, in Covenant Theology, has the primacy. 'It is the Word that gives, as it were, voice to the sacraments, so that without that interpreting and illuminating voice they are dumb signs that do not instruct or edify', comments Finlayson.[18] The sacraments confirm the truth which believers have already received. Separation of word from sacrament is the first step on the road to sacramentalism, and consequently the Reformed tradition has insisted on preaching accompanying the administration of the sacraments, as laid down, for example, in *The Directory for the Publick Worship of God* drafted by the Westminster Assembly. G. C. Berkouwer sums up the position which we are setting out in this way: 'The significance of the sacrament lies in the divine act in which God directs our attention again to the trustworthiness of his Word, upon which man can depend without fear and with great boldness.'[19]

The sacraments are thus not 'bare signs', a view vigorously opposed by the Reformers, among others. When used by the Holy Spirit they truly are 'sealing ordinances' and means of grace. This is expressed memorably by Robert Bruce in one of a series of sermons preached in St Giles, Edinburgh, in 1589, when he says that 'the Lord has appointed the Sacraments as hands to deliver and exhibit the things signified'.[20] This statement comes at the end of a vivid passage on the true nature of the sacraments which deserves to be quoted in full. Sacraments, Bruce says, are not bare signs, since

if they did nothing but represent or signify a thing absent, then any picture or image would be a Sacrament, for with every picture, the thing signified comes into your mind. For example, at the sight of a picture of the King, the King will come into your mind, and it will signify to you that that is the King's picture. If therefore, the sign of the Sacrament did no more than that, all pictures would be Sacraments, but the Sacrament exhibits and delivers the thing that it signifies to the soul and heart, as soon as the sign is delivered to the mouth ... No picture of the King will deliver the King to you.[21]

From a covenantal perspective, it is most important to remember that through the sacraments believers feed spiritually on Christ and find their covenant fellowship with Him strengthened. This is well summed up in a comment by R. S. Wallace on Calvin's sacramental theology, noting the Reformer's concern 'to preserve the idea that grace is not a substance, but the personal presence of Christ offering men a personal relationship even in uniting them to Himself.'[22] Robert Bruce likewise keeps the Mediator at the centre when he says that 'the Sacrament is a potent instrument appointed by God to deliver to us Christ Jesus for our everlasting salvation'.[23] In the sacraments, therefore, Christ is spiritually present, a truth which, as we will note below, has been debated at length in discussions of the Lord's Supper.

As signs of the covenant, the sacraments contain both command and promise. Here we are thinking of more than the command of Christ to observe the sacraments, which is referred to in the Westminster Confession of Faith (XXVII.3). Along with the promises of grace which are made visible in the sacraments, we also hear the Lord's summons to a response of obedience. As J. van Genderen says, in relation to baptism, 'We receive the richest promises from God the Father, Son and Holy Spirit. We are also called and obliged to a new obedience.'[24] The same holds true for the Lord's Supper: partaking of the sacrament makes demands on the way we live, both in preparation for partaking ('a man ought to examine himself') and after partaking. The nourishment provided by the Supper is with a view to godly living and active service. Thus van Genderen concludes, 'We should seriously consider that by eating the bread and drinking the wine of the Lord's Supper we are renewing the covenant of God, thus binding ourselves more closely to it as with a new seal, resolved that we will abide by its terms.'[25] We may link this idea of covenant renewal with Calvin's comment about the sacraments, 'They are also marks and as it were badges of our profession.'[26] Rededication to the Lord is a testimony to the world.

Covenant theologians have been careful to stress that in order to profit from the sacraments the recipients must exercise faith. In no sense are these ordinances means of grace for the unsaved or the non-elect. The Shorter Catechism, for example, makes this clear. In Q91 the efficacy of the sacraments is ascribed to 'the blessing of Christ, and the working of His Spirit in them that *by faith* receive them'. Similarly, in Q92, in defining a sacrament, we read, 'Christ, and the benefits of the New Covenant, are represented, sealed and applied *to believers.*' There is no magical operation in the sacraments. Beza, too, holds the same view, stating that 'he who does not bring faith cannot receive the reality signified in the Sacraments, and he who brings true faith receives the reality in the genuine manner.'[27] From the Scottish tradition William Cunningham states forcefully that 'there is no adequate ground for counting upon [the sacraments] exerting their appropriate influence in individual cases, apart from the faith which the participation in them ordinarily expresses, and which must exist before participation in them can be either warrantable or beneficial.'[28]

It does have to be kept in mind that the exercise of faith and the reception of blessing need not be tied to the point in time when the sacrament is received. Sign and reality may be separated by a lengthy period of time. This is the case with an unbeliever who falsely professes faith and is baptized, yet is not converted until years afterwards. It is also very relevant to the baptism of covenant children where the same separation of sign and reality often occurs. Those who use this separation to argue against infant baptism must be consistent in denying the validity of adult baptism in the case first cited, although few would in fact do so. On the other hand, covenant theologians acknowledge 'the sovereignty of the Spirit to establish the connection between sign and that which is signified in the fulness of life as a whole, but not necessarily at the very beginning of life.'[29]

The Reformed and covenantal view of the sacraments, historically speaking, was hammered out in conscious opposition to the position held by Rome. Thus the Reformers cited the necessity for sacraments to have been instituted by Christ as signs and seals of covenant grace to reject Rome's five extra 'sacraments' (orders, marriage, penance, confirmation and extreme unction). Many modern Roman Catholic theologians in fact argue that in a wider sense a sacrament is 'any finite reality through which the divine is perceived to be disclosed and communicated, and through which our human response to the divine assumes some measure of shape, form, and structure.'[30] On this view, many things unconnected with Christianity could be considered 'sacramental'.

Traditionally Rome has held that the sacraments confer grace 'ex opere operato', i.e. 'by the power of the completed sacramental rite'.[31] As long as the prescribed form is observed, regardless of the disposition of the celebrant, sacramental grace is available. The *Catechism of the Catholic Church* adds, 'Nevertheless, the fruits of the sacraments also depend on the disposition of the one who receives them.'[32] In the case of adults, faith is required, or at least the absence of any obstacle to the sacrament's working, but in the case of the baptism of infants saving grace is automatically conferred.[33]

In accordance with the decrees of the Council of Trent, Rome officially holds that 'for believers the sacraments of the New Covenant are necessary for salvation.'[34], a position vigorously rejected by Covenant Theology. Some modern Roman Catholic theologians also reject such a necessity, but on the grounds that God already works graciously in every person. Thus McBrien asserts that 'everybody does not strictly "need" baptism to become a child of God and an heir of heaven. Every human person, by reason of birth and God's universal offer of grace, is already called to be a child of God and an heir of heaven... The sacraments signify, celebrate, and effect what God is, in a sense, already doing everywhere and for all.'[35]

Before turning to give individual attention to baptism and the Lord's Supper, we should note a further fundamental principle of Covenant Theology's view of the sacraments, which will be of great significance in relation to baptism in particular. That principle is the unity of meaning between the sacraments of the Old Testament and those of the New Testament. The Westminster Confession states, 'The sacraments of the Old Testament, in regard of the spiritual things thereby signified and exhibited, were, for substance, the same with those of the new' (XXVII.5). Thus Wollebius argues, 'Baptism corresponds, by analogy, to circumcision, and the Lord's Supper corresponds to the paschal lamb.'[36] This is the position universally held by covenant theologians and defended in the following pages. It is an essential element of their sacramental theology. The roots of the New Testament sacraments are to be found in the Old Testament.

The sacrament of baptism

It is agreed by evangelicals in general that the sacrament of baptism is symbolic of the beginning of the Christian life and marks reception into the visible fellowship of the Church. Thus, as Robert Letham says, 'the outset of the Christian life is marked by faith on the one hand and baptism on the other, so that the two are integrally related.'[37] Drawing on what we have said about the nature of sacraments in the previous section, we can understand why the Reformers and their theological descendants rejected Rome's view of baptism as actually effecting the saving transformation that it portrays. That the Roman Catholic view has not changed is evident from the statement of the *Catechism of the Catholic Church*: 'Through Baptism we are freed from sin and reborn as sons of God; we become members of Christ, are incorporated into the Church and made sharers in her mission.'[38] At a later point it is stated, 'Justification is conferred in Baptism, the sacrament of faith.'[39] The work of the Holy Spirit, which will be considered below, is here erroneously ascribed to the sacrament.

What, then, does Covenant Theology hold the meaning of baptism to be? In order to discern what is central to the meaning of baptism we must turn to the institution of the sacrament by Christ in Matthew 28:19. In this text the mission of the Church is stated to be making disciples of all nations, and ancillary to that task is teaching them to observe what Christ has revealed and (literally) 'baptising them *into* the name of the Father and of the Son and of the Holy Spirit'. The preposition 'into' is most significant. It is used in 1 Corinthians 10:2 ('baptised into Moses') and 1 Corinthians 1:13 ('baptised into the name of Paul'). Regarding its significance, John Murray is correct to observe, 'It is apparent that it expresses a relationship to the person into whom or into whose name persons may have been baptised. It is this fact of relationship that is basic.'[40]

The nature of that relationship is established by appeal to a number of texts which speak of union with Christ, and which have occupied our attention in a previous chapter. Thus we may note, for example, Paul's statement in Galatians 3:27-8 that 'all of you who were baptised into Christ have clothed yourselves with Christ ... you are all one in Christ Jesus', and this should be linked with his acknowledgement in Galatians 2:20 that 'I have been crucified with Christ and I no longer live, but Christ lives in me.' The same thought is expressed in Colossians 2:11-12 ('In him you were circumcised, in the putting off of the sinful nature ... with the circumcision done by Christ, having been buried with him in baptism and raised with him through your faith in the power of God, who raised him from the dead.').

A crucial passage is Romans 6:1ff., where Paul asks rhetorically, 'Or don't you know that all of us who were baptised into Christ Jesus were baptised into his death? We were therefore buried with him through baptism into death in order that, just as Christ was raised from the dead through the glory of the Father, we too may live a new life. If we have been united with him in his death, we will certainly also be united with him like this in his resurrection' (v. 3-5). Commenting particularly on verse 3, C. E. B. Cranfield considers the claim of Paul that Christian baptism is essentially baptism into Christ's death thus:

Not that it actually relates the person concerned to Christ's death, since this relationship is already an objective reality before baptism takes place, having been brought into being by God's gracious decision, [here he refers to 'for us' in 5:8], but that it points to, and is a pledge of, that death which the person concerned has already died – in God's sight.[41]

On the basis of such texts we can conclude that the fundamental fact portrayed in baptism is the saving union of believers with Christ in the Covenant of Grace. The entrance of God's people into the enjoyment of the blessings of that covenant is given visual form in the sacrament of baptism. Believers are united to Christ in His crucifixion, death, burial and resurrection. Recalling Matthew 28:19, we must not forget that the union in view also includes the Father and the Holy Spirit. Baptism is explicitly related to the Trinity. Believers are united to the three Persons, as John Murray puts it, 'both in the unity expressed by their joint possession of the one name and in the richness of the distinctive relationship which each person of the Godhead sustains to the people of God in the economy of the covenant of grace.'[42]

Another element in the meaning of baptism may be deduced from the use of water as the sacramental element. The symbolism of cleansing from sin is clear, and has specific biblical support in both Old and New Testaments. A good example is the promise of the Lord in Ezekiel 36:25, 'I will sprinkle clean water on you, and you will be clean; I will cleanse you from all your impurities and from all your idols.' Note how this is accompanied by the covenant promise, 'you will be my people, and I will be your God' (v. 28). This theme is taken up in the New Testament, for example when Jesus says that 'no-one can enter the kingdom of God unless he is born of water and the Spirit [parallel to 'born again']' (John 3:5). The imagery of washing also occurs in 1 Corinthians 6:11 ('You were washed, you were sanctified, you were justified') and Titus 3:5 ('He saved us through the washing of rebirth and renewal by the Holy Spirit'). Calvin indeed makes cleansing from sin the chief significance of baptism. Although we disagree with this, his summary of its purification symbolism is apt:

> Scripture declares that baptism first points to the cleansing of our sins, which we obtain from Christ's blood; then to the mortification of our flesh, which rests upon participation in his death and through which believers are reborn into newness of life and into the fellowship of Christ.[43]

The latter part of Calvin's definition may be linked with a third element of the significance of baptism. As Robert Reymond points out, 'because the very name of the ordinance is what it is, namely, baptism ... it obviously symbolises the only spiritual work given that name in Holy Scripture, namely, Christ's work of baptizing his people with the Holy Spirit.'[44] The importance of this aspect of Christ's work is underlined by the recording of John the Baptist's reference to it in each of the Gospels: Matthew 3:11; Mark 1:8; Luke 3:16; John 1:33. After the resurrection, Christ promises His disciples that 'in a few days you will be baptised with the Holy Spirit' (Acts 1:5) and all believers are described by Paul as recipients of this baptism in 1 Corinthians 12:13 ('For we were all baptised by one Spirit into one body ... and we were all given the one Spirit to drink'). This is the inner spiritual baptism which is to match the outer water baptism, resulting in regeneration and sanctification.

Given that all these covenant blessings are symbolized in the sacrament of baptism, we can see the appropriateness of this ordinance to serve as a sign and seal of the Covenant of Grace and as the means of admission into the visible fellowship of the covenant community of the Church.

the Abrahamic covenant and circumcision
Earlier in this study we alluded to the view, expressed by all covenant theologians and enshrined in the Reformed Confessions, that the New Testament sacraments are the same in substance as the sacraments of the Old Testament. Thus Covenant Theology asserts that baptism is the equivalent of the rite of circumcision first required by God in the covenant established with Abraham. This is a vital element in Covenant Theology's defence of infant baptism.

It is essential to establish at the outset that the Abrahamic covenant is fundamentally a spiritual covenant, a stage in the revelation of the everlasting Covenant of Grace. Careful attention to the Scriptural material relating to the Abrahamic covenant will show clearly its spiritual nature and, as Donald Macleod says, 'the terms of the Abrahamic covenant make it plain that it was understood by Abraham himself in spiritual terms.'[45]

Genesis 17:1ff. is a crucial passage for understanding this covenant. It is immediately clear that the central promise given to Abraham is exactly the same as that which characterizes the whole history of the Covenant of Grace. Thus we read in Genesis 17:7, 'I will establish my covenant as an everlasting covenant between me and you and your descendants after you for the generations to come, to be your God and the God of your descendants after you.' What could be more spiritual than a promise of covenant fellowship with God? On this account Romans 4:11 can speak, with regard to Abraham, of 'the righteousness that he had by faith'. Abraham was a man justified by faith, whose hope was of a spiritual inheritance to be provided by the Lord. As Hebrews 11:10 says, 'he was looking forward to the city with foundations, whose architect and builder is God.'

There are, of course, other promises made to Abraham, chiefly of numerous descendants and possession of the land, which on the face of it are entirely material. We must also take into account, however, the statements of Paul in Galatians. Thus in Galatians 3:16 we are shown that ultimately the 'seed' of Abraham is fulfilled in Christ and His redemptive work. (It is unfortunate that the NIV tends not to use the term 'seed' in Genesis, obscuring this link.) Galatians 3:29 is also very significant regarding all who are in union with Christ: 'If you belong to Christ, then you are Abraham's seed, and heirs according to the promise.' The promise has a spiritual fulfilment. So also with regard to the promise of the land, since through Christ 'the meek ... will inherit the earth' (Matt. 5:5) and when the new heavens and the new earth are ushered in as the eternal home for God's people, the same covenant promise is repeated: 'Now the dwelling of God is with men, and he will live with them. They will be his people, and God himself will be with them and be their God' (Rev. 21:3). Abraham will of course have a share in that blessing.

This is not to deny that there were material aspects to the promises, namely numerous physical descendants and the possession of Canaan. John Murray, however, puts these in a proper biblical perspective when he says,

It is indeed true that the spiritual blessing of the covenant made with Abraham carried with it external privileges and it marked off the chosen people as a distinct national and racial entity ... But these external blessings and national privileges accrued from the spiritual blessings which the covenant embodied and imparted.[46]

Viewing the whole of the Old Testament period, Calvin comes to the same conclusion:

It is quite certain that the primary promises, which contained that covenant ratified with the Israelites by God under the Old Testament, were spiritual and referred to eternal life; then, conversely, that they were received by the fathers spiritually (as was fitting) in order that they might gain therefrom assurance of the life to come, to which they aspired with their whole heart.[47]

Thus the land of Canaan, for example, was never an end in itself, but was to draw the thoughts of the covenant people to the 'city with foundations'.

Support for this assertion can be drawn from passages such as Ezekiel 36:24ff., where covenant blessings provided in Christ make use of the the the language of material blessings used in, for example, Deuteronomy 28. Thus the promise 'I will give you a new heart and put a new spirit in you' (v. 26) is alongside one such as 'I will call for the corn and make it plentiful and will not bring famine upon you' (v. 29).

Covenant Theology, therefore, argues for a fundamental covenant unity between the Abrahamic and the New Covenants, a fact rejected by many Baptist theologians. G. R. Beasley-Murray, for example, claims that the major mistake of the covenant theologians 'is their one-sided stressing of the elements of unity in the Covenant, Gospel and Church of both dispensations, and their ignoring of the equally clear elements of discontinuity, elements which, in fact, often take the attention of the New Testament writers more than the elements of unity because they are so overwhelming.'[48] Whilst he does go on to show that the blessings of the New Covenant are richer, his arguments do not in any way disprove that the core of the covenants is the same and that, consequently, the elements of unity are in fact 'over-whelming'.

That the Abrahamic covenant is a vital part of the single covenant purpose of God is clear in a text such as Galatians 3:14, 'He redeemed us in order that the blessing given to Abraham might come to the Gentiles through Christ Jesus, so that by faith we might receive the promise of the Spirit.' Verse 29 has already been quoted: 'If you belong to Christ, then you are Abraham's seed, and heirs according to the promise.' The promise to Abraham was one of worldwide blessing: 'In your seed all the nations of the earth shall be blessed' (Gen. 22:18 NASB). The Great Commission of Matthew 28:19 regarding making disciples of 'all nations' marks the beginning of the fulfilment of that promise in the New Testament Church, the book of Acts traces its early progress and at the end God will have gathered 'a great multitude that no-one could count, from every nation, tribe, people and language' (Rev. 7:9).

The sign of admission to the covenant in Old Testament days was circumcision, a sign which spoke of cleansing and the removal of sin. Covenant theologians argue that according to Scripture circumcision is not merely, or even chiefly, a sign of racial identity but a sign of membership of a covenant whose spiritual nature has been set out above. Thus appeal can be made to Romans 4:11-12, regarding Abraham: 'And he received the sign of circumcision, a seal of the righteousness that he had by faith while he was still uncircumcised. So then, he is the father of all who believe but have not been circumcised, in order that righteousness might be credited to them. And he is also the father of the circumcised who not only are circumcised but who also walk in the footsteps of the faith that our father Abraham had before he was circumcised.' Circumcision is unmistakably a spiritual sign. The fact that it marked the ethnic group to whom the land of Canaan was given is ancillary to this key principle.

Nevertheless, as the record of Genesis 17 shows, the *spiritual* sign was to be applied to the *physical* seed of Abraham: both Isaac and Ishmael were to be circumcised, even though Ishmael would show himself not to be among the elect. As Donald Macleod says,

'It is not the elect who receive the sign. It is not the born again who receive the sign. It is the physical seed.'[49] This reflects what we may term the 'organic' and 'historic' character of God's covenant. The Lord delights to work graciously in succeeding generations of His people, bringing the children to the faith of their fathers. As history unfolds, so does God's saving purpose. As Pierre Marcel expresses it, 'It is not simply individuals, separate from each other, who are saved, but rather, through Christ, the organism of humanity and of the universe itself which is saved in the person of the elect.'[50] The practice of circumcision, with its generational pattern, aptly depicts God's promise 'to be your God and the God of your descendants [seed] after you' (Gen. 17:7).

Possessing the sign of circumcision did not in any way prove that a person was regenerate or, indeed, elect. Scripture makes this abundantly clear, particularly in Romans 9:6-8: 'It is not as though God's word had failed. For not all who are descended from Israel are Israel. Nor because they are descendants are they all Abraham's children. On the contrary, "It is through Isaac that your offspring will be reckoned". In other words, it is not the natural children who are God's children, but it is the children of the promise who are regarded as Abraham's offspring.' Thus faith in the God of the covenant is necessary for the enjoyment of the blessings of the covenant. Men cannot, of course, read the heart and decide who is elect or regenerate, and the sign is to be applied to all the physical seed and all are to be counted within the circle of the covenant. It is significant that when Jesus was speaking to Nicodemus the Pharisee, a circumcised descendant of Abraham, he said, 'You [plural] must be born again' (John 3:7). The message was for all the circumcised: the new birth is essential for the reception of the spiritual blessings of the covenant.

the baptism of covenant children
The principles that we have laid down thus far lead covenant theologians to the conclusion that the children of at least one believing parent are to be baptized. Those within the circle of the covenant are to receive the sign of the covenant.

It is clear from Scripture that baptism has replaced circumcision as the sacrament of entrance into the covenant. Thus the Heidelberg Catechism refers to 'Circumcision, in place of which in the New Testament Baptism is appointed' (Q74). The crucial link is made in Colossians 2:11-13: 'in Him you were also circumcised with a circumcision made without hands, in the removal of the body of the flesh by the circumcision of Christ; having been buried with Him in baptism, in which you were also raised up with Him through faith in the working of God, who raised Him from the dead. When you were dead in your transgressions and the uncircumcision of your flesh, He made you alive together with Him' (NASB). Here Paul uses 'circumcision' to refer to the regeneration, union with Christ and cleansing which God grants to His people: the same blessings which are signified by the sacrament of baptism. The two rites have the same meaning. In Calvin's words, 'Baptism, therefore, is a sign of the thing exhibited, which when it was absent was figured by circumcision.'[51]

Baptist theologians have responded to this position in various ways. Beasley-Murray, for example, argues that 'the spiritual circumcision promised under the old covenant has become a reality under the new through baptism', but concludes from this that baptism is so vastly superior to circumcision that 'there is no *a priori* case for postulating an identity of administration of the two rites' and he can speak of 'this utter newness of baptism'.[52] A self-consciously Reformed Baptist like David Kingdon argues that circumcision finds its fulfilment in regeneration, not in baptism, and so concludes, 'No New Testament proof can be found for the contention that baptism and circumcision are identical.'[53] Neither really addresses Covenant Theology's realization that the spiritual significance of both rites is the same. It is noteworthy that another Baptist, Paul Jewett, does recognize that the two rites 'symbolize the same inner reality in Paul's thinking', and concludes that 'circumcision may fairly be said to be the Old Testament counterpart of Christian baptism'.[54]

Covenant Theology also argues that the position of the children of believers with respect to covenant privileges has not changed with the inauguration of the New Covenant. In John Murray's words, 'If infants are excluded now, it cannot be too strongly emphasised that this change implies a complete reversal of the earlier divinely instituted practice.'[55] In many respects the blessings poured out on God's people in the New Covenant are greater, as we saw with regard to the work of the Holy Spirit, and it is unimaginable that the place of covenant children within the circle of the covenant would be withdrawn.

The children of believers ought therefore to receive the sign of the covenant, the sacrament of baptism. They are baptized because of the status they possess: they are covenant children. Baptism does not make them such, and indeed the absence of baptism does not prevent them from being such. In the language of 1 Corinthians 7:14, 'they are holy' – set apart for God, with the responsibility to be faithful to the demands of the covenant. Scripture provides no support for the view known as 'presumptive regeneration', a view held by Abraham Kuyper and other eminent covenant theologians such as B. B. Warfield.[56] There is no warrant for such a position: covenant children may be regenerate, but the administration of baptism passes no judgment on the subject.

It is important to stress that in the case of covenant children, baptism has exactly the same meaning as for adults. It is still a sign speaking of union with Christ, purification from sin and the baptism of the Holy Spirit. The sacrament must still be matched by faith in order to be a means of grace, although often in the case of children that faith may follow at a later point in their lives. As the Westminster Confession states, 'The efficacy of Baptism is not tied to that moment of time wherein it is administered; yet, notwithstanding, by the right use of this ordinance, the grace promised is not only offered, but really exhibited, and conferred, by the Holy Ghost, to such (whether of age or infants) as that grace belongeth unto, according to the counsel of God's own will, in His appointed time' (XXVII.6). It is interesting that many who deny that baptism can be meaningful when it includes infants who cannot exercise faith, do not have the same problem with the fact which none can deny, namely that sometimes baptism is administered to adults who do not really have faith.

The familiar covenant pattern is thus maintained in the New Covenant: the spiritual sign is given to the physical seed. There are no grounds for arguing, as Paul Jewett does, that the sign is to be given only to the 'true seed' of Abraham, which in the age of fulfilment is made up only of those who truly believe.[57] Even on this view, Baptists baptize some adults who are not the 'true seed'.

The covenant children of believers are placed in a position of great privilege, with the promises of God and the prayers and nurture of the covenant community. In the promises, Christian parents have great encouragement to pray for and seek the salvation of their children. Among covenant theologians there has been a range of views as to how covenant children should be regarded. Some who would reject the administration of baptism on the ground of presumptive regeneration nevertheless believe that those who have been baptized should be treated as regenerate until they consciously reject their covenant obligations, another version of 'presumptive regeneration'. This is reflected in Murray's statement, 'Baptized infants are to be received as the children of God and treated accordingly.'[58] Similarly H. Westerink says, 'If the parents are blessed, then the children are also blessed. Their children, already at birth, are not excluded from citizenship in Israel; they are not aliens to the covenant of promise, without Christ, without God, and without hope in the world ... Children, with their parents, have been brought near by the blood of Christ.'[59]

Other covenant theologians would avoid such statements, 'being satisfied to affirm merely that there is a seed for the Lord among the seed of believers'.[60] Such a cautious approach has been taken by, for example, James Henley Thornwell and Robert L. Dabney.[61] In the same vein, William Cunningham argues that 'neither parents nor children, when the children come to be proper subjects of instruction, should regard the fact that they have been baptized, as affording of itself even the slightest presumption that they have been regenerated.' He goes on the say that 'nothing should ever be regarded as furnishing any evidence of regeneration, except the appropriate proofs of an actual renovation of moral nature, exhibited in each case individually.'[62]

Without in any way minimizing the encouragement which the covenant promises give to believing parents, it seems to us that the covenant gives no ground for presumption regarding covenant children. They must be told that God has put the sign of the covenant on them and so they should be His and ought to respond to the call of the gospel and the demands of the covenant. The need for the new birth must be impressed lovingly upon them, as Jesus impressed it upon Nicodemus, and their responsibilities as well as their privileges must be made clear to them. The great privileges which they have within the fellowship of the covenant community make their responsibilities all the greater. The unregenerate who have been baptized, whether as adults or infants, sin against a greater measure of the light of God's truth and their guilt is consequently increased. Herman Hanko compares the position of elect and reprobate who receive the same covenant nurture in this way: 'God wills that this be so. But His purpose is thus: that the elect may manifest themselves as elect even as herbs become manifest as herbs, and that reprobate manifest themselves as reprobate even as thistles manifest themselves as thistles.'[63] Such is the Lord's amazing sovereign purpose.

As far as the question of which parents have a right to baptism for their children is concerned, practice among Reformed churches has varied. All agree that members of the Church who are faithfully keeping their covenant commitment to the Lord (as far as outward, visible conduct is concerned) have a right to baptism for their covenant children. Differences arise over those who may be termed 'adherents', people perhaps baptized as infants who have not made a public profession of faith. Some theologians argue in favour of the baptism of the children of such since they have not repudiated the covenant openly. As John Murray points out, however, the Church should be teaching such adherents 'that the necessary implicate of the covenant relation, sealed by their baptism in infancy, is the open avowal and embrace of that covenant and the public confession of Christ as their only Saviour and Lord.'[64] He concludes that those who are not willing, or ready, to embrace the covenant fully are not in a fit state to receive baptism for their children.

For those who say that their baptism as infants is now a distant and meaningless event, we can do no better than direct them to the Larger Catechism's description of the 'needful but much neglected duty of improving our baptism' (Q167). This is carried out, we are told,

> by serious and thankful consideration of the nature of it, and of the ends for which Christ instituted it, the privileges and benefits conferred and sealed thereby, and our solemn vow made therein; by being humbled for our sinful defilement, our falling short of, and walking contrary to, the grace of baptism, and our engagements; by growing up to assurance of pardon of sin, and of all other blessings sealed to us in that sacrament; by drawing strength from the death and resurrection of Christ, into whom we are baptized, for the mortifying of sin, and quickening of grace; and by endeavouring to live by faith, to have our conversation in holiness and righteousness, as those that have therein given up their names to Christ; and to walk in brotherly love, as being baptized by the same Spirit into one body.

the mode of baptism

In opposition to Baptists, who claim that immersion is the only valid mode of baptism, covenant theologians have generally agreed that pouring, sprinkling and immersion are all equally valid modes. Such arguments have included discussions of the Greek terminology for baptism, concluding that it does not require immersion, and these can be found in standard treatments of the subject, such as that by John Murray.[65]

Without denying the validity of immersion, however, we wish to argue that the covenantal significance of baptism in fact makes pouring or sprinkling more appropriate modes.[66] It is significant, to begin with, that in Old Testament covenantal ceremonies the blood of the sacrifice was sprinkled, as recorded for example in Exodus 24: 'Moses took half of the blood and put it in bowls, and the other half he sprinkled on the altar. Then he took the Book of the Covenant and read it to the people. They responded, "We will do everything the Lord has said; we will obey." Moses then took the blood, sprinkled it on the people and said, "This is the blood of the covenant that the Lord has made with you..."' (vv. 6-8). The Jews would thus be thoroughly familiar with *sprinkling* in a covenant context.

The same symbolism is used with reference to the work of the Messiah in Isaiah 52:15, 'so will he sprinkle many nations'. The same is true of God's promise in Ezekiel 36:25, 'I will sprinkle clean water on you, and you will be clean', a promise followed in verse 28 by the covenant promise, 'you will be my people and I will be your God'. It therefore comes as no surprise that the application of the atonement effected by Christ is frequently described in terms of the sprinkling of His blood: 'let us draw near to God ... having our hearts sprinkled to cleanse us from a guilty conscience' (Heb. 10:22); 'chosen ... for obedience to Jesus Christ and sprinkling by his blood' (1 Pet. 1:2).

Baptists often appeal to the symbolism of burial in Romans 6 in support of immersion. Aside from the fact that Paul is there describing the living union of believers with Christ by the power of the Holy Spirit (which baptism can only symbolize), it must be remembered that Paul states, 'don't you know that all of us who were baptised into Christ Jesus were baptised into his death?' (v. 3). That death was as a result of his being lifted up on a cross, and as Jay Adams says, 'Immersion in no sense symbolizes crucifixion.'[67] That death was followed by burial in a tomb above ground level, not in a grave in the earth. Immersion cannot adequately portray union with Christ.

Baptism also depicts the baptism of the Holy Spirit, and the terminology associated with the pentecostal outpouring of the Spirit is *pouring*. Thus in Acts 2:17 Peter quotes the prophetic words of Joel 2:28: 'In the last days, God says, I will pour out my Spirit on all people.'

As a sign of the Covenant of Grace, baptism is appropriately administered by sprinkling or pouring water on the candidate.

The Lord's Supper

At the institution of the Lord's Supper its covenantal significance was made clear by the Lord Jesus Christ: 'This is my body given for you; do this in remembrance of me ... This cup is the new covenant in my blood, which is poured out for you' (Luke 22:19-20). In the elements of bread and wine the atoning death of the Mediator is symbolized, the shedding of blood which is essential to the establishment of the Covenant of Grace. As the Lord 'gave thanks' before breaking the bread, so the Church 'gives thanks' for His redemptive work, giving rise in some circles to the name 'eucharist' applied to the sacrament. As the Lord's people feed physically on bread and wine, so they are to feed spiritually on Him. The body and blood of Christ are, sacramentally, 'spiritual food and drink'.[68]

Thus the Westminster Confession states that the Lord's Supper is to be observed 'for the perpetual remembrance of the sacrifice of Himself in His death; the sealing all benefits thereof unto true believers, their spiritual nourishment and growth in Him, their further engagement in and to all duties which they owe unto Him; and, to be a bond and pledge of their communion with Him, and with each other, as members of His mystical body' (XXIX.1).

At the heart of the Lord's Supper is the union of Christ the Mediator with His covenant people. As in baptism the beginning of that union is symbolized, so in the Lord's Supper the strengthening of the union and nourishing of the relationship is depicted. There is a spiritual and covenantal communion between Christ and His people which must grow and develop. Thus Paul can ask rhetorically, 'Is not the cup of thanksgiving for which we give thanks a participation in the blood of Christ? And is not the bread that we break a participation in the body of Christ?' (1 Cor. 10:16).

The spiritual reality of which the Lord's Supper is a sign is set out by the Lord in John 6:22-58, his 'Bread of Life' discourse. The discourse is *not* an exposition of the sacrament, but describes the believer's relationship to the Lord in terms of feeding upon Him: 'I tell you the truth, unless you eat the flesh of the Son of Man and drink his blood, you have no life in you. Whoever eats my flesh and drinks my blood has eternal life' (vv. 53-4). This clearly refers to the sinner's saving union with Christ which no sacrament can confer. It seems clear, however, that this union is symbolized in the elements and actions of the Lord's Supper.

The covenant people need to be receiving a regular supply of spiritual nourishment. As George Hutcheson comments on John 6:35 ('He who comes to me will never go hungry, and he who believes in me will never be thirsty'): 'This promise of being delivered from hunger and thirst is but begun to be accomplished here, and daily going on, and shall be perfected hereafter, when believers shall enjoy complete and total satisfaction throughout eternity.'[69]

The symbolism of a sacramental meal was thoroughly familiar to the people of God in Old Testament days in the form of the Passover and it is profoundly significant that Christ instituted the Lord's Supper in the setting of the Passover. Robert Reymond is correct to draw attention to the fact that 'our Lord used elements already normally employed in the Passover celebration'.[70] Indeed, as Roger Beckwith observes, 'The only new thing which Christ instituted was his interpretation of the elements, i.e. his words of institution; for the thanksgivings, breaking of the bread and distributing of the elements took place at any formal meal, as the rabbinical literature shows.'[71]

The Passover commemorated the deliverance of the covenant people from God's judgment on Egypt through the shedding of the blood of the lamb. Thus when Paul states in 1 Corinthians 5:7 'Christ, our Passover lamb, has been sacrificed', he indicates that it is Christ in His sacrificial, atoning work who ultimately fulfils the Passover symbolism. The Passover directed the attention of God's people to the Lamb of God who truly takes away sin. Richard Vines, a member of the Westminster Assembly, sums up, after comparing the Passover and Christ's atonement,

And so much for the Passover as referring to Christ our Sacrifice, for that it does so is plain by this: that which is said of the Paschal lamb in Exodus 12:46 is expressly applied to and fulfilled in Christ in John 19:36 ['Not one of his bones will be broken.']. So much for the Passover as a sacrifice, or as the figure of our sacrifice and theirs, Christ Jesus.[72]

Covenant theologians, in opposition to Rome, assert that the sacrament itself cannot be a sacrifice. The traditional Roman Catholic position, restated in the *Catechism of the Catholic Church* (1994), is as follows: 'In this divine sacrifice which is celebrated by the Mass, the same Christ who offered himself once in a bloody manner on the altar of the cross is contained and is offered in an unbloody manner.'[73] However such statements have been explained or qualified, covenant theologians have recognized in the doctrine of the Mass a fatal undermining of Christ's sacrifice at Calvary, and an ascription to the sacrament of powers which find no support in Scripture. This is perhaps most clear with reference to those who have already died: 'The Eucharistic sacrifice is also offered for the faithful departed who "have died in Christ but are not yet wholly purified" [quoting Trent], so that they may be able to enter into the light and peace of Christ.'[74] On such grounds covenant theologians have labelled the Mass blasphemous.

As a seal of the Covenant of Grace, however, the sacrament is truly a means of grace for believers. Edmund Calamy, one of the English Presbyterians at the Westminster Assembly, says, 'As certainly as bread and wine are put into the devout communicant's hands, so certainly is he invested in all gospel benefits. God gives Himself, His Son, His Spirit, His grace, His favour, and all that can be reasonably desired or truly wanted to the believing soul.'[75] Where true faith is present, blessing can be expected. Along with the word, which must accompany the observance of the sacrament in order to explain its meaning, the Lord's Supper serves to strengthen believers and confirm their assurance of a share in the Covenant of Grace.

Historically, debate has raged over the nature of Christ's presence in the Lord's Supper, the 'real presence' as it is termed. Many Baptists, arguing that the sacrament is no more than a memorial of the work of Christ, hold that there is no real presence in the Supper. The 'negativism' of this view is noted by Baptist theologian Millard Erickson, who warns, 'Out of zeal to avoid the conception that Jesus is present in some sort of magical way, some have sometimes gone to such extremes as to give the impression that the one place where Jesus most assuredly is not to be found is the Lord's Supper.'[76] Erickson quotes another Baptist as terming this 'the doctrine of the real absence' of Christ. Along with this view, covenant theologians also reject Rome's doctrine of transubstantiation (the bread and wine actually change into the body and blood of Christ) and the Lutheran doctrine of consubstantiation (the body and blood of Christ are present under and along with the bread and wine).[77] What then is the correct view?

It has to be admitted that there have been differences among covenant theologians and at times their views have not been entirely clear. All are agreed that Christ is present spiritually, by means of the ministry of the Holy Spirit. Some, however, wish to include Christ's bodily human nature in His presence, although they seek to avoid any crassly materialistic presence. Wollebius, for example, says that 'in addition to his being present by his divine person and his Holy Spirit, he is also present by his body and blood, not locally but sacramentally.'[78] Calvin, too, spoke along similar lines when, in appealing to John 6, he asks, 'Now who does not see that communion of Christ's flesh and blood is necessary for all who aspire to heavenly life.'[79] He acknowledges that the manner of such feeding is mysterious, but claims that nevertheless it takes place.

Such language, however, seems dangerous and open to misunderstanding. William Cunningham described Calvin's position as 'perhaps, the greatest blot in the history of Calvin's labours as a public instructor'.[80] Although such a statement is perhaps excessive, we have to agree with Robert Reymond's assessment that 'Calvin, by his language, though not by intention, comes perilously close to suggesting the Godhead's apotheosizing of Christ's humanity and to transferring, at least in the Lord's Supper, the saving benefits of Christ's atoning death directly to his human nature now localized in heaven.'[81] Although recognizing an element of mystery in the subject, we agree with Finlayson's cautious statement:

> Though the presence of Christ is held to be real in the Supper, yet it is not in any sense different from that in which we regard His presence elsewhere. It was plainly enough the belief of the disciples that as the bodily presence of Christ departed from among them the Spirit came to minister that presence. Thus in the blessed agency of the Spirit Christ is present in the Supper as a Person, and not merely in the elements as such.[82]

The Lord's Supper is clearly a sacrament for the Lord's covenant people. No one can feed spiritually on Christ who has not previously been savingly united to Him. The Supper in fact reaffirms the covenant bonds between Christ and His people, and their bonds with one another as the covenant community. The verse quoted previously from 1 Corinthians 10 speaks of 'participation' in the body and blood of Christ (v. 16), and the following verse draws out the implication for believers' unity: 'Because there is one loaf, we, who are many, are one body, for we all partake of the one loaf' (v. 17).

As far as believers' renewal of their vows to God is concerned, Edmund Calamy makes this valuable link between baptism and the Lord's Supper:

> Our vow in baptism indeed binds us fast to God, and our owning its obligation on us tends to increase its force. Yet God thinks it fit to require and take new security of us, and orders us to come to His table that we may there strengthen our obligations, and not only own again and again that we are His by right, but be guided by the awful and affecting considerations there presented to us to new resolutions and engagements and solemn vows to lead a life of holy devotedness. And in requiring this of us, He very much considers our benefit.[83]

As far as the unity of believers is concerned, Theodore Beza cites 1 Corinthians 10:17 (and 12:13) and comments, 'This, I say, shows us the bond and union which ought to exist between us all who are the mystical Body of Jesus Christ, our Head, according to the common public confession which we make.'[84]

The biblical exhortation 'Let a man examine himself' (1 Cor. 11:28 NASB) excludes the unsaved from participation in the Lord's Supper since such are unable to 'discern the Lord's body' (however that phrase is to be understood). Most covenant theologians have also held that covenant children are thereby also excluded. This is reflected in the Larger Catechism's reference to the limitation of participation 'only to such as are of years and ability to examine themselves' (Q177). Although in recent years some within the Reformed family have argued for 'paedocommunion', for example by drawing a close analogy between the Passover and the Lord's

Supper, the traditional position seems most consistent with Scripture. Those who receive the Lord's Supper are clearly required to engage in spiritual activity, namely self-examination, in contrast to the basic passivity that characterizes baptism, whether adult or infant. This is well summed up by Edmund Clowney when he states, 'The decisive difference between the two sacraments is that the Supper requires active and discerning participation. Indeed, communicants who take and eat in remembrance of Christ's death are performing the sacrament as well as receiving it.'[85] This is reflected in the old Scottish practice of the communicants serving each other at the table. We might also note that Larger Catechism Q175 lists numerous duties to be performed by Christians after they have received the sacrament, all of which require self-examination in considerable depth.

In 1 Corinthians 11:26 we read, 'For whenever you eat this bread and drink this cup, you proclaim the Lord's death until he comes.' The Lord's Supper looks forward as well as back, forward to a day when it will no longer be required. The sacrament points us to the consummation of God's covenantal purpose at the return of Christ, and to that glorious subject we now turn.

Notes

1. Theodore Beza, *The Christian Faith*, 1558 edition, translated by James Clark (Lewes, 1992) 4.51.

2. Johannes Wollebius, *Compendium of Christian Theology* (1626) in *Reformed Dogmatics*, translated and edited by John W. Beardslee III (Grand Rapids, 1977), p. 120.

3. R. A. Finlayson, 'The Reformed Doctrine of the Sacraments' in *Reformed Theological Writings* (Fearn, 1996), p. 152.

4. ibid.

5. John Calvin, *Institutes of the Christian Religion*, 1559 edition, translated by Ford Lewis Battles (Philadelphia, 1960), IV.xiv.3.

6. John Calvin, *Institutes*, IV.xiv.6.

7. Wilhelmus à Brakel, *The Christian's Reasonable Service*, 1700 edition, translated by Bartel Elshout (Ligonier, 1992), vol. 2, ch. 38, p. 474.

8. Louis Berkhof, *Systematic Theology* (Edinburgh, 1958), p. 618.

9. R. A. Finlayson, op. cit., p. 158.

10. Theodore Beza, op. cit., 4.44.

11. John Calvin, *The Catechism of the Church of Geneva* (1545) in *Calvin: Theological Treatises*, edited by J. K. S. Reid (Philadelphia, 1954), p. 131.

12. Robert L. Reymond, *A New Systematic Theology of the Christian Faith* (Nashville, 1998), p. 922.

13. W. P. Stephens, *The Theology of Huldrych Zwingli* (Oxford, 1986), p. 187.

14. Both are readily available in *Zwingli and Bullinger*, edited by G. W. Bromiley (Philadelphia, 1953).

15. Millard J. Erickson, *Christian Theology*, 2nd edition (Grand Rapids, 1998), p. 1114.

16. John Calvin, *Institutes*, IV.xiv.7.

17. Wilhelmus à Brakel, op. cit., vol. 2, ch. 38, pp. 477-8.

18. R. A Finlayson, op. cit., p. 156.

19. G. C. Berkouwer, *The Sacraments*, translated by Hugo Bekker (Grand Rapids, 1969), p. 53.

20. Robert Bruce, *The Mystery of the Lord's Supper*, translated and edited by Thomas F. Torrance (London, 1958), p. 44.

21. ibid.

22. R .S .Wallace, *Calvin's Doctrine of the Word and Sacrament* (Edinburgh, 1953), pp. 153-4.

23. Robert Bruce, op. cit., p. 44.

24. J. van Genderen, *Covenant and Election* (Neerlandia, 1995), p. 72.

25. J. van Genderen, op. cit., p. 73.

26. John Calvin, *Catechism*, p. 138.

27. Theodore Beza, op. cit., 4.46.

28. William Cunningham, *The Reformers and the Theology of the Reformation*, 1862 edition (Edinburgh, 1979), p. 245.

29. G. C. Berkouwer, op. cit., p. 180.

30. Richard P. McBrien, *Catholicism*, 2nd edition (New York, 1994), p. 788.

31. Ludwig Ott, *Fundamentals of Catholic Dogma* (Rockford, 1974), p. 329.

32. *Catechism of the Catholic Church* (Dublin, 1994), para. 1128.

33. *Catechism*, para. 1250.

34. *Catechism*, para. 1129.

35. Richard P. McBrien, op. cit., p. 794.

36. Johannes Wollebius, op. cit., p. 126.

37. Robert Letham, *The Work of Christ* (Leicester, 1993), p. 82.

38. *Catechism*, para. 1213.

39. *Catechism*, para. 1992.

40. John Murray, *Christian Baptism* (Philadelphia, 1962), p. 6.

41. C. E. B. Cranfield, *The Epistle to the Romans*, 2 volumes (Edinburgh, 1975-9), ad. loc.

42. John Murray, op. cit., p. 7.

43. John Calvin, *Institutes*, IV.xvi.2.

44. Robert L. Reymond, op. cit., p. 926.

45. Donald Macleod, *A Faith to Live By* (Fearn, 1998), p. 215.

46. John Murray, op. cit., p. 49.

47. John Calvin, *Institutes*, IV.xvi.11.

48. G. R. Beasley-Murray, *Baptism in the New Testament* (Exeter, 1972), p. 337.

49. Donald Macleod, op. cit., p. 216.

50. Pierre Ch Marcel, *The Biblical Doctrine of Infant Baptism*, translated by Philip Edgcumbe Hughes (Cambridge, 1953), p. 106.

51. John Calvin, *The Epistles of Paul the Apostle to the Galatians, Ephesians, Philippians and Colossians*, translated by T. H. L. Parker (Edinburgh, 1965), on Colossians 2:12.

52. G. R. Beasley-Murray, op. cit., 341-2.

53. David Kingdon, *Children of Abraham* (Worthing, 1973), p. 34.

54. Paul K. Jewett, *Infant Baptism and the Covenant of Grace* (Grand Rapids, 1978), p. 89.

55. John Murray, op. cit., p. 52.

56. B. B. Warfield, 'The Polemics of Infant Baptism' in *Studies in Theology* (New York, 1932).

57. Paul K. Jewett, op. cit., p. 236.

58. John Murray, op. cit., p. 59.

59. H. Westerink, *A Sign of Faithfulness*, translated by J. Mark Beach (Neerlandia, 1997), p. 121.

60. Robert L. Reymond, op. cit., p. 947.

61. James Henley Thornwell, *Collected Writings*, 1875 edition (Edinburgh, 1974), 4.333-41; Robert L. Dabney, *Systematic Theology*, 1871 edition (Edinburgh, 1985), pp. 792-5.

62. William Cunningham, op. cit., p. 291.

63. Herman Hanko, *We and Our Children* (Grand Rapids, 1981), p. 89.

64. John Murray, op. cit., p. 82.

65. John Murray, op. cit., p. 9ff.

66. A useful, short, study of the subject is *The Meaning and Mode of Baptism* by Jay E. Adams (Phillipsburg, 1980).

67. Jay E. Adams, op. cit., p. 28.

68. Johannes Wollebius, op. cit., p. 133.

69. George Hutcheson, *The Gospel of John*, 1841 edition (London, 1972), ad. loc.

70. Robert L. Reymond, op. cit., p. 957.

71. R. T. Beckwith, 'Eucharist' in *New Dictionary of Theology*, edited by Sinclair B. Ferguson and David F. Wright (Leicester/Downers Grove, 1988), p. 236.

72. Richard Vines, 'The Passover. Its Significance, and the Analogy Between it and Christ our Passover' in *The Puritans on the Lord's Supper* by Richard Vines, et al (Morgan, 1997), p. 13.

73. *Catechism*, para. 1368.

74. *Catechism*, para. 1371.

75. Edmund Calamy, 'The Lord's Supper Is a Federal Ordinance' in *The Puritans on the Lord's Supper*, p. 25.

76. Millard J. Erickson, op. cit., p. 1130.

77. Brief summaries of these views are provided by e.g. R. A. Finlayson, op. cit., pp. 162-3.

78. Johannes Wollebius, op. cit., p. 122.

79. John Calvin, *Institutes*, IV.xvii.9.

80. William Cunningham, op. cit., p. 240.

81. Robert L. Reymond, op. cit., p. 963. Reymond goes on to refute Calvin's use of John 6.

82. R. A. Finlayson, op. cit., p. 163. .

83. Edmund Calamy, op. cit., p. 23. Another sermon by Calamy in the same volume is entitled 'The Express Renewal of Our Christian Vows Every Time We Come to the Holy Communion, and Directions about the Right Management of It'.

84. Theodore Beza, op. cit., 4.50.

85. Edmund P. Clowney, *The Church* (Leicester, 1995), p. 284.

11

The Final Triumph

The God of the covenant is a God who is sovereign and whose decrees are always fulfilled in every detail. He is the God who declares, 'I make known the end from the beginning, from ancient times, what is still to come. I say: My Purpose will stand, and I will do all that I please' (Isa. 46:10). Thus the beginning and the end of human history as the unfolding of God's sovereign purpose are bound inextricably together. The risen and exalted Christ proclaims in Revelation 22:13, 'I am the Alpha and the Omega, the First and the Last, the Beginning and the End.'

This is vital to bear in mind when we come to consider the consummation of God's redemptive covenant work at the end of human history. The events to be considered normally come under the heading of 'eschatology', the study of the 'last things', which includes, for example, death, the intermediate state, the return of Christ and the resurrection. These matters, however, must not be treated as something 'tagged on' at the end of theological textbooks, without any major connection with all that has gone before. Robert Doyle, in his recent study of eschatology, sums up the biblical perspective accurately in these words: 'God's end-time purposes and activities operate from creation onward, and find expression at key points in the history of Israel and the world.'[1]

The 'last things' should be thought of in terms of *consummation*: the summing up and completing of all that has gone before or, better, of all that God has done before. The trajectory of God's saving purpose runs from Eden to the new heavens and the new earth, embracing all of history in between these crucial points. At the centre stands the cross of the Mediator (inseparable from the empty tomb), the focal point which shapes all of history from Eden onwards and which determines the path to final glory. As A. A. Hoekema says, 'The Bible, therefore, teaches us to see human history as completely dominated by Jesus Christ. History is the sphere of God's redemption, in which he triumphs over man's sin through Christ and once again reconciles the world to himself'.[2]

Many threads link the end to the beginning. Doyle highlights three: promise, the kingdom of God and mediatorial kingship.[3] He fails to mention, however, the theme of covenant, and it is surprising that no mention is made in his study of the importance of covenant for eschatology. All the areas of Covenant Theology that we have considered so far reach their God-ordained consummation with the return of the Mediator in glory. As we shall see, covenant is integral to a biblical understanding of eschatology.

The 'last days'

A question commonly asked in Christian circles is, 'Are we living in the last days?' Some invest a great deal of effort in trying to find parallels between biblical prophecies and contemporary events in pursuit of an answer to this question. Amid the often confused and confusing debates about prophecy, however, one thing in Scripture is clear: the 'last days' began with the incarnation of Christ. On the day of Pentecost Peter quotes from Joel 2, 'In the last days, God says, I will pour out my Spirit on all people', and points to the fulfilment of the prophet's words in the outpouring of the Holy Spirit (Acts 2:16ff.). The same perspective is to be found in the statement of Hebrews 1:2 that 'in these last days [God] has spoken to us by his Son', and we should also note the similar language of 1 John 2:18, 'Dear children, this is the last hour'. In biblical terms, therefore, the first coming of Christ marked the beginning of the last days.

This fact is reflected in Jesus' preaching of the kingdom of God. As New Testament scholars have demonstrated,[4] Jesus proclaimed that in Him the kingdom (or Reign) of God had really come, yet not in its final glorious form. The kingdom was present because the King was at work: 'But if I drive out demons by the finger of God, then the kingdom of God has come to you' (Luke 11:20). Already sinners are entering the kingdom and the gift of salvation is being bestowed, but Jesus also speaks of a future coming of the kingdom which is bound up with His return to earth at some point after His triumphant resurrection. Ridderbos is correct to observe that 'the great orientation-point given us in Jesus's speeches about the coming epoch is before all else to be found in the as yet unfulfilled *parousia* of the Son of Man'.[5] (The *parousia* is a New Testament term for the coming of Christ.) In the terms that have become standard in discussions of this subject, 'already' the kingdom has come, but 'not yet' in its final form.

It is in these terms that we should understand the work of the Mediator of the Covenant. The Covenant of Redemption established within the Trinity in eternity made provision for the salvation of the elect, from the incarnation of the Son through to the final glorification of the elect. As this provision unfolds in the course of history, the Mediator makes atonement for the sins of His people and by the working of the Holy Spirit sinners are regenerated and brought into the Covenant of Grace. God has 'begun a good work' in them, to use the language of Philippians 1:6. That work will not be allowed to fail. As Romans 8:29-30 demonstrates, those foreknown and predestined by God will ultimately be glorified. The salvation of the covenant people, embracing both body and soul, has still to be brought to completion, but its completion is certain. The Covenant of Grace secures the glory of all those for whom Christ died, and so Paul can be confident regarding the good work that God 'will carry it on to completion until the day of Christ Jesus' (Phil. 1:6).

An illustration which is often used to clarify this already/not yet dynamic was first suggested by the German theologian Oscar Cullmann in his book *Christ and Time*.[6] The illustration, drawing on the later stages of the Second World War, distinguishes between D-Day, when the decisive Allied blow was struck at Normandy and V-Day, when victory was finally celebrated. After D-Day the destruction of the Nazi regime was in sight, but the battles had to be fought to subdue the enemy completely. In theological terms, the decisive blow has been struck at Calvary and the final triumphant outcome has been rendered certain, yet for a time the Church is engaged in warfare as the enemy tries to do as much damage as possible. The results of the work of Christ are of course certain in a sense that could not be applied to the progress of the war from D-Day to V-Day (at least from a human perspective), but the main point of Cullmann's illustration is apposite.

In chapter 5 we thought of Christ as Mediatorial King, presently exercising 'all authority in heaven and on earth' (Matt. 28:18), specifically 'for the church' (Eph. 1:22). At present many refuse to recognize the King and 1 Corinthians 15:25 states that 'he must reign until he has put all his enemies under his feet'. This is in harmony with the Father's words to the Son recorded in Psalm 110:1, 'Sit at my right hand until I make your enemies a footstool for your feet'. The mediatorial reign of Christ is moving towards a triumphant consummation when 'every knee [shall] bow' (as Phil. 2:10 envisages). Raymond Zorn sums up this truth helpfully:

> Christ's victory will not be complete until the usurpers, sin, Satan and death have been subdued under him (Phil. 3:21b). The conflict with these usurpers which began at the incarnation, which was victoriously determined on the cross in ransom for sin and which is now since the resurrection and ascension carried on in the heavenly realm, will be concluded only when his triumph is universal. And that triumph awaits the cataclysm of the consummation for its accomplishment.[7]

We will note the various aspects of Christ's triumph as our study unfolds.

Death and beyond

(i) the certainty of death
The consequences of breaking the Covenant of Works were spelled out clearly by the Lord: 'from the tree of the knowledge of good and evil you shall not eat, for in the day that you eat from it you will surely die' (Gen. 2:17, NASB). This translation appears to reflect the insight of Geerhardus Vos that the Hebrew expression 'in the day that' is an idiomatic way of expressing the certainty of the outcome.[8] As we noted in chapter 4, Adam and Eve did die spiritually as soon as they broke the covenant. As Zorn puts it, man 'being ethically alienated from God, is to suffer the separation of his very being from God in a spiritual death of which the physical

is but an image'.[9] Physical death follows later but equally certainly as part of the Lord's sentence: 'dust you are and to dust you will return' (Gen. 3:19). In the fullest sense it can be said that 'in Adam all die' (1 Cor. 15:22). If the sinner's condition is not reversed by the grace of God he will eventually experience the 'second death' of Revelation 20:6, 14, which is eternal separation from God. To this we will return later in our study.

Death is clearly an intruder into God's good creation. Had the Covenant of Works not been violated, the human race would have had no experience of death. There is no scriptural support for a view such as that of Karl Barth, that in some sense death is part of that good creation. Alongside an acknowledgment of the judgment aspect of death, Barth can assert, 'In itself, therefore, it is not unnatural but natural for human life to run its course to this *terminus ad quem*, to ebb and fade, and therefore to have this forward limit.'[10] Even less acceptable, and rather curious, is the statement by radical Dutch theologian Hendrikus Berkhof, 'Death is included in the renewal process as a fermenting element.'[11] Death is always 'the last enemy', as 1 Corinthians 15:26 states. Whilst on occasion death may bring relief from suffering, it is, even for believers, an enemy, a profoundly unnatural intruder.

We may wonder, however, why God's covenant people, those in saving union with Christ the Mediator, still have to pass through the experience of physical death. Might they not be spared such a trial in the way that Enoch was? (Gen. 5:24). The Heidelberg Catechism provides an answer in these terms: 'Our death does not pay the debt of our sins. Rather it puts an end to our sinning and is our entrance into eternal life' (Q42). God has chosen to bring His people into the full experience of fellowship with Him through the doorway of the death of the body. The Larger Catechism states that 'it is out of God's love, to free them perfectly from sin and misery, and to make them capable of further communion with Christ in glory, which they then enter upon' (Q85).

All this is thoroughly biblical. Believers can look beyond death to the glory that God has prepared for them, knowing that Christ has triumphed over death and that in union with Him they too share in His triumph, as Paul makes clear in 1 Corinthians 15. Nevertheless we must address the fact that God leads His people through an experience that may involve protracted suffering and indignity. Why should He do this? We surely see in the experience of death a further trial by which God sanctifies His people. As in all trials, we are thrown back on the resources of the Lord for grace that will be sufficient to cope with whatever death entails. Once again, the believer finds that Hebrews 13:5 is true – God never leaves him nor forsakes him. Even in the final hours of earthly life progress in sanctification can take place as earthly things are let go and glory becomes more real. Death is no exception to the principle of Romans 5:3, 'we also exult in our tribulations, knowing that tribulation brings about perseverence; and perseverence, proven character; and proven character, hope; and hope does not disappoint, because the love of God has been poured out within our hearts through the Holy Spirit who was given to us' (NASB). As à Brakel puts it, 'Death will be as the dreadful lion killed by Samson which, after having been killed, yielded sweet honey'.[12]

(ii) immortality
The phrase 'immortality of the soul' is never found in Scripture, perhaps, as Robert Morey suggests, in order to avoid pagan connotations such as pre-existence or transmigration.[13] The Greek words translated as 'immortality' in the Authorized Version are *athanasia* meaning 'incapable of death', used of the resurrection body in 1 Corinthians 15:43,53, and *aphtharsia* meaning 'incapable of corruption'. The latter word is applied to God in Romans 1:23 and to the resurrection body in 1 Corinthians 15:42, 50, 52-54. It is mistranslated as 'immortality' in the AV renderings of 1 Timothy 1:17 and 2 Timothy 1:10. These terms clearly relate to the state of believers after the bodily resurrection, not to their state immediately after death. Does Scripture teach that the soul of man survives death?

The Jehovah's Witnesses are in no doubt about the correct answer to this question: 'God did not create man with a soul. Man is a soul. So, as we would expect, when man dies, his soul dies.'[14]

Increasingly it is being argued that man is a unity of body and soul in such a way that the soul does not survive the death of the body. Some argue that the soul is not naturally immortal and that God confers immortality only on believers, whilst others deny even that concession.[15] Immortality is said to be derived more from Plato than from the Bible.

A closer look at the biblical evidence indicates that Scripture does not *argue* for the continued existence of the soul after death but simply *assumes* it. There are no philosophical speculations about the inherent indestructibility of the soul such as some theologians have offered. However much Platonic notions may have influenced some early Christian thinkers, they find no place in Scripture. Rather, as with belief in the existence of God, belief in the continued existence of the soul is, in Loraine Boettner's words, 'assumed as an undeniable postulate'.[16]

As we might expect, in the Old Testament we do not find a fully articulated doctrine of immortality, yet the fact of immortality is clearly revealed, for example in the common description of death as being 'gathered to one's people', as in Genesis 15:15, 25:8 (Abraham), Genesis 35:29 (Isaac) and Genesis 49:33 (Jacob). Other passages in the Old Testament speak of a future existence, but Psalm 16:10-11 is interpreted in the New Testament in terms of resurrection (Acts 2:31). Continued existence after death but before the resurrection does appear to be envisaged, however, in Psalm 73:24 'You guide me with your counsel and afterwards you will take me into glory.'

The immortality of the soul is revealed more fully in the New Testament. It is often claimed that 'immortality' is a Greek idea, in contrast to Hebraic ideas of 'resurrection',[17] and that early Christian thinking was influenced away from the biblical position by Greek philosophy. In a study written in 1976, however, Murray Harris has demonstrated that Judaism in the New Testament period was fully conversant with the concept of immortality, and he concludes, 'No longer can anyone maintain that "resurrection" is Hebraic and "immortality" Greek'.[18]

As far as the New Testament is concerned, there is no support whatsoever for any theory of 'soul sleep' nor any indication that men cease to exist at death. On the contrary, in His debate with the Sadducees Jesus referred to Abraham, Isaac and Jacob as 'the living', even before their resurrection at the last day. That it is not only the covenant people of God who continue to exist after death is evident from the description of the rich man and Lazarus in Luke 16:19-31. Even when we allow for the parabolic form of the story, it is 'legitimate to deduce from the setting of this story the basic characteristics of the post mortem state of Christians and non-Christians'.[19] It is clear that after death the rich man's powers of reasoning and perception have improved.

The focus of the New Testament material, however, is on the confidence of those who share in the Covenant of Grace that the 'eternal life' which Christ gives to them entails unbroken conscious fellowship with God. Thus Paul can express a preference 'to be away from the body and at home with the Lord' (2 Cor. 5:8) and a desire 'to depart and be with Christ, which is better by far' (Phil. 1:23). No gap between leaving the body and being present with the Lord is envisaged. Like Jesus after His death, the spirits of believers are safe in God's hands (cf. Luke 23:46 'into your hands I commit my spirit'). They 'live according to God in regard to the spirit' (1 Pet. 4:6, specifically with reference to those 'now dead'). The martyrs under the altar in God's presence can cry to him for vindication (Rev. 6:9-10). As the Shorter Catechism expresses it, 'The souls of believers are at their death made perfect in holiness and do immediately pass into glory' (Q37). The believer does not look forward to a gap in his consciousness after death as his soul 'sleeps'[20] but to a more glorious experience of covenant fellowship with his Lord.

The Bible is not concerned with immortality as an abstract concept. The continued existence of the soul is simply assumed and attention is given mainly to the quality of that existence. Does the soul continue to enjoy covenant fellowship with God or does it begin to experience the wrath of God on those guilty of breaking the Covenant of Works?

(iii) the intermediate place

As we have noted, the Bible's concern is chiefly with the *state* of people after death, but brief reference needs to be made to their *location*. The texts to which reference was made in the previous section indicate that at death God's people enter into His presence: in other words, they are in heaven. This is explicit in the vision of the souls under the altar (Rev. 6:9-10), where the setting is undeniably heaven. The state of believers is one of blessedness, enjoying the presence of their Lord. Of the supposed fires of Purgatory, still spoken of in the *Catechism of the Catholic Church*, Scripture knows nothing.[21]

There is a great deal of scholarly debate about two words, one Hebrew (Sheol) and one Greek (Hades), which also apply to the place of the dead after leaving this present world.

Regarding Sheol, it has become common to claim that it refers to a shadowy world into which both righteous and wicked descend after death, reflecting the fact that as yet clear revelation regarding the afterlife had not been given. This view is argued at length, from a Reformed perspective, by Robert Morey, who argues that there are only hints of the glory awaiting believers in the Old Testament.[22] On the other hand Old Testament scholar R. Laird Harris contends that Sheol is simply the grave, into which all descend.[23] To complete the range of options offered, we may add that W. G. T. Shedd believes that Sheol is the place of punishment into which only the wicked go,[24] a view to which Desmond Alexander inclines;[25] Loraine Boettner holds that it refers generally to the grave and sometimes to the place of punishment;[26] A. A. Hoekema believes that it has a variety of meanings.[27] Whilst acknowledging the difficulties in coming to firm conclusions on the subject, we suggest that Sheol is best understood as a term for the realm of death, a state rather than a 'geographical' place, not an underworld, even one with separate places for righteous and unrighteous. The unrighteous should fear entering Sheol, whilst the righteous have the confidence of Psalm 73:24 that through death they are going to be with the Lord.

As far as the term Hades in the New Testament is concerned, its meaning is similarly debated. A passage such as Luke 16:19-

31, dealing with the torment of the rich man 'in this fire', would indicate that Hades can refer to the penultimate place of punishment for the wicked. At other times it would appear to refer to the state of death or the grave, as in Acts 2:27, 31, with reference to Christ. It seems that some diversity in meaning must be allowed for.[28]

What is clear is that none of the terms used in Scripture regarding the intermediate state or location implies any break in the covenant fellowship between God and his people. After death the promise still holds true: 'I will walk among them and be their God.'

The Mediator returns
Before going to the cross Christ promised His disciples, 'I will come back and take you to be with me that you also may be with me where I am' (John 14:3). After His resurrection and ascension the promise was stated in these terms: 'this same Jesus, who has been taken from you into heaven, will come back in the same way you have seen him go into heaven' (Acts 1:11). The New Testament is full of references to the return of Christ and, on occasion, provides some idea of what it will entail. The Mediator's redemptive work was not completed at His first coming. As Hebrews 9:28 says, '[Christ] will appear a second time, not to bear sin, but to bring salvation to those who are waiting for him.'

For some Christians, mention of the return of Christ at once raises the question of the millennium, the thousand-year reign of Christ spoken of in Revelation 20. Will Christ return before His millennial reign on earth (Premillennialism)? Will He return at the end of a thousand years of unprecedented progress for the gospel throughout the world (Postmillennialism)? Is the millennial reign in fact a way of describing the whole period between the comings of Christ (Amillennialism)? It is interesting that Covenant Theology has been able to accommodate all of these views and the great Reformed confessions do not require one particular view. Due to this fact, and on account of the complexity of the issues involved, we will not discuss the millennial question here. A few covenant theologians, such as the great Scottish preacher Robert

Murray McCheyne, have been premillennial in outlook. Many, including most of the Puritans, have held a postmillennial position and derived great missionary impetus from their beliefs.[29] In recent years it has been defended by theologians such as John Jefferson Davis and Keith A. Mathison.[30] The amillennial view has grown in influence over the years and has been most ably defended by A. A. Hoekema.[31] The one view which is incompatible with Scripture and with Covenant Theology is Dispensational Premillennialism which will be evaluated in an appendix to this study.[32]

If the reader insists on knowing the present author's view, we willingly admit to an amillennial position as expounded by Hoekema and others. The premillennial view of Christ reigning on earth over a kingdom that includes resurrected saints, still living saints and the unregenerate is, in our view, impossible to square with the biblical evidence. On the other hand, however attractive the postmillennial vision of a substantially converted world may be, we cannot reconcile it with Scripture's insistence on the intermixing of wheat and weeds right to the end, and its descriptions of the growth of evil alongside the spread of the gospel until the Lord returns. It is important to note that the return of Christ is depicted in Scripture as a sudden, cataclysmic inbreaking into the course of history, which appears to be incompatible with the premillennial position. As Donald Macleod says, 'The final phase of the kingdom of God will not be established by gradual and imperceptible evolution from the present or by factors already operating in the world, but by a fresh, unprecedented intrusion of the glory of God.'[33]

Whatever their view of the millennium, covenant theologians have consistently asserted that Christ will certainly return to this earth. The Belgic Confession of Faith speaks of it in these terms:

> Finally, we believe, according to the Word of God, when the time appointed by the Lord (which is unknown to all creatures) is come and the number of the elect complete, that our Lord Jesus Christ will come from heaven corporally and visibly, as He ascended, with great glory and majesty to declare Himself Judge of the living and the dead, burning this old world with fire and flame to cleanse it (Article XXXVII).

The Mediator will return *once* more – personally, visibly, gloriously. Scripture knows nothing of a secret, invisible return to 'rapture' the Church. He will return to complete what He began at His first coming. Having paid the price for the redemption of His people, He must bring them to an enjoyment of the full blessings that He purchased for them. The covenant work of Christ must be brought to a triumphant climax.

The main Greek words used to designate the return of Christ in the New Testament indicate something of its nature.[34] It is termed the *parousia*, a word used in Greek to refer to the 'arrival' of a ruler. The return of Christ will be the coming of the Mediatorial King in whose hands is all authority in heaven and on earth. The term *apokalypsis* indicates the 'unveiling' of Christ. At present He is seen only with the eyes of faith: at the last day He will be revealed to all. As Revelation 1:7 states, 'every eye will see him, even those who pierced him', and so terrible will be the sight for the unregenerate that 'all the peoples of the earth will mourn because of him'. The third term is *epiphaneia* which denotes the 'manifestation' of the Lord's glory. No longer will His glory be hidden from the world: it will be manifested to all. Thus Paul speaks of the Church waiting 'for the blessed hope, the glorious appearing of our great God and Saviour, Jesus Christ' (Tit. 2:13). Each word shows why believers look forward to the return of Christ with anticipation and joy. The day they have longed for will have come: they will see the Lord face to face in their resurrected bodies.

The resurrection of the body
The covenant people of God are united to a risen Saviour. He is the one who said, 'I am the resurrection and the life' (John 11:25). Not only has He triumphed over sin and the powers of evil, He has triumphed over death. As Peter states in Acts 2:24, 'it was impossible for death to keep its hold on him'. Christ did not merely live on in some spiritual realm after His death: He rose from the dead and the tomb was empty. As author Frank Morison discovered when he set out to write a book disproving the resurrection, the fact of the empty tomb cannot be explained away, and he ended

up writing a book in defence of the resurrection.[35]

The resurrection of Christ is crucial to the gospel. Not only does it demonstrate the true identity of the one who died on the cross, so that He was 'declared with power to be the Son of God by His resurrection from the dead' (Rom. 1:4), but it is itself part of his redemptive work. The resurrection is a central element in the theology and preaching of the New Testament Church because of its implications for those whom Christ saves.[36] Because Christ has risen in triumph, those brought into union with Him experience a spiritual resurrection from spiritual death. Thus Paul can say, 'God raised us up with Christ and seated us with him in the heavenly realms in Christ Jesus' (Eph. 2:6). As Richard Gaffin puts it, 'Jesus is raised in his specific identity as the second Adam'.[37] Thus all who are regenerated and united to Him in the Covenant of Grace share in the benefits of His resurrection.

More is entailed for believers, however, than just this spiritual resurrection. The Lord saves *people* – bodies as well as souls. The whole person shares in the benefits of His resurrection. The Shorter Catechism is correct to say that '[believers'] bodies, being still united to Christ, do rest in their graves till the resurrection' (Q37). When Paul speaks of Christ being 'the firstfruits of those who have fallen asleep' (1 Cor. 15:20) he indicates the certainty that believers have of sharing in bodily resurrection. As we have seen in considering immortality, believers (and unbelievers) continue to exist apart from the body after death, but the full hope of believers is of bodily resurrection, and it is on this that the New Testament concentrates.

It is because of what Christ has done as Surety, bearing the burden of His people's punishment, that they will rise. 'The kind of resurrection that believers will experience, a resurrection in glory, has been secured by and will be determined by what Christ did on the cross of Calvary. The believer's resurrection body will be as glorious as the obedience of God's own Son deserves,' says Donald Macleod.[38] In addition, believers share in the very life of Christ: they are united indissolubly to a risen Saviour and so, in ways beyond our understanding, their bodies will share in His glory.

The resurrection of believers is the work of the Triune God. In John 5:21 Jesus speaks of the Father as the one who 'raises the dead and gives them life', whilst in verses 28 and 29 He says that 'a time is coming when all who are in their graves will hear [the Son of Man's] voice and come out'. The role of the Holy Spirit is indicated by Paul when he says that 'he who raised Christ from the dead will also give life to your mortal bodies through his Spirit, who lives in you' (Rom. 8:11).

For some Christians the nature of the resurrection body holds great fascination, yet the biblical material on the subject is limited, perhaps by our lack of capacity to understand more. In his expansive study *The Nature of the Resurrection Body*, J. A. Schep considers first the indirect evidence afforded by Scripture and concludes that the resurrection body will consist of 'glorified flesh'.[39] He goes on to state, however, that 'When we wish to consider the *direct* New Testament references to the nature of the resurrection-body, we find hardly any.'[40] The only relevant passage cited is 1 Corinthians 15.

It is possible to deduce from Scripture some basic characteristics of the resurrection bodies of believers since we know that Christ 'will transform our lowly bodies so that they will be like his glorious body' (Phil. 3:21), and several qualities are mentioned in 1 Corinthians 15:42-44. Most obviously, believers' bodies will be glorious. They will manifest perfectly the image of the Lord, into which they are being transformed according to 2 Corinthians 3:18. At the resurrection their bodies will share in the perfection previously enjoyed by their souls. It would seem that the resurrection body will also be radiant, in view of the statement of Matthew 13:43, 'Then the righteous will shine like the sun in the kingdom of their Father.' Francis Turretin cites the examples of Moses' radiance after his meeting with the Lord (Exod. 34:29) and Christ's radiance at the transfiguration (Matt. 17:2) and concludes that 'it will be nothing else than the irradiation of God's glory, from which the bodies will be made to shine'.[41]

Paul in 1 Corinthians 15:42 also indicates that the resurrection body will be characterized by 'incorruption' (*aphtharsia*). Death, disease and suffering will be no more. As Paul says, 'Death has been swallowed up in victory' (v. 54). Still entirely dependent on the Lord, the body will be imperishable. With the abolition of sin will come the abolition of death. 'Thus the saints will be confirmed in good so that they cannot sin and being thus confirmed in life that they cannot die,' says Turretin.[42] The picture of perfection painted in Revelation 21:4 will therefore be realised: 'There will be no more death or mourning or crying or pain.'

Linked with this characteristic of incorruption is the 'power' that Paul refers to in 1 Corinthians 15:43. All causes of weakness will be removed from the resurrection bodies and they will exhibit the full vigour of which they are capable. As the resurrection body of Christ evidently had heightened and even new capacities, so it will be for His resurrected people. Donald Macleod expresses this helpfully: 'The body is going to have more energy, more physical capability, more stamina, more athleticism, more speed, more co-ordination, more durability than it ever, ever had because we're not going to need the body less, we're going to need it more and use it more.'[43] We will think more of this when considering the renewal of creation.

The resurrection body is also a 'spiritual' body according to Paul. We must not misunderstand what he is saying. The body is not one changed into 'spirit' and so no longer material. It is quite clear that Christ's body was material and could be touched and examined (see e.g. Luke 24:39). Granted, Paul shows us that the body is not 'flesh and blood' as we now understand it, since 'flesh and blood cannot inherit the kingdom of God' (1 Cor. 15:50), so the body will certainly be 'changed' (v. 51). The key is our understanding of 'spiritual' (*pneumatikōs*). The word is always being used in the New Testament with reference to the Holy Spirit and His work. Since this is so, it appears that Simon Kistemaker's comments on the verse are accurate: '[Paul] describes our bodies raised from the dead as being completely Spirit-filled and Spirit-governed ... The resurrected body will be completely filled with the Spirit of glory. This glorified body is not immaterial but rather has spiritual aspects that lift it to a supernatural level.'[44]

We have spent some time considering the resurrection body, not in order to provoke unbiblical speculation, but because it is such an important aspect of Christian hope. The Covenant of Grace provides a future for God's people which embraces both the spiritual aspects and the physical aspects of our being. Nothing is left out or denied. Believers look forward to a future which has solidity, shape and colour, which is a testimony to the re-creative grace of God.

Scripture also teaches that the reprobate will also be raised. Paul speaks of his hope that 'there will be a resurrection of both the righteous and the wicked' (Acts 24:15). Nothing is said about the nature of their bodies, although we can be sure that they will have none of the glorious characteristics of the bodies of the redeemed. Jesus indicates in John 5:29 the purpose of their resurrection – 'those who have done evil will rise to be condemned.' No more needs to be known. At the last day the unsaved will have more to worry about than the nature of their resurrection bodies.

The final reckoning

In Athens Paul confronted his listeners with the fact that God 'has set a day when he will judge the world with justice by the man he has appointed' (Acts 17:31). The identity of the judge is made explicit in 2 Corinthians 5:10, 'For we must all appear before the judgment seat of Christ, that each one may receive what is due to him for the things done while in the body, whether good or bad.'

Christ the Mediator of the covenant will be the judge of all men, as well as of the angels. As the great New England theologian Jonathan Edwards pointed out in his (undated) discourse 'The Final Judgment', it is a testimony to the marvellous wisdom of God that this should be the case. In the first place, men are to be judged by one who shared their nature. 'God seeth fit, that those who have bodies, as all mankind will have at the day of judgment, should see their judge with their bodily eyes, and hear him with their bodily ears.'[45] Edwards goes on to argue that Christ is given the honour of judging the world as a reward for His redemptive suffering and that this is part of His exaltation. Among the various points that Edwards makes, including the comfort that it should be to believers knowing that Christ is to be their judge, perhaps the most important is that Christ's judging the world is necessary for His finishing the work of redemption. Christ is to be a complete redeemer of His people. This involves His making atonement for sinners, but also consists, in great measure,

> in converting sinners to the knowledge and love of the truth, in carrying them on in the way of grace and true holiness through life, and in finally raising their bodies to life, in glorifying them, in pronouncing the blessed sentence upon them, in crowning them with honour and glory in the sight of men and angels, and in completing and perfecting their reward.[46]

Edwards' words serve to remind us that a 'judge' in biblical terminology is one who brings deliverance and secures justice. The Old Testament judges performed such functions, reflecting the almighty judge who helps His covenant people (see e.g. Judg. 11:27 and 2 Sam. 18:31). According to the Old Testament, God judges the nations and will ultimately destroy all ungodliness (see e.g. Isa. 2:12-18; Amos 1–2, where Israel and Judah are not spared God's evaluation). The New Testament shows that God's judgment will be performed through Christ, the Judge who took the punishment due to His people. On this account the Lord's people can look forward to the judgment, knowing that it will mark the completion of their deliverance. There is no room for complacency among professing Christians, however, since 'it is time for judgment to begin with the family of God; and if it begins with us, what will the outcome be for those who do not obey the gospel of God?' (1 Pet. 4:17).

By now it is becoming clear why a final judgment is necessary. Some wonder about this since immediately after death individuals are either in a state of blessedness or torment. Surely the final judgment is superfluous? The relevant section of the Westminster Confession of Faith demonstrates that the final judgment above all serves to glorify God: 'The end of God's appointing this day is for the manifestation of the glory of his mercy in the eternal salvation of the elect, and of his justice in the damnation of the reprobate who are wicked and disobedient' (XXXIII. 2). The judgment will manifest to all rational beings (men, angels and demons), the mercy and the justice of God and so His name will be glorified. Those brought within the Covenant of Grace will be eternal testimonies to God's grace. Thus Paul states in Ephesians 2:7 that believers are saved 'in order that in the coming ages he might show the incomparable riches of his grace, expressed in his kindness to us in Christ Jesus'. As Calvin comments, 'it was the will of the Lord to hallow in all ages the remembrance of so great goodness.'[47] The reprobate, too, will glorify God, albeit unwillingly, since they will be testimonies to His perfect justice.

At the last day all will appear before Christ to be judged. Scripture gives no support for any idea of a 'second chance' to believe in Christ after death. Such false ideas are held, for example, by Jehovah's Witnesses, who believe that all will be raised at Judgment Day, and during that 'day' (really a long period) they will be judged on the basis of their conduct *then*, not on the basis of past sins. As one Jehovah's Witness publication states, 'During Judgment Day all the people will learn about Jehovah, and they will be given every opportunity to obey and serve him.'[48]

In recent years from within the evangelical camp the voice of Clark Pinnock has been raised in support of what he terms 'a postmortem encounter with Christ'.[49] He claims that 'Scripture does not require us to hold that the window of opportunity is slammed shut at death',[50] and goes on to argue that since God remains a God of grace, when sinners stand before Him at the last day salvation will be available if they are willing to have it. 'One group that will have a grace-filled postmortem encounter with Christ consists of those who sought God during their earthly lives and loved him, though they had not heard of Jesus.'[51] In defence of his position Pinnock can offer only two texts. One is 1 Peter 3:19-20, which he claims indicates the possibility that the dead were given a chance to respond to salvation by Christ preaching to them. The best view of the text, however, is that Christ through Noah preached to those alive before the Flood who are now dead.[52] Pinnock also claims that Hebrews 9:27 ('Just as man is destined to die once, and after that to face judgment ...') does not exclude postmortem decisions to believe, a view which biblical descriptions of postmortem existence and of judgment rule out. It should also be remembered that Pinnock holds an Arminian view of the power of man's unaided will in relation to salvation, not the biblical view of sovereign divine grace, defended by Covenant Theology. Pinnock thus has no difficulty allowing for unforeseen changes of mind by sinners after death.

The standard of judgment is made clear in Scripture: it is the revealed will of God. Those who have the written word of God or who have heard the gospel will be judged by that knowledge of the will of God available to them. Those who have not had these privileges will be judged by the knowledge of God's will available to them from natural revelation and conscience. Romans 1:19-20 deals with the former: 'what may be known about God is plain to them, because God has made it plain to them. For since the creation of the world God's invisible qualities – his eternal power and divine nature – have been clearly seen, being understood from what has been made, so that men are without excuse.' Romans 2:14-15 deals with the latter: 'Indeed, when Gentiles, who do not have the law, do by nature things required by the law, they are a law for themselves, even though they do not have the law, since they show that the requirements of the law are written on their hearts, their consciences also bearing witness, and their thoughts now accusing, now even defending them.' Sinners will not be judged by what they have not heard. God will judge 'in righteousness' (Ps. 9:8).

These Scriptures provide an answer to the question often posed, 'What about those who never heard the gospel?' We must also say, however, that the Bible does not hold out any hope for those who do not consciously respond to Christ. We considered this in chapter 5, dealing with the person and work of Christ, and we must reiterate it here. Apart from faith in Christ, sinners who have had the gospel fail to live up to the knowledge of God's will that it provides, sinners who have had the light of nature and conscience fail to live up to that knowledge. As Paul says in Romans 2:12 'All who sin apart from the law will also perish apart from the law, and all who sin under the law will be judged by the law.' Old Testament believers had faith in Christ who was to come; after the first coming of Christ, believers have faith in Christ who has come. We must therefore reject the assertion of missiologist Peter

Cotterell that 'an overt knowledge of Christ or of the work of Christ was not a condition of salvation under the Old Covenant and is not a condition of salvation under the New Covenant'.[53] Without faith in Christ, sinners will fail the test.

It must not be forgotten that God's covenant people are among the 'we all' who must 'appear before the judgment seat of Christ' (2 Cor. 5:10). At stake will not be believers' salvation, since 'it is by grace you have been saved, through faith ... not by works' (Eph. 2:8-9) but the evaluation of their works. This sobering fact is set out in 1 Corinthians 3:10-15. The 'building' that believers do will be tested by fire: 'his work will be shown for what it is, because the Day will bring it to light. It will be revealed with fire, and the fire will test the quality of each man's work' (v. 13). Two possibilities are presented: 'If what he has built survives, he will receive his reward. If it is burned up, he will suffer loss; he himself will be saved, but only as one escaping through the flames' (vv. 14-15).

The weighty responsibility resting on believers, especially preachers and teachers, is clear from those verses. Our work matters to God, and it will be tested. That is a great stimulus to faithfulness. We must not, however, misinterpret Paul's words to suggest that believers may be punished at the final judgment, and that the day is therefore a cause of anxiety or fear. The main focus of Scripture is on the rewards to be given to faithful believers, without forgetting that rewards may be forfeited. Philip Hughes correctly observes, 'The judgment pronounced is not a declaration of doom, but an assessment of worth.'[54]

The giving of rewards to believers is a mark of the abundance of the covenant grace of God. We can never do more than He requires: 'when you have done everything you were told to do, [you] should say, "We are unworthy servants; we have only done our duty"' (Luke 17:10). There are no 'works of supererogation' as taught by Rome. Nevertheless God will reward His faithful people, probably with differing capacities to enjoy fellowship with Him. That there will be degrees of reward is clear from passages such as Jesus' parable of the ten minas in Luke 19:12ff. Bavinck suggests that God's purpose in giving different rewards is that 'on earth as in heaven, there would be profuse diversity in the believing community and that in that diversity the glory of his attributes would be manifest'.[55]

For the reprobate there will also be degrees of punishment, reflecting individual guilt, particularly regarding the degree of light rejected in the course of life. This aspect of judgment is stated by Jesus, using the illustration of servants failing to prepare for their master's return, in Luke 12:47-48: 'That servant who knows his master's will and does not get ready or does not do what his master wants will be beaten with many blows. But the one who does not know and does things deserving punishment will be beaten with few blows. From everyone who has been given much, much will be demanded; and from the one who has been entrusted with much, much more will be asked.' In the same way Jesus warns those Jews who had witnessed His miracles that 'it will be more bearable for Sodom on the day of judgment than for you' (Matt. 11:24). The serious implications for those who sit under gospel preaching for years without responding are inescapable.

The sentence of condemnation

According to Matthew 25:41, Christ at the last day will say to the unsaved (those on his left), 'Depart from me, you who are cursed, into the eternal fire prepared for the devil and his angels', and the outcome of his sentence is stated in verse 46, 'they will go away to eternal punishment.'

The Bible leaves us in no doubt that the unrepentant will be punished for their sins. All who have broken the Covenant of Works in Adam and who remain outside the Covenant of Grace will bear the consequences of their transgressions. As Surety, Christ bore His people's guilt and sin; all others will bear their own guilt and sin as they face the Judge. The unrepentant will be punished on account of what they have done, not on account of their not being elected by God. There is nothing arbitrary or capricious about the judgment of God.

Covenant Theology rightly emphasizes that the condemnation of the wicked is a consequence of the nature of God. He is a God of infinite holiness and perfect justice. Throughout Scripture we have copious testimony to this fact. 'Holy, holy, holy is the Lord Almighty', cry the seraphim according to Isaiah 6:3; 'Righteousness and justice are the foundation of your throne' (Ps. 89:14). Such a God must respond to sin with righteous wrath, if He is not to deny His own nature. 'Your eyes are too pure to look on evil; you cannot tolerate wrong' (Hab. 1:13). As a consequence, we must say that, in relation to sin, 'our God is a consuming fire' (Deut. 4:24; Heb. 12:29). The penalty for breaking God's law is His wrath and curse. This is stated in covenant language in Deuteronomy 7:9-10 'Know therefore that the Lord your God is God; he is the faithful God, keeping his covenant of love to a thousand generations of those who love him and keep his commands. But those who hate him he will repay to their face by destruction; he will not be slow to repay to their face those who hate him.' As Robert Morey says, 'The punishment of God must be endured either by the person or his substitute in order to satisfy fully the just penalty of the curse of God for disobedience.'[56] God is not to be thought of as coldly indifferent or vindictive towards sinners. He does not gloat over their punishment. As He says in Ezekiel 33:11, 'As surely as I live, ... I take no pleasure in the death of the wicked, but rather that they turn from their ways and live.' Nevertheless, since He is a just and holy God, if the wicked do not turn, they will experience His righteous wrath on their sins in hell.

The word used in the New Testament for the eternal abode of the unsaved – 'Gehenna' – gives some indication of what hell will be like. 'Gehenna' is the Greek equivalent for the Hebrew term 'valley of Hinnom'. It was the place where apostate Jews offered human sacrifices to pagan deities, according to 2 Kings 23:10 and 2 Chronicles 28:3, 33:6. By New Testament times this hated and 'unclean' place had become the rubbish dump for Jerusalem. There rubbish was burned in fires that never went out. This provides the background for the use of Gehenna as a name for the place of final punishment. Christ, who spoke more about this matter than anyone else in Scripture, indicates that it is a place where both body and soul are punished: 'be afraid of the one who can destroy both body and soul in hell' (Matt. 10:28). He gives a graphic description of hell in Mark 9:43-49, where He speaks of it as a place 'where the fire never goes out' and where 'their worm does not die' (quoting Isa. 66:24). It is clearly a place of suffering and grief.

In answering the question 'What is Hell?' R. A. Finlayson helpfully identified four aspects of hell:[57]

a) it is the fixation of moral character: change is no longer possible;

b) it is an encounter with the will and character of God. 'The unregenerate soul finds himself at the last in radical and implacable conflict with the will of God';

c) it is an unending process of spiritual disintegration;

d) it means that character and environment must be in harmony. In a real sense people will spend eternity in the place which matches their spiritual condition, whether holy or evil. As Finlayson says, 'The wicked in nature and character have an affinity to the place to which they go.'

In the history of the Church there have always been those, very few in number, who taught a doctrine of 'universalism', the view that ultimately all men will be saved.[58] In modern times, the view of divine election held by Karl Barth appears to lead to universalism, although Barth himself denied that he was a universalist. On one occasion he stated, 'I don't believe in universalism, but I do believe in Jesus Christ, the reconciler of all.'[59] As we noted in chapter 3, in Barth's view Christ is both elect and reprobate on behalf of all men, with the result that all men are elect in Christ and none is reprobate, Christ having himself taken the 'No' of God's rejection. In Barth's view, therefore, 'What is laid up for man is eternal life in fellowship with God.'[60] There appears to be no way of avoiding the conclusion that all will be saved, even though Barth would not say so explicitly. Cornelius Van Til correctly sums up Barth's position in these words: 'There is no eternal punishment awaiting those who are not in Christ [because] there are no men who are not in Christ.'[61]

More common among professed evangelicals, particularly in recent years, is the view that only the redeemed will enjoy eternal existence and that others will simply be annihilated by God after the final judgment. This view is variously designated 'conditional immortality' or 'annihilationism', and its modern popularity is traced back by Eryl Davies to 1974, the year he terms 'a watershed in the contemporary history of the doctrine of eternal punishment'.[62] In that year *The Goodness of God* by John Wenham was published by Inter-Varsity Press, a book voicing the author's profound doubts about eternal punishment and cautiously suggesting conditional immortality as a more biblical alternative.[63] Since then other prominent evangelicals have expressed a similar view. In dialogue with the liberal theologian David Edwards, John Stott stated his belief that 'the ultimate annihilation of the wicked should at least be accepted as a legitimate, biblically founded alternative to their conscious torment'.[64] Other prominent defenders of this view include Philip Edgcumbe Hughes, E. Earle Ellis and Edward William Fudge.[65]

Covenant theologians, in common with the majority of evangelicals, have defended the view that hell involves everlasting conscious suffering under the righteous wrath of God. An older work, recently reprinted, is W. G. T. Shedd's *The Doctrine of Endless Punishment*, and in more recent years defences of the doctrine have been provided by writers such as John Blanchard and Robert A. Peterson.[66]

Careful exegesis of all the relevant biblical texts, taken in their immediate and wider contexts, demonstrates that the Bible's understanding of hell is of a place where the unsaved endure the wrath of God, suffering consciously for eternity. The imagery employed, such as the undying worm and ever-burning fire (Mark 9:43-49), the exclusion from God's presence, the weeping and the gnashing of teeth (Luke 13:25-28), indicates that the unsaved are not annihilated. As Eryl Davies comments, 'The Bible consistently speaks of suffering and loss rather than annihilation after death for unbelievers. Furthermore, the fact that there are degrees of punishment in hell is incompatible with annihilation.'[67] The term 'eternal' (*aiōnios* in Greek) is applied to both the blessedness of the saved and the punishment of the lost in Matthew 25:46. It is not possible to evade the fact that whatever qualitative connotations the term may have, it also has temporal (or quantitative) connotations. Eternal punishment will last as long as eternal blessedness. As J. C. Ryle states, 'It is clearly revealed in Scripture: the eternity of God, and heaven, and hell, all stand on the same foundation. As surely as God is eternal, so surely is heaven an endless day without night, and hell an endless night without day.'[68]

Covenant theologians acknowledge that the thought of hell is a terrible one, and its horror must never be minimized. It does, however, indicate the sinfulness of sin against a holy God. For those who remain outside the Covenant of Grace, this will be the recompense that their sins have earned. In his famous sermon 'Sinners in the hands of an angry God', preached in 1741, Jonathan Edwards stated,

> God certainly has made no promises either of eternal life, or of any deliverance or preservation from eternal death, but what are contained in the covenant of grace, the promises that are given in Christ, in whom all the promises are yea and amen. But surely they have no interest in the promises of the covenant of grace who are not the children of the covenant, who do not believe in any of the promises, and have no interest in the Mediator of the covenant.[69]

As Edwards goes on to point out, it is only by the forbearance of God that sinners are not immediately plunged into hell.

The covenant people of God do not need to fear such a terrible experience, since Christ as their Surety has already taken their punishment. Calvin explains the phrase 'he descended into hell' in the Apostles' Creed in these terms. Having shown that Christ suffered all the punishments that His people deserved, Calvin continues, 'No wonder, then, if he is said to have descended into hell, for he suffered the death that God in his wrath had inflicted on the wicked.'[70] The people of God can never experience hell. Some have wondered if the redeemed will be aware of the suffering of those in hell and have wondered how their joy could be complete if friends and relatives are thus suffering. Jonathan Edwards in 'The End of the Wicked contemplated by the Righteous',[71] argued that the elect would rejoice over the lost, citing Revelation 18:20 ('Rejoice over her, O heaven! Rejoice, saints and apostles and prophets! God has judged her for the way she treated you'). If there is an awareness of the sufferings of the lost, there is no doubt that thoughts of the holiness and the justice of God's action will fill the minds of His people, and their perspective will be very different from what it now is.

The consummation of redemption

The return of Christ will mark the final stage of God's plan of redemption. The work which has been unfolding since Eden, up to Calvary and beyond, will be brought to a triumphant conclusion, with all the glories provided for in the Covenant of Redemption fully realized. Nothing will be lacking with regard to the fulfilment of the divine decrees. The elect will enter fully into the blessings of the Covenant of Grace. By the grace of God, each one of the elect will persevere until the end of life and will receive his reward. The golden chain of Romans 8:29-30 leads inevitably from 'those God foreknew' to 'those he justified, he also glorified'. Paul goes on to exult in the fact that nothing in the whole creation 'will be able to separate us from the love of God that is in Christ Jesus our Lord' (Rom. 8:39). Christ Himself has promised that 'no-one can snatch them out of my hand' (John 10:28). It is certainly true that believers must persevere in the faith and must pursue holiness without which 'no-one will see the Lord' (Heb. 12:14). By the sovereign grace of God, they will so persevere.

All the people of God will be gathered to receive the inheritance spoken of in 1 Peter 1:4, both Jews and Gentiles. There have been those in recent years who have claimed that God has two covenants, one for Jews and a different one for Gentiles, an unbiblical view ably refuted by covenant theologians such as David Holwerda.[72] God has *one* covenant people. Many covenant theologians have concluded that towards the end of history there will be a great ingathering of the Jews to Christ, citing Romans 11:23-27. Some, like Herman Bavinck,[73] reject this position, but the exegesis of commentators such as John Murray and Thomas Schreiner seems to offer good grounds for such a hope. It must be stressed, however, that the Jews who share in the glories to come are those who believe in Christ for salvation. As Schreiner says, 'Just as God has chosen to extend mercy upon the Gentiles in the present era, so too in conformity with his ancient promises he pledges to shower his grace upon Israel in the future.'[74]

So much that is said in the Bible about the return of Christ deals with themes of completion and perfection. Already believers are adopted into the family of God, and yet Romans 8:23 indicates that in a sense adoption will only be completed at the resurrection. Paul writes that 'we ourselves, who have the firstfruits of the Spirit, groan inwardly as we wait eagerly for our adoption as sons, the redemption of our bodies.' Glorified in body and soul, believers will live as the children of God for ever. The process of sanctification will also be completed at that time. They will be fully 'conformed to the likeness of his Son' (Rom. 8:29), they will 'appear with him in glory' (Col. 3:4). As John expresses our Christian hope, 'we know that when he appears, we shall be like him, for we shall see him as he is' (1 John 3:2). It is significant that sonship and sanctification are inextricably interwoven in such passages. Believers will be glorified along with and on account of their 'elder brother'. A. A. Hoekema is correct to say, 'Union with Christ was planned from eternity, and is destined to continue eternally.'[75]

A constant theme throughout our study has been the covenant promise, 'I will walk among you and be your God, and you will be my people.' This promise of covenant fellowship, as we have seen, is realized in a measure in this present life and remains unbroken by death. The perfect fulfilment will be enjoyed by God's children after the return of Christ. With the removal of sin, all obstacles to fellowship are removed. Thus at the consummation, as described in Revelation 21, the covenant promise is repeated (verse 3). The fellowship that believers will enjoy will be as intimate as it is possible for finite creatures to have. Bavinck is right to stress the superiority of the knowledge and fellowship enjoyed by believers after the resurrection over anything experienced in this present world. As he says, 'They will all know him, each in the measure of his mental capacity ... directly, immediately, unambiguously, and purely. Then they will receive and possess everything they expected here only in hope. Thus contemplating and possessing God, they enjoy him, and are blessed in his fellowship: blessed in soul and body, in intellect and will.'[76] Thus 'man's chief end' according to the Shorter Catechism Q1 will be realized: 'to glorify God and enjoy him for ever.'

At the last day the mediatorial reign of Christ will have achieved its goal of 'bringing many sons to glory' (Heb. 2:10). Having appeared once as the Suffering Servant, Christ will appear again as the glorious and triumphant King. As Psalm 110:1 indicates, all His enemies will be made a footstool for His feet. His victory will be total. As Raymond Zorn says, 'That Christ is able to enforce the decrees of just condemnation on all his implacable foes, from the greatest to the least, is but another exhibition of that power by which he shall bring his total victory to its proper consummation.'[77] On the other hand, 'the righteous will shine like the sun' (Matt. 13:43), reflecting the radiance of their glorious Lord. Whether willingly, by God's grace, or unwillingly, in fruitless rebellion, every knee will bow to King Jesus (Phil. 2:10).

Will the mediatorial kingship of Christ come to an end with his second coming? According to 1 Corinthians 15:24-25, 'Then the end will come, when he hands over the kingdom to God the Father after he has destroyed all dominion, authority, and power. For he must reign until he has put all his enemies under his feet.' Verse 28 continues, 'When he has done this, then the Son himself will be made subject to him who put everything under him, so that God may be all in all.' Some covenant theologians, such as George Gillespie,[78] have argued that this mediatorial kingship will end and that in eternity Christ will reign simply as Son of God, along with the Father and Holy Spirit. Many others, particularly among Continental Reformed theologians, argued that, although Christ's meritorious activity for the elect will eventually cease (otherwise it would be imperfect), His mediatorial reign will be eternal. They accepted that its form and manner of administration might change, its substance would not. The Scottish Covenanter William Symington, writing in 1840, argued at length for the eternity of Christ's mediatorial kingship. He cites Scriptures speaking of the eternity of the Messiah's reign, demonstrates how an eternal reign is a fitting reward for Christ, emphasizes that the relationship between the Redeemer and the redeemed is perpetual and notes that the redeemed require the continuing work of the Mediator.[79] Although the consummation will no doubt bring changes in Christ's reign, of which we cannot now conceive, it seems best to conclude that His mediatorial reign will be eternal.[80]

The renewed creation

In Romans 8:19ff. Paul indicates that the whole creation 'waits in eager expectation for the sons of God to be revealed' since the completion of their redemption will deliver the creation from its 'bondage to decay' resulting from the divine curse pronounced in Genesis 3. The whole creation will share 'the glorious freedom of the children of God'. Similarly Peter speaks of the believer's hope in these terms: 'in keeping with his promise we are looking forward to a new heaven and a new earth, the home of righteousness' (2 Pet. 3:13).

The scope of the covenant work of Christ is indeed universal, not in the sense that all people will be saved, but in the sense that He will bring about the renewal of the entire cosmos. This is reflected in some significant words that are used in the New Testament.[81] The word *palingenesia* means 'renewal, restoration, regeneration' and is used in Matthew 19:28 ('the renewal of all things') and Titus 3:5. The latter refers to individual regeneration whilst the former refers to the Messiah's renovation of the cosmos. The second word is *apokatastasis*, used in Acts 3:21 ('to restore everything'), which has the same significance as *palingenesia*. The third term is *anakephalaiōsis* which designates the 'summing up' of all things in Christ as their head, and is used in Ephesians 1:10. All three terms indicate the cosmic scope of Christ's work at the last day.

Just as the elect are renewed in body and soul, so the creation is renewed to provide a suitable dwelling place for them. Whilst Lutherans have generally held that the creation will be destroyed and recreated, covenant theologians have generally held that Christ will renew the creation.[82] Destruction of the old creation would, it was held, have represented a measure of success for Satan.

The people of God will thus inhabit a renewed creation, returned to its original perfection and perhaps in many respects surpassing its glories. Old Testament descriptions of a perfect world, such as Isaiah 11:6ff., need not be spiritualized away: they will have a literal fulfilment in the new creation. Christianity does not despise the material world: it is God's world and He will give it a glorious eternal existence. As Abraham Kuyper says, 'Cosmical life has regained its worth not at the expense of things eternal, but by virtue of its capacity as God's handiwork and as a revelation of God's attributes.'[83]

Christians look forward, not to a colourless, ethereal, purely spiritual existence, but to an eternal embodied life in a world that will be full of beauty and activity. It is described as a 'Sabbath rest' in Hebrews 4:9, rest from labour, trials and suffering, but not the rest of inactivity. In Eden Adam and Eve had work to do. On the new earth there will be work that will stimulate and satisfy every aspect of our being. All will be done in a spirit of praise to the Lord, who will walk among His covenant people, and there will be no sense of frustration or failure. Throughout eternity there will always be more work to do and discover, above all deeper and fuller knowledge of the Lord to enjoy. It is an exciting prospect. As Donald Macleod observes, 'The scenario is a thrilling one: brilliant minds in powerful bodies in a transformed universe.'[84] The covenant community will rejoice in God's presence for ever.

Christian hope

The predominant biblical note with regard to the 'last things' is one of hope in Christ, and as Paul says, 'hope does not disappoint us' (Rom. 5:5). Biblical hope is certain and unshakeable because grounded in Christ. Many modern theologians have given renewed attention to 'eschatology' (the study of the last things) but often their views diverge considerably from Scripture.[85] Covenant theology embodies that hope in a way that is faithful to God's inerrant revelation, and finds in that hope the capstone of the Lord's redemptive covenant work.

Far from encouraging idleness or carelessness, a right understanding of Christian hope provides a great stimulus to godly living and faithful service. As John says, 'Everyone who has this hope in him purifies himself, just as he is pure' (1 John 3:3). A holy covenant people await the glorious revelation of their holy covenant Lord.

Notes

1. Robert C. Doyle, *Eschatology and the Shape of Christian Belief* (Carlisle, 1999), p. 25.

2. A. A. Hoekema, *The Bible and the Future* (Exeter, 1979), p. 29.

3. Robert C. Doyle, op. cit., pp. 25ff.

4. One of the most helpful treatments of this subject is *The Coming of the Kingdom* by Herman Ridderbos, translated by H. de Jongste (Philadelphia, 1962).

5. Herman Ridderbos, op. cit., p. 468.

6. Oscar Cullmann, *Christ and Time*, 3rd edition, translated by Floyd V. Filson (London, 1962).

7. Raymond O. Zorn, *Christ Triumphant* (Edinburgh, 1997), p. 113.

8. Geerhardus Vos, *Biblical Theology* (Grand Rapids, 1948), pp. 48-9.

9. Raymond Zorn, op. cit., p. 119.

10. Karl Barth, *Church Dogmatics* (Edinburgh, 1960), III/2, p. 632.

11. Hendrikus Berkhof, *Christian Faith*, revised edition, translated by Sierd Woudstra (Grand Rapids, 1986), p. 488.

12. Wilhelmus à Brakel, *The Christian's Reasonable Service*, 1700 edition, translated by Bartel Elshout (Ligonier, 1992), vol. 4, ch. 100, p. 311.

13. Robert A. Morey, *Death and the Afterlife* (Minneapolis, 1984), p. 95.

14. Watchtower Bible and Tract Society, *You Can Live Forever in Paradise on Earth* (New York, n.d.), p. 78.

15. See the quotations provided by Eryl Davies in *An Angry God?* (Bryntirion, 1991), pp. 121-2.

16. Loraine Boettner, *Immortality* (Philadelphia, 1956), p. 78. Boettner does, however, offer arguments such as the necessity of immortality to vindicate the moral order.

17. See e.g. *Immortality of the Soul or Resurrection of the Dead?* by Oscar Cullman (London, 1958).

18. Murray J. Harris, 'Resurrection and immortality: eight theses' in *Themelios* 1:2, Spring 1976, p. 53.

19. Murray J. Harris, 'The New Testament view of life after death' in *Themelios* 11:2, January 1986, p. 48. Harris provides a good survey of the New Testament evidence.

20. It is interesting that one of Calvin's earliest works was a refutation of 'soul sleep'. See his *Psychopannychia* (1534) in *Selected Works of John Calvin. Tracts and Letters*, edited by Henry Beveridge and Jules Bonnet (Edinburgh, 1851), vol. 3, pp. 413ff.

21. 'All who die in God's grace and friendship, but still imperfectly purified, are indeed assured of their eternal salvation; but after death they undergo purification, so as to achieve the holiness necessary to enter the joy of heaven ... The tradition of the Church, by reference to certain texts of Scripture, speaks of a cleansing fire.' *Catechism of the Catholic Church* (Dublin, 1994), para. 1030-1.

22. Robert A. Morey, op. cit., pp. 72-81.

23. R. Laird Harris, 'Sheol' in *Theological Wordbook of the Old Testament*, edited by R. Laird Harris et. al. (Chicago, 1980), pp. 892-3.

24. W. G. T. Shedd, *Dogmatic Theology*, 1889-94 edition (Nashville, 1980), vol. 2, pp. 625-33.

25. Desmond Alexander, "The Old Testament view of life after death" in *Themelios* 11:2, January 1986, pp. 42-44.

26. Loraine Boettner, op. cit., p. 101.

27. A. A. Hoekema, op. cit., pp. 95-9.

28. Morey, Boettner and Hoekema provide the necessary exegetical discussion.

29. See *The Puritan Hope* by Iain Murray (Edinburgh, 1971).

30. John Jefferson Davis, *Christ's Victorious Kingdom. Postmillennialism Reconsidered* (Grand Rapids, 1986); Keith Mathison, *Postmillennialism. An Eschatology of Hope* (Phillipsburg, 1999).

31. A. A. Hoekema, op. cit.

32. Representatives of all four views state their case in *The Meaning of the Millennium*, edited by Robert G. Clouse (Downers Grove, 1977).

33. Donald Macleod, *A Faith To Live By* (Fearn, 1998), p. 259.

34. Comprehensive studies of these words are to be found in the *New International Dictionary of New Testament Theology*, edited by Colin Brown (Carlisle, 1986).

35. Frank Morison, *Who Moved the Stone?* (London, 1930).

36. A most helpful study of this area of theology is *The Centrality of the Resurrection. A Study in Paul's Soteriology* by Richard B. Gaffin (Grand Rapids, 1978).

37. Richard B. Gaffin, op. cit., p. 60.

38. Donald Macleod, op. cit., p. 281.

39. J. A. Schep, *The Nature of the Resurrection Body* (Grand Rapids, 1964), p. 184.

40. ibid.

41. Francis Turretin, *Institutes of Elenctic Theology*, translated by G. M. Giger (Phillipsburg, 1992-7), Locus 20, Q9, para. 7 (3. 619).

42. Francis Turretin, op. cit., Locus 20, Q9, para. 4 (3. 618).

43. Donald Macleod, op. cit., p. 277.

44. Simon J. Kistemaker, *Exposition of the First Epistle to the Corinthians* (Grand Rapids, 1993), ad. loc.

45. Jonathan Edwards, 'The Final Judgment' in *The Works of Jonathan Edwards*, 1834 edition (Edinburgh, 1974), vol. 2, p. 193.

46. ibid.

47. John Calvin, *The Epistles of Paul the Apostle to the Galatians, Ephesians, Philippians and Colossians*, translated by T. H. L. Parker (Edinburgh, 1965), ad. loc.

48. Watchtower Bible and Tract Society, *You Can Live Forever in Paradise on Earth*, p. 178.

49. Clark H. Pinnock, *A Wideness in God's Mercy* (Grand Rapids, 1992), p. 168.

50. Clark H. Pinnock, op. cit., p. 171.

51. ibid.

52. See e.g. Herman Bavinck's treatment of the text in *The Last Things*, translated by John Vriend (Grand Rapids/Carlisle, 1996), pp. 60-4.

53. Peter Cotterell, *Mission and Meaninglessness* (London, 1990), p. 81.

54. Philip E. Hughes, *The Second Epistle to the Corinthians* (Grand Rapids, 1962), on 2 Corinthians 5:10.

55. Herman Bavinck, op. cit., p. 169.

56. Robert Morey, op. cit., p. 107.

57. R. A. Finlayson, *Reformed Theological Writings* (Fearn, 1996), pp. 180-1.

58. A useful summary of the history of universalist thinking is provided by Robert Morey, op. cit., pp. 223-31.

59. Eberhard Busch, *Karl Barth. His life from letters and autobiographical texts*, translated by John Bowden (London, 1976), p. 394.

60. Karl Barth, *Church Dogmatics* (New York and Edinburgh, 1936-69), II/2, p. 319.

61. Cornelius Van Til, *Karl Barth and Evangelicalism* (Philadelphia, 1965), p. 38.

62. Eryl Davies, op. cit., p. 10.

63. John W. Wenham, *The Goodness of God* (London, 1974). More recently Wenham has defended his view in 'The Case for Conditional Immortality' in *Universalism and the Doctrine of Hell*, edited by Nigel M. de S. Cameron (Carlisle/Grand Rapids, 1992), pp. 161ff.

64. David L. Edwards and John Stott, *Essentials. A liberal-evangelical dialogue* (London, 1988), p. 320.

65. Philip Edgcumbe Hughes, *The True Image* (Grand Rapids/Leicester, 1989), ch. 37; E. Earle Ellis, 'New Testament Teaching on Hell' in *The reader must understand*, edited by K. E. Brower and M. W. Elliott (Leicester, 1997), pp. 199ff; Edward William Fudge, *The Fire that Consumes*, revised edition (Carlisle, 1994).

66. W. G. T. Shedd, *The Doctrine of Endless Punishment*, 1885 edition (Edinburgh, 1986); John Blanchard, *Whatever happened to hell?* (Darlington, 1993); Robert A. Peterson, *Hell on Trial: The Case for Eternal Punishment* (Phillipsburg, 1995).

67. Eryl Davies, op. cit., p. 119.

68. Quoted by Davies, op. cit., p. 119.

69. Jonathan Edwards, 'Sinners in the hands of an angry God' in *Works*, vol. 2, p. 9.

70. John Calvin, *Institutes of the Christian Religion*, 1559 edition, translated by Ford Lewis Battles (Philadelphia, 1960), II. xvi. 10.

71. Jonathan Edwards, *Works*, vol. 2, pp. 207-12.

72. David E. Holwerda, *Jesus and Israel. One Covenant or Two?* (Grand Rapids/Leicester, 1995).

73. Herman Bavinck, op. cit., pp. 104-7.

74. Thomas R. Schreiner, *Romans* (Grand Rapids, 1998), p. 622.

75. A. Hoekema, *Saved by Grace* (Grand Rapids/Exeter, 1989), p. 64.

76. Herman Bavinck, op. cit., p. 162.

77. Raymond O. Zorn, op. cit., p. 116.

78. George Gillespie, *Aaron's Rod Blossoming*, Book 2, ch. 5, p. 92, in *The Presbyterian's Armoury* edition (Edinburgh, 1846).

79. William Symington, *Messiah the Prince*, 2nd edition (Edinburgh, 1840), ch. 10.

80. Robert Doyle, op. cit., pp. 32-3, suggests that the handing over of the 'kingdom' in 1 Corinthians 15 should be understood as Christ's handing his glorified people to the Father.

81. Robert Doyle, op. cit., pp. 22-5.

82. For the traditional Lutheran view see *Doctrinal Theology of the Evangelical Lutheran Church* by Heinrich Schmid, 3rd edition, translated by Charles A. Hoy and Henry E. Jacob (Minneapolis, 1899), p. 656. Among covenant theologians, Wollebius held that the old creation will be destroyed.

83. Abraham Kuyper, *Lectures on Calvinism* (Grand Rapids, 1931), p. 120.

84. Donald Macleod, op. cit., p. 298.

85. Useful surveys of modern eschatology are to be found in David Fergusson's chapter 'Eschatology' in *The Cambridge Companion to Christian Doctrine* edited by Colin E. Gunton (Cambridge, 1997) and in chapter 9 of Robert Doyle's book cited above.

12

Covenant Response Today

In our study thus far we have noted that the Covenant of Grace requires a response from men and women: from unconverted sinners it requires a response of repentance and saving faith in the Lord Jesus Christ; from the people of God it requires a life of willing and joyful obedience to the Lord's covenant law. Those who have been saved by grace are in covenant with the triune God.

Many covenant theologians have also recognized the value of believers' renewing their covenant commitment to the Lord as a means of strengthening their resolve to live for Him. This theme has been particularly prominent among the Scottish Covenanters of the seventeenth century and their spiritual descendants in Reformed Presbyterian Churches in places such as Scotland, Ireland, North America and Australia.[1] We may note three aspects of such covenant response, or covenant renewal:

(i) personal covenanting
There is great value in a believer's renewing his covenant commitment to the Lord from time to time. In doing so he is not taking upon himself any new obligations, but is again accepting the obligations which, according to Scripture, already rest upon him. As it is sometimes put, a covenant additionally binds, but it does not bind to anything additional. Nothing is to be added to scriptural duties.

Covenant renewal can serve to stir up a believer to renewed zeal for the Lord and for holiness as he considers afresh what he has received from the Lord and what the Lord requires of him. Herman Witsius, in speaking of such covenant renewal, makes a comparison with soldiers swearing allegiance to their general. He argues that at the very least covenant renewal will be of use '1st. To restrain the soul from sin, by being put in mind of its late promise. 2nd. To quicken its indolence into zeal. 3rd. To raise it when fallen and teach it to mourn for its sins, with more than ordinary bitterness, especially as the guilt of treachery and perjury is added to all the rest.'[2] In a similar vein, Scottish theologian John Cunningham, writing near the middle of the nineteenth century, includes in his list of specific duties that are embraced in covenant renewal, 'Abstinence from besetting sins, increased diligence in the use of the means of grace, positive benevolent or religious services, the exercise of all the christian [sic] graces, and whatever observance the enlightened mind may apprehend as peculiarly incumbent'.[3]

It is interesting to find the famous commentator Matthew Henry recording on several occasions in his diary a rededication of himself to the Lord. It would seem that this was his usual practice on 1st January. On 1st January 1714, for example, he notes with thankfulness 'the many mercies of the year past', he goes on to express his sorrow and shame regarding 'my manifold defects, and short-comings in holy duties', and then he writes, 'I this morning renewed the dedication of myself to God, my own self, my whole self, body, soul and spirit. Father, I give thee my heart; use me for thy glory this year; employ me in thy service; fit me for thy will.'[4]

Far from being an outdated practice, covenant renewal is of the greatest significance in a post-modern culture in which 'choice' is seen as supremely important and enduring commitment is devalued. John Benton accurately sums up the attitude that is so common in western societies today: 'In a society where people idolise choice, then keeping one's options open as much as possible becomes the order of the day. Commitment to one cause or course of action therefore becomes a currency which is of diminishing value in most people's eyes.'[5] Christians follow a Lord who requires and deserves total commitment. They are to swim against the tide of the surrounding culture. Thus in the twenty-first century covenant renewal is a bold counter-cultural act and a powerful testimony to a disintegrating culture.

(ii) church covenanting

What the believer is to do as an individual by way of covenant renewal, the covenant community may do as a body. We have previously noted the centrality of the Church in God's redemptive purpose and so it is appropriate that the Church, or different parts of it, should enter into covenant renewal. In so doing the people of God are further strengthened in their commitment to the Lord and the biblical unity of the Church, so sadly fragmented in the present day, is enhanced. In the words of John Cunningham,

> One in opinion regarding her doctrine, worship, discipline, and government, her members having one origin, upheld by the same grace, designed for one end, called to the same privileges, enjoined to perform the same duties, expectants of the same glorious consummation, and harmonious in their sentiments regarding special incumbent duties, and concerning the manner of performing them, come forward, and as one body in this unite.[6]

Covenant renewal is thus an important element in promoting the true unity of God's covenant people.

On a number of occasions Reformed Presbyterian Churches in Scotland and Ireland have renewed the covenants which are an integral part of their history, the National Covenant of Scotland (1638) and the Solemn League and Covenant of the Three Kingdoms (1643). Although the national governments had no interest in such renewal, the churches entered into covenant renewal from time to time. A useful account of some of these renewals is provided by the Irish Reformed Presbyterian Thomas Houston in his *Memorial of Covenanting*, and his conclusion is, 'The act of covenant-renovation tended to foster deeply in the minds of those who engaged in it a sense of the value of the principles of the testimony of Christ, and to bind them to their faithful maintenance and general diffusion.'[7]

(iii) national covenanting

It has always been a part of the testimony of Covenanters and Reformed Presbyterians, right down to the present day, that rulers and the nations they rule should acknowledge the supremacy of

Christ as King of kings and Lord of lords, and that His law should
be their guide for national life. Much was made of texts such as
Psalm 2:11-12, where rulers in their official capacity are addressed
thus: 'Serve the Lord with fear and rejoice with trembling. Kiss
the Son, lest he be angry and you be destroyed in your way.' Space
does not permit a defence of this view here, but the arguments are
set out in the works by Cunningham and Houston already
mentioned, and by others such as William Symington in Scotland
and Alexander McLeod in the United States.[8]

Indeed Reformed Presbyterians saw in the covenants of 1638
and 1643 examples of such biblical national covenanting. Many
have held that the letter of these covenants still binds the nations
which accept them, whilst others hold that the biblical principles
contained in them are what still bind the nations.

It is often claimed that national covenanting entails forcing
Christian beliefs on unwilling citizens. In response it may be
pointed out that covenanting of this kind would be possible only
in a context of a great movement of the Holy Spirit bringing
national revival. Only then would rulers and citizens be in a
position to make a true covenant response to the Lord. Furthermore,
the laws of every nation reflect a particular religious outlook, even
if it be only that of the secular humanism so prevalent in western
culture. Laws must embody some values: Christians must pray
and work for the embodiment of biblical principles in national
laws. Although these may offend the consciences of secular
humanists, the present laws of many nations offend the consciences
of Christians. Some belief system must prevail. National
covenanting, flowing from revival, would simply acknowledge
the only true Lawgiver and Judge. The covenant people of God
cannot settle for any lesser goal.

Notes

1. A brief popular history of the Covenanters is *The Scottish Covenanters* by J. G. Vos (Pittsburgh, 1940). The subject of covenanting is examined biblically and theologically by F. S. Leahy in *The Theological Basis for Covenanting* (Pittsburgh, 1979).

2. Herman Witsius, *The Economy of the Covenants between God and Man*, 1677 edition, Translated by William Crookshank (Escondido, 1990), III.12.114.

3. John Cunningham, *The Ordinance of Covenanting* (Glasgow, n.d.), p. 44.

4. J. B. Williams, *The Lives of Philip and Matthew Henry* (Edinburgh, 1974), vol. 2, p. 161.

5. John Benton, *Christians in a Consumer Culture* (Fearn, 1999), p. 120. The whole of chapter 7, 'The Currency of Commitment', is most helpful on this issue.

6. John Cunningham, op. cit., p. 45.

7. Thomas Houston, *Memorial of Covenanting* in *Works Doctrinal and Practical*, 4 volumes (Edinburgh, 1876), vol. 3, p. 345.

8. William Symington, *Messiah the Prince*, 2nd edition (Edinburgh, 1840); Alexander McLeod, *Messiah, Governor of the Nations of the Earth*, 1803 edition (Elmwood Park, 1992).

Appendix

Covenant Theology and Dispensationalism

Covenant Theology is a system which claims to provide the 'big picture' as far as God's revelation in the Bible is concerned. In the course of our study we have sought to show how the theme of 'covenant' relates to all the major areas of theology, and indeed how it is integral to them all. Among evangelicals the main alternative to Covenant Theology is Dispensationalism, a system which, in its developed form, arose in the latter part of the nineteenth century. Dispensationalism, which has become very influential in many parts of the world, differs radically from Covenant Theology at a number of crucial points and, in our opinion, distorts the meaning of Scripture, particularly with regard to God's redemptive dealings with the human race. Although a detailed examination of Dispensationalism is not possible in the space available here, we must nevertheless note briefly some of its main features and indicate the points at which it differs from Covenant Theology and from Scripture.

The System of Dispensationalism[1]
The system of biblical interpretation which has come to be known as Dispensationalism was originated by John Nelson Darby (1800-82), a Dubliner who in 1827 left the Anglican priesthood and became associated with a group later to be known as the Plymouth Brethren. Darby's premillennial views of prophecy, particularly in relation to Israel's place in the purposes of God, were developed in a systematic fashion by a number of American Fundamentalists, of whom the most significant was the Congregationalist Cyrus I. Scofield. What may be termed 'Classical Dispensationalism' was given its definitive form in the *Scofield Reference Bible*, an edition of the Authorised Version with study notes by Scofield, published in 1909 and in a revised edition in 1917. The influence of Dispensationalism spread widely through the non-denominational

Bible Conference movement in the USA and in many fundamentalist circles its dominance is unquestioned. Among more recent leaders of the movement have been men such as Lewis Sperry Chafer, Harry A. Ironside, William Kelly, J. Dwight Pentecost, Charles C. Ryrie and John F. Walvoord.

Dispensationalism is not a monolithic movement and there are significant differences among its leading theologians. Nevertheless several distinctive elements may be identified and are to be found, with varying emphases, in all dispensational writers:

(i) the dispensations
All Dispensationalists accept some scheme of dividing history into 'dispensations'. Although the term is used by others, and is to be found in the Westminster Confession of Faith VII.6, Dispensationalists use it in a particular, unique way. It refers, according to Scofield, to 'a period of time during which man is tested in respect of obedience to some specific revelation of the will of God', tests which in each dispensation man has failed. According to Scofield, there were seven dispensations: Innocency, Conscience, Human Government, Promise, Law, Grace, Kingdom (i.e. Millennium).

In past dispensations, it is argued, people were tested regarding their obedience to God and were given promises of *earthly* life. Men's failures meant that these promises were not obtained in any lasting sense, but those who did trust God will be given (unexpected) *heavenly* salvation. It is only in the present dispensation (Grace) that believers consciously seek a heavenly salvation. In the future dispensation (Millennium) God will resume his earthly purpose.

(ii) Israel and the Church
Dispensationalists argue for a radical separation between Israel and the Church, claiming that God has separate purposes for each of them. The Church is said to be a 'parenthesis' in history, interrupting God's earthly purpose for Israel, a period not foreseen by the Old Testament prophets. In the Dispensationalist scheme, God has two different redemptive plans, one relating to earth and

involving Israel, the other relating to heaven and involving the Church. Older Dispensational writers spoke of a heavenly people of God, embracing the redeemed who died before the Millennium, and an earthly people who will be eternally distinct and will not receive resurrection bodies.

More recent writers have abandoned this division, regarding Israel and the Church as two (mutually exclusive) groups who receive the same salvation but who still remain eternally distinct. Their eternal existence is placed by some on earth (Pentecost) and by others in heaven (Walvoord, Ryrie). The result of this way of thinking is, as Robert Reymond puts it, 'Two distinct ages with two distinct contents of faith, and as a result two distinct peoples of God with two distinct destinies'.[2] Essential to Dispensationalism is a premillennial eschatology, which differs from other premillennial views in teaching a pre-tribulation rapture of the Church from the earth.

(iii) literal interpretation
Dispensationalists often claim that their views result from the application of a literalist hermeneutic to the Bible, and they charge covenant theologians and others with 'spiritualizing' away the plain meaning of God's Word. At the simplest level, they claim that in the Bible words mean what they appear to say. This method of interpretation is termed by Ryrie 'literal ... normal or plain'.[3] Dispensationalists therefore claim to take prophetic language about Israel consistently literally, and so they argue for a political future for Israel on earth. For this reason men like Jerry Falwell and Pat Robertson have been zealous supporters of Zionism.

Such a position is in fact impossible to maintain consistently. In the description of the 'rebuilt Temple' in Ezekiel 40-48 we are told that sacrifices will be offered again and they are specifically described as 'sin offerings' that make atonement (see e.g. Ezek. 45:15, 17). Taken literally, this would contradict what the Book of Hebrews teaches about the finality and completeness of Christ's atonement, and at such points Dispensationalists are forced to overlook Ezekiel's statements about the atoning nature of the sacrifices.

In more recent years a number of writers, including Craig Blaising and Darrell Bock, have developed what is termed 'Progressive Dispensationalism'.[4] In this version of Dispensationalism the breaking down of the rigid separation of Israel and the Church which has been evident in some dispensational writers is taken even further and a more unified view of the biblical covenants is sought. Some discern in these changes a movement towards Covenant Theology. It may be that eventually some Progressive Dispensationalists will embrace a form of Covenant Theology, but at this point we must agree with the verdict of Keith Mathison that 'Progressive dispensationalism is not dispensationalism. But neither is it Reformed. Still unchanged are a number of its doctrines of salvation. For now, "progressive dispensationalism" is a generic form of premillennial, modified Arminianism.'[5]

The response of Covenant Theology
Recognizing their fundamental differences with Dispensationalism, many covenant theologians have sought to expose the weakness of the system and to provide a more biblical alternative. Book-length treatments of the subject include the classic work by Oswald T. Allis of Westminster Seminary, *Prophecy and the Church* and, at a more popular level, the recent work of Keith Mathison *Dispensationalism. Rightly Dividing the People of God?* Other covenant theologians have devoted a portion of larger studies to refuting Dispensationalism, some of the most recent and useful being A. A. Hoekema, Palmer Robertson and Robert Reymond.[6]

Dispensationalism is vulnerable at a number of points, not least in its concept of 'dispensations'. Space permits us to consider only two issues which are particularly pertinent to our foregoing study, namely the unity of the Covenant of Grace and, consequent upon this, the unity of the people of God.

(i) the unity of the Covenant of Grace[7]
The first gospel promise of grace followed immediately upon the fall of man and the pronouncing of the divine sentence. In Genesis 3:15 God states, 'I will put enmity between you and the woman,

and between your seed and her seed; he shall bruise you on the head, and you shall bruise him on the heel' (NASB). Here we have the inauguration of the Covenant of Grace and in subsequent chapters we see people such as Abel (Gen. 4:4; Heb. 11:4), Enoch (Gen. 5:22-3; Heb. 11:5) and Noah (Gen. 6:8-9) receiving grace and salvation from the Lord.

God's establishing His covenant with Abraham marks a significant advance in the unfolding of the Covenant of Grace which was 'definitive for all time to come'.[8] In the Abrahamic covenant (Gen. 12:1-3, 13:14-16, 15:18-21, 17:1-16, 22:16-18) God makes promise of salvation blessings for 'all peoples on earth'. All that God does subsequently for the salvation of sinners flows from this covenant. The promise of salvation is so central to the Abrahamic covenant, and other earthly promises regarding the possession of land are subsidiary to that. The promise of the land will be fulfilled in the new creation described in, for example, Romans 8:19-23, and Abraham himself, according to Hebrews 11:10, was looking forward to 'the city with foundations, whose architect and builder is God'. Verse 16 of the same chapter makes it clear that he sought 'a better country – a heavenly one' and the city in view is the New Jerusalem of Revelation 21. The covenant promises given to Abraham can be traced all the way through history to their fulfilment in the final consummation at the return of Christ.

It is noteworthy that the same covenant is confirmed with Isaac (Gen. 17:19, 26:3-4) and with Jacob (Gen. 28:13-15, 35:12). The events of the Exodus flow from God's covenant promises to Abraham, Isaac and Jacob, according to Exodus 2:24 and 4:5. In the course of the history of Israel in the Old Testament God's showing grace and mercy to His people is regularly ascribed to His keeping His covenant promises to Abraham. 'I will remember my covenant with Jacob and my covenant with Isaac and my covenant with Abraham' (Lev. 26:42). 'You will be true to Jacob and show mercy to Abraham, as you pledged on oath to our fathers in days long ago' (Mic. 7:20). References could be multiplied many times over to these covenant promises.

From the very outset the work of Christ is described in the

New Testament in terms of the promises to Abraham. Mary says, '[the Mighty One] has helped his servant Israel, remembering to be merciful to Abraham and his descendants for ever, even as he said to our fathers' (Luke 1:54-55) and Zechariah says, 'Praise be to the Lord, the God of Israel, because he has come ... to remember his holy covenant, the oath he swore to our father Abraham' (Luke 1:68, 72-3). Clearly they recognize that the Abrahamic covenant is fulfilled in Christ. He himself is able to say that 'Abraham rejoiced at the thought of seeing my day; he saw it and was glad' (John 8:56).

The rest of the New Testament testifies to the same truth. In Acts 3:25-26, for example, Peter describes Christ's work of turning sinners from their wicked ways in terms of the fulfilment of God's covenant promise of worldwide blessing given to Abraham in Genesis 12:3 and elsewhere. Paul refers to the same promise in Galatians 3:8-9 and interprets it in terms of God's justifying the Gentiles through faith in Christ. Later in the same chapter he speaks of Christ dying on the cross and bearing the curse of the law 'in order that the blessing given to Abraham might come to the Gentiles through Christ Jesus, so that by faith we might receive the promise of the Spirit' (Gal. 3:14). Lest there be any misunderstanding, Paul then stresses that the giving of the Law through Moses several centuries later 'does not set aside the covenant previously established by God [with Abraham] and thus do away with the promise' (Gal. 3:17), and he is able to conclude in verse 29 'If you belong to Christ, then you are Abraham's seed, and heirs according to the promise'. In Romans 4:11-12 Abraham is said to be 'the father of all who believe', both the circumcised and the uncircumcised.

Such passages make it clear that there is one covenant of grace which raises up one redeemed people of God from Eden until the last day. The blessings which New Testament believers receive are founded on God's covenant with Abraham and, behind that, the covenant promise in Genesis 3:15. As Reymond concludes, 'This is just to say that the Abrahamic covenant, in the specific prospect it holds forth of the salvation of the entire church of God, is identical with the soteric program of the covenant of grace, indeed, is identical with the covenant of grace itself.'[9] There is no place in the biblical picture for the dual divine purpose that is central to Dispensationalism.

(ii) the unity of the people of God

What we have said about the unity of the Covenant of Grace would lead us to expect that the people of God will be described in Scripture as a single body. This is precisely what we find. There has only ever been one Church, embracing the people of God under the Old Covenant as well as under the New Covenant. Most obviously this is demonstrated in the repeated application to the Church by New Testament writers of language used of Israel in the Old. As Peter says in 1 Peter 2:9, 'you are a chosen people, a royal priesthood, a holy nation, a people belonging to God', drawing on the language of texts such as Exodus 19:6. It is no surprise, therefore, to find baptism described in the language of circumcision in Colossians 2:11-12, or to find Christian worship and service described in the language of sacrifice in Hebrews 13:15-16.

It is clear that the apostles came to grasp this truth at an early stage. At the Council of Jerusalem (Acts 15), dealing with the admission of the Gentiles to the Church, James cites Amos 9:11-12, which speaks of God rebuilding David's fallen tent, and sees it being fulfilled in the bringing of Gentiles to faith in Christ. Amos spoke of the building of the Church in a way which indicates that it is the continuation of the true spiritual Israel.

In an earlier chapter we noted that in Romans 11:11-24 Paul shows that there is but one good olive tree. In the Old Testament it included believing and unbelieving Israelites (cf. Isa. 17:4-6; Jer. 11:16). Natural branches representing unbelieving Israelites have been broken off and onto the olive tree have been grafted 'wild' branches, representing believing Gentiles. Contrary to the requirements of Dispensationalism, no tree of unbelieving Israel is left.

We may also note Paul's description in Ephesians 2:11-19 of the condition of the Gentiles before and after conversion. Verse 12 shows that, among other things, they were 'excluded from citizenship in Israel and foreigners to the covenants of the promise'. In total five elements of their plight are listed and all are reversed by their union with Christ. There are no exegetical grounds for denying that the relationship to Israel and the covenants are not reversed in Christ. The implication is clear: if Gentile believers are no longer separate from Christ, they are no longer excluded from Israel and they are no longer foreigners to the covenants of the promise. It is for such a reason that the writer to the Hebrews says that the Old Testament giants of the faith will be 'made perfect' only together with New Testament believers (Heb. 11:39-40). They all form one body in Christ.

At the final consummation, as Revelation 21:9-14 shows, the Bride of Christ, the Church, will be revealed in her full glory. As verse 12 shows, the names of the twelve tribes of Israel are written on the gates, and in verse 14 we are told that the names of the twelve apostles are written on the foundation stones. The Bride is composed of all believers, Jew and Gentile, from all ages.

While acknowledging the love for the Lord and zeal for His cause that many Dispensationalists manifest, we must respectfully say that their system is not that of Scripture.

Notes

1. A concise history of the system is to be found in Stephen R. Spencer's article 'Dispensationalism' in *The Encyclopedia of Christianity*, edited by Erwin Fahlbusch et al. (Grand Rapids/Cambridge, 1999), vol. 1, pp. 854-5. A fuller account is provided by Craig A. Blaising and Darrell L. Bock in *Progressive Dispensationalism* (Wheaton, 1993), Part 1.

2. Robert L. Reymond, *A New Systematic Theology of the Christian Faith* (Nashville, 1998), p. 511.

3. Charles C. Ryrie, *Dispensationalism Today* (Chicago, 1965), p. 45.

4. For details of this view, consult the book by Blaising and Bock cited above.

5. Keith A. Mathison, *Dispensationalism. Rightly Dividing the People of God?* (Phillipsburg, 1995), p. 137.

6. Oswald T. Allis, *Prophecy and the Church* (Philadelphia, 1945); Keith A. Mathison, op. cit; A. A. Hoekema, *The Bible and the Future* (Exeter, 1979), ch. 15; O. Palmer Robertson, *The Christ of the Covenants* (Grand

Rapids, 1980), ch. 11; Robert L. Reymond, op. cit., ch. 14.

7. We gladly acknowledge our indebtedness to the work of Robert Reymond in this section. His consideration of the subject (op. cit., pp. 512-8) is most helpful.

8. Robert L. Reymond, op. cit., p. 513.

9. Robert L. Reymond, op. cit., pp. 517-8.

BIBLIOGRAPHY

Jay E. Adams. *The Meaning and Mode of Baptism*. Phillipsburg 1980

Desmond Alexander. 'The Old Testament view of life after death'. *Themelios* 11:2. January 1986

Oswald T. Allis. *Prophecy and the Church*. Philadelphia 1945

Thomas J. J. Altizer. *The Contemporary Jesus*. London 1998

William Ames. *The Marrow of Theology*. Trans. from the Latin edition, 1629, and ed. by John D. Eusden. Durham, N.C. 1983

Thomas Aquinas. *Summa Theologica*. Trans. by the Fathers of the English Dominican Province. 5 vols. New York 1948

Gustaf Aulén. *Christus Victor*. Trans. by A. G. Herbert. London 1931

Greg L. Bahnsen. *By This Standard*. Tyler 1985

Greg L. Bahnsen. *Theonomy in Christian Ethics*. Phillipsburg 1984

Greg L. Bahnsen. *Van Til's Apologetic*. Phillipsburg 1998

D. Douglas Bannerman. *The Scripture Doctrine of the Church*. 1887 edition. Grand Rapids 1976

James Bannerman. *The Church of Christ*. 1869 edition. London 1960

William S. Barker and W. Robert Godfrey (eds.). *Theonomy. A Reformed Critique*. Grand Rapids 1990

Karl Barth. *Church Dogmatics*. 12 vols. New York/Edinburgh. 1936-69

Herman Bavinck. *The Last Things*. Trans. by John Vriend. Grand Rapids/ Carlisle 1996

Herman Bavinck. *Our Reasonable Faith*. Trans. by Henry Zylstra. Grand Rapids 1956

J. H. Bavinck. *An Introduction to the Science of Missions*. Philadelphia 1960

G. R. Beasley-Murray. *Baptism in the New Testament*. Exeter 1972

Roger T. Beckwith and Wilfred Stott. *This is the Day*. London 1978

John Benton. *Christians in a Consumer Culture*. Fearn 1999

Hendrikus Berkhof. *Christian Faith*. Revised ed. Trans. by Sierd Woudstra. Grand Rapids 1986

Louis Berkhof. *Systematic Theology*. Edinburgh 1958

G. C. Berkouwer. *The Church*. Trans. by James E. Davison. Grand Rapids 1976

G. C. Berkouwer. *The Sacraments*. Trans. by Hugo Bekker. Grand Rapids 1969

R. J. Berry. *God and Evolution*. London 1988

Theodore Beza. *The Christian Faith*. 1558 edition. Trans. by James Clark. Lewes 1992

Craig A. Blaising and Darrell L. Bock. *Progressive Dispensationalism.* Wheaton 1993

John Blanchard. *Whatever happened to hell?* Darlington 1993

Loraine Boettner. *Immortality.* Philadelphia 1956

Thomas Boston. *Human Nature in its Fourfold State.* 1850 ed. London 1964

Thomas Boston. *A View of the Covenant of Grace.* 1734 ed. Lewes 1990

Wilhelmus à Brakel. *The Christian's Reasonable Service.* 1700 ed. Trans. by Bartel Elshout. 4 vols. Ligonier 1992-5

Gerald Bray. *The Personal God.* Carlisle 1998

Jerry Bridges. *True Fellowship.* New Malden 1986

G. W. Bromiley (ed.). *Zwingli and Bullinger.* Philadelphia 1953.

K. E. Brower and M. W. Elliott (eds.). *The reader must understand.* Leicester 1997

Colin Brown. *Karl Barth and the Christian Message.* London 1967

Colin Brown (ed.). *New International Dictionary of New Testament Theology.* 4 vols. Carlisle/Grand Rapids 1986

Robert Bruce. *The Mystery of the Lord's Supper.* Trans. and ed. by Thomas F. Torrance. London 1958

Mark T. Bube. 'The Principles of Reformed Missions'. *Proceedings of the International Conference of Reformed Churches*, October 15-23, 1997, Seoul, South Korea. Neerlandia/Pella 1997

James Buchanan. *The Doctrine of Justification.* 1867 ed. Grand Rapids 1977

John Bunyan. *All Loves Excelling.* Edinburgh 1998

Alex Burns. 'Will androids dream of electric sheep?' *21-C.* 1.97, pp. 22-7

Eberhard Busch. *Karl Barth. His life from letters and autobiographical texts.* Trans. by John Bowden. London 1976

Michael Bushell. *The Songs of Zion.* Pittsburgh 1980

John Calvin. *Commentaries on the First Book of Moses called Genesis.* Trans. by John King. Grand Rapids 1948

John Calvin. *Concerning the Eternal Predestination of God.* Trans. by J. K. S. Reid. London 1961

John Calvin. *The Epistles of Paul the Apostle to the Galatians, Ephesians, Philippians and Colossians.* Trans. by T. H. L. Parker. Edinburgh 1965

John Calvin. *A Harmony of the Gospels of Matthew, Mark and Luke.* Trans. by T. H. L. Parker. Edinburgh 1972

John Calvin. *Institutes of the Christian Religion.* 1559 ed. Trans. by Ford Lewis Battles. Philadelphia 1960

John Calvin. *Selected Works of John Calvin. Tracts and Letters.* Ed. and trans. by Henry Beveridge. 1849 ed. 7 vols. Grand Rapids 1983

Nigel M. de S. Cameron (ed.). *Universalism and the Doctrine of Hell.* Carlisle/Grand Rapids 1992

Iain D. Campbell. *The Doctrine of Sin.* Fearn 1999

Robert S. Candlish. *A Commentary on I John.* 1870 ed. Edinburgh 1993

Robert S. Candlish. *The Fatherhood of God.* 3rd ed. Edinburgh 1866

D. A. Carson (ed.). *The Church in the Bible and the World.* Exeter/Grand Rapids 1987

D. A. Carson (ed.). *From Sabbath to Lord's Day.* Grand Rapids 1982

D. A. Carson. *The Gospel according to John.* Leicester 1991

Catechism of the Catholic Church. Dublin 1994

Robert G. Clouse (ed.). *The Meaning of the Millennium.* Downers Grove 1977

Edmund P. Clowney. *The Church.* Leicester 1995

Leonard J. Coppes. *Who Will Lead Us?* Phillipsburg 1977

Peter Cotterell. *Mission and Meaninglessness.* London 1990

C. E. B. Cranfield. *The Epistle to the Romans.* 2 vols. Edinburgh 1975-9

Oscar Cullmann. *Christ and Time.* 3rd ed. Trans. by Floyd V. Filson. London 1962

Oscar Cullmann. *Immortality of the Soul or Resurrection of the Dead?* London 1958

John Cunningham. *The Ordinance of Covenanting.* Glasgow n.d.

William Cunningham. *The Reformers and the Theology of the Reformation.* 1862 ed. Edinburgh 1979

Robert L. Dabney. *Systematic Theology.* 1871 ed. Edinburgh 1985

Eryl Davies. *An Angry God?* Bryntirion 1991

John Jefferson Davis. *Christ's Victorious Kingdom. Postmillennialism Reconsidered.* Grand Rapids 1986

Richard Dawkins. *The Blind Watchmaker.* London 1986

P. Y. de Jong. *The Church's Witness to the World.* 2 vols. St Catharines 1980

Bruce Demarest. *General Revelation.* Grand Rapids 1982

Daniel Dennett. *Darwin's Dangerous Idea.* Harmondsworth 1995

Richard R. de Ridder. *Discipling the Nations.* Grand Rapids 1975

J. D. Douglas. *Light in the North.* Grand Rapids 1964

Robert C. Doyle. *Eschatology and the Shape of Christian Belief.* Carlisle 1999

W. J. Dumbrell. *Covenant and Creation.* Exeter 1984

James Durham. *The Dying Man's Testament to the Church of Scotland or A Treatise Concerning Scandal.* 1990 revision of 1680 ed. Dallas 1990

Eknath Easwaran. *The Upanishads.* London 1988

Brian Edwards (ed.). *Men, Women and Authority.* London 1996

David L. Edwards and John Stott. *Essentials. A liberal-evangelical dialogue.* London 1988

Jonathan Edwards. *The Works of Jonathan Edwards*. 1834 ed. 2 vols. Edinburgh 1974

Ron Elsdon. *Greenhouse Theology*. Tunbridge Wells 1992

Allen Emerson and Cheryl Forbes. *The Invasion of the Computer Culture*. Leicester 1989

Millard J. Erickson. *Christian Theology*. 2nd ed. Grand Rapids 1998

Philip H. Eveson. *The Great Exchange*. London 1996

Erwin Fahlbusch et al. *The Encyclopedia of Christianity*. Grand Rapids/ Cambridge 1999-

Marilyn Ferguson. *The Aquarian Conspiracy*. London 1982

Sinclair Ferguson. *The Holy Spirit*. Leicester 1996

Sinclair B. Ferguson and David F. Wright (eds.). *New Dictionary of Theology*. Leicester/Downers Grove 1988

R. A. Finlayson. *Reformed Theological Writings*. Fearn 1996

John Flavel. *The Fountain of Life*. 1671 ed. Grand Rapids 1977

John Frame. *Worship in Spirit and in Truth*. Phillipsburg 1996

James Fraser. *A Treatise on Sanctification*. 1897 ed. Audubon 1992

Anthony Freeman. *God in Us*. London 1993

Edward William Fudge. *The Fire that Consumes*. Revised ed. Carlisle 1994

Richard B. Gaffin, Jr. *The Centrality of the Resurrection. A Study in Paul's Soteriology*. Grand Rapids 1978

Richard B. Gaffin, Jr. *Perspectives on Pentecost*. Phillipsburg 1979

Mahatma Gandhi. *Christian Missions*. Ahmedabad 1941

George Gillespie. *The Works of Mr. George Gillespie* in *The Presbyterian's Armoury*. Vols. 1 and 2. Edinburgh 1846

John L. Girardeau. *Discussions of Theological Questions*. 1905 ed. Harrisonburg 1986

John L. Girardeau. *Instrumental Music in the Public Worship of the Church*. 1888 ed. Haverton 1983

Thomas Goodwin. *The Work of the Holy Spirit in our Salvation*. Edinburgh 1979

Douglas Groothuis. *Confronting the New Age*. Downers Grove 1988

Douglas Groothuis. *The Soul in Cyberspace*. Grand Rapids 1997

Douglas Groothuis. *Unmasking the New Age*. Downers Grove 1986

Wayne Grudem. 'Does *kephal* ("Head") Mean "Source" or "Authority Over" in Greek Literature? A Survey of 2,336 Examples.' *Trinity Journal* 6NS 1985

Wayne Grudem. *Systematic Theology*. Leicester/Grand Rapids 1994

Colin E. Gunton (ed.). *The Cambridge Companion to Christian Doctrine*. Cambridge 1997

Herman Hanko. *We and Our Children*. Grand Rapids 1981

Murray J. Harris. 'The New Testament view of life after death'. *Themelios* 11:2. January 1986

Murray J. Harris. 'Resurrection and immortality: eight theses'. *Themelios* 1:2. Spring 1976

R. Laird Harris et al. (eds). *Theological Wordbook of the Old Testament.* 2 vols. Chicago 1980

Stephen W. Hawking. *A Brief History of Time.* London 1988

William Hendriksen. *Ephesians.* Edinburgh 1972

William Hendriksen. *Philippians.* Edinburgh 1962

John Hick and Paul F. Knitter (ed.). *The Myth of Christian Uniqueness.* London 1987

A. A. Hodge. *The Confession of Faith.* 1869 ed. London 1958

Charles Hodge. *A Commentary on the Epistle to the Ephesians.* 1856 ed. Grand Rapids 1980

Charles Hodge. *Commentary on the Epistle to the Romans.* 1886 ed. Grand Rapids 1947

Charles Hodge. *A Commentary on I and II Corinthians.* Edinburgh 1974

Charles Hodge. *Systematic Theology.* 1871-73 ed. 3 vols. Grand Rapids 1977

Zane C. Hodges. *Absolutely Free! A Biblical Reply to Lordship Salvation.* Grand Rapids 1989

A. A. Hoekema. *The Bible and the Future.* Exeter 1979

A. A. Hoekema. *Saved by Grace.* Grand Rapids/Exeter 1989

Herman Hoeksema. *Reformed Dogmatics.* Grand Rapids 1966

David E. Holwerda. *Jesus and Israel. One Covenant or Two?* Grand Rapids/Leicester 1995

Michael Horton *In the Face of God.* Dallas 1996

Thomas Houston. *Works Doctrinal and Practical* 4 vols. Edinburgh 1876

Philip E. Hughes. *The Second Epistle to the Corinthians.* Grand Rapids 1962

Philip Edgcumbe Hughes. *The True Image.* Grand Rapids/Leicester 1989

Gretchen Gaebelein Hull. *Equal to Serve.* London 1989

James B. Hurley. *Man and Woman in Biblical Perspective.* Grand Rapids 1981

George Hutcheson. *The Gospel of John.* 1841 ed. London 1972

Paul K. Jewett. *Infant Baptism and the Covenant of Grace.* Grand Rapids 1978

Mark Johnston. *Child of a King.* Fearn 1997

Hywel R. Jones. *Only One Way.* London 1996

Christopher B. Kaiser. *The Doctrine of God.* London 1982

Ernest F. Kevan. *The Grace of Law.* Grand Rapids 1976

David Kingdon. *Children of Abraham.* Worthing 1973

Simon J. Kistemaker. *Exposition of the First Epistle to the Corinthians.* Grand Rapids 1993

Simon Kistemaker. *James and I-III John.* Welwyn 1987

Fred H. Klooster. *The Significance of Barth's Theology.* Grand Rapids 1961

R. B. Kuiper. *For Whom did Christ die?* Grand Rapids 1959

R. B. Kuiper. *The Glorious Body of Christ.* London 1967

R. B. Kuiper. *God-Centred Evangelism.* Grand Rapids 1961

Paul Kurtz (ed.). *Humanist Manifestos I and II.* New York 1973

Abraham Kuyper. *Lectures on Calvinism.* Grand Rapids 1931

Abraham Kuyper. *The Work of the Holy Spirit.* Trans. by Henri de Vries. 1900 ed. Grand Rapids 1975

F. S. Leahy. *The Theological Basis for Covenanting.* Pittsburgh 1979

Francis Nigel Lee. *The Covenantal Sabbath.* London n.d.

Robert Letham. *The Work of Christ.* Leicester 1993

John F. MacArthur. *The Gospel according to Jesus.* 2nd ed. Grand Rapids 1994

Richard P. McBrien. *Catholicism.* 2nd ed. New York 1994

Thomas McCrie. *The Unity of the Church.* 1989 revision of 1821 ed. Dallas 1989

Sallie McFague. *Models of God.* London 1987

Alister E. McGrath. *Iustitia Dei.* 2nd ed. Cambridge 1998

Alister McGrath. *Understanding Doctrine.* London 1990

Alister McGrath. *Understanding the Trinity.* Eastbourne 1987

W. D. J. McKay. *An Ecclesiastical Republic.* Carlisle 1997

Donald K. McKim and David F. Wright (eds.). *Encyclopedia of the Reformed Faith.* Louisville/Edinburgh 1992

Shirley MacLaine. *Dancing in the Light.* New York 1985

Shirley MacLaine. *Going Within.* New York 1989

Alexander McLeod. *Messiah, Governor of the Nations of the Earth.* 1803 ed. Elmwood Park 1992

Donald Macleod. *A Faith to Live By.* Fearn 1998

Donald Macleod (ed.). *Hold Fast Your Confession.* Edinburgh, 1978

J. Douglas MacMillan. *Jesus – Power Without Measure.* Bryntirion 1990

John Macpherson. *The Doctrine of the Church in Scottish Theology.* Edinburgh 1903

J. Gresham Machen *The Virgin Birth of Christ.* London 1958

Thomas Manton. *Complete Works.* Worthington n.d.

Pierre Ch. Marcel. *The Biblical Doctrine of Infant Baptism.* Trans. by Philip Edgcumbe Hughes. Cambridge 1953

Hugh Martin. *The Atonement.* Edinburgh 1976

Keith A. Mathison. *Dispensationalism. Rightly Dividing the People of God?* Phillipsburg 1995

Keith Mathison. *Postmillennialism. An Eschatology of Hope.* Phillipsburg 1999

Elliot Miller. *A Crash Course in the New Age Movement.* Eastbourne 1989

Robert A. Morey. *Death and the Afterlife.* Minneapolis 1984

Leon Morris. *The Apostolic Preaching of the Cross.* Leicester 1965

Leon Morris. *The Atonement.* Leicester 1983

Leon Morris. *The Gospel According to Matthew.* Grand Rapids/Leicester 1992

Frank Morrison. *Who Moved the Stone?* London 1930

Alec Motyer. *The Message of James.* Leicester 1985

Alec Motyer. *The Message of Philippians.* Leicester 1984

Iain Murray. *The Puritan Hope.* Edinburgh 1971

John Murray. *Christian Baptism.* Philadelphia 1962

John Murray. *Collected Writings of John Murray.* 4 vols. Edinburgh 1976-82

John Murray *The Epistle to the Romans* 2 vols. London 1967

John Murray. *The Imputation of Adam's Sin.* Grand Rapids 1959

John Murray. *Redemption Accomplished and Applied.* Grand Rapids 1955

Harold A. Netland. *Dissonant Voices. Religious Pluralism and the Question of Truth.* Leicester 1991

A. Noordtzij. *Leviticus.* Trans. by Raymond Togtman. Grand Rapids 1982.

Ludwig Ott. *Fundamentals of Catholic Dogma.* Rockford 1974

John Owen. *The Works of John Owen.* Ed. by William H. Goold, 1850-53 ed. 16 vols. Edinburgh 1965

J. I. Packer. *Evangelism and the Sovereignty of God.* London 1961

J. I. Packer. *God's Words.* Leicester 1981

Edwin H. Palmer. *The Person and Ministry of the Holy Spirit.* Grand Rapids 1974

J. Barton Payne. *The Theology of the Older Testament.* Grand Rapids 1962

Robert A. Peterson. *Hell on Trial: The Case for Eternal Punishment.* Phillipsburg 1995

Clark Pinnock et al. *The Openness of God.* Downers Grove/Carlisle 1994

Clark H. Pinnock and Robert C. Brow. *Unbounded Love.* Carlisle/Downers Grove 1994

Clark Pinnock. *A Wideness in God's Mercy.* Grand Rapids 1992

Joseph A. Pipa. *The Lord's Day.* Fearn 1997

John Piper and Wayne Grudem (eds.). *Recovering Biblical Manhood and Womanhood.* Wheaton 1991

Vern S. Poythress. *The Shadow of Christ in the Law of Moses.* Phillipsburg 1981

Anne Primavesi. *From Apocalypse to Genesis*. Tunbridge Wells 1991
James Rachels. *Created from Animals*. Oxford 1990
James Redfield. *The Celestine Prophecy*. London 1994
Reformed Presbyterian Church of North America. *The Biblical Doctrine of Worship*. Pittsburgh 1974
J. K. S. Reid (ed.). *Calvin: Theological Treatises*. Philadelphia 1954
Ernest C. Reisinger. *Lord and Christ*. Phillipsburg 1994
Robert L. Reymond. *Jesus, Divine Messiah: The Old Testament Witness*. Fearn 1990
Robert L. Reymond. *A New Systematic Theology of the Christian Faith*. Nashville 1998
Herman Ridderbos. *The Coming of the Kingdom*. Trans. by H. de Jongste. Nutley 1962
Herman Ridderbos. *Paul: An Outline of his Theology*. Trans. by John R. de Witt. London 1977
O. Palmer Robertson. *The Christ of the Covenants*. Grand Rapids 1980
Robert Rollock. *A Treatise of God's Effectual Calling*. 1603 ed. Trans. by H. Holland in *Select Works of Robert Rollock*. Edinburgh 1849
Rousas J. Rushdoony. *The Institutes of Biblical Law*. Nutley 1973
Samuel Rutherford. *The Covenant of Life Opened*. Edinburgh 1655
Samuel Rutherford. *The Trial and Triumph of Faith*. 1645 ed. Glasgow 1845
Charles Ryrie. *Balancing the Christian Life*. Chicago 1969
Charles C. Ryrie. *Dispensationalism Today*. Chicago 1965
Carl Sagan. *Cosmos*. London 1981
Francis Schaeffer. *The Finished Work of Christ*. Leicester 1998
Francis A. Schaeffer. *The God Who is There*. London 1968
Philip Schaff (ed.). *The Creeds of Christendom*. 6th ed. 1931 Grand Rapids 1983
J. A. Schep. *The Nature of the Resurrection Body*. Grand Rapids 1964
Heinrich Schmid. *Doctrinal Theology of the Evangelical Lutheran Church*. 3rd ed. Trans. by Charles A. Hoy and Henry E. Jacob. Minneapolis 1899
Thomas R. Schreiner. *Romans*. Grand Rapids 1998
Scots Confession, 1560, and Negative Confession, 1581, with Introduction by G. D. Henderson. Edinburgh 1937
K. M. Sen. *Hinduism*. Harmondsworth 1961
W. G. T. Shedd. *The Doctrine of Endless Punishment*. 1885 ed. Edinburgh 1986
W. G. T. Shedd. *Dogmatic Theology*. 1889-94 ed. 3 vols. Nashville 1980
Robert J. Sheehan *The Word of Truth*. Darlington 1998
Peter Singer. *Practical Ethics*. 2nd ed. Cambridge 1993
James Sire. *The Universe Next Door*. 2nd ed. Leicester 1988

George Smeaton. *Christ's Doctrine of the Atonement.* 1871 ed. Edinburgh 1991

George Smeaton. *The Doctrine of the Holy Spirit.* 1889 ed. Edinburgh 1974

Frank J. Smith and David C. Lachman (eds.). *Worship in the Presence of God.* Greenville 1992

Wayne Spear. 'Rediscovering the Foundations'. *Covenanter Witness.* July/ August 1999

R. C. Sproul. *By Faith Alone.* London 1995

R. C. Sproul. *The Gospel of God.* Fearn 1999

Gordon J. Spykman. *Reformational Theology.* Grand Rapids 1992

W. P. Stephens. *The Theology of Huldrych Zwingli.* Oxford 1986

John Stott. *The Cross of Christ.* Leicester 1986

R. S. Sugirtharajah (ed.). *Asian Faces of Jesus.* London 1993

William Symington. *Messiah the Prince.* 2nd ed. Edinburgh 1840

James Henley Thornwell. *Collected Writings.* 1875 ed. 4 vols. Edinburgh 1974

Carl Trueman. *The Claims of Truth.* Carlisle 1998

Tim Trumper. 'The Metaphorical Import of Adoption: A Plea for Realisation. I: The Adoption Metaphor in Biblical Usage'. *Scottish Bulletin of Evangelical Theology,* 14:2. Autumn 1996

Francis Turretin. *Institutes of Elenctic Theology.* Trans. by G. M. Giger. 3 vols. Phillipsburg 1992-7

Zacharias Ursinus. *Commentary on the Heidelberg Catechism.* Trans. by G. W. Williard. 1852 ed. Phillipsburg n.d.

J. van Genderen. *Covenant and Election.* Neerlandia 1995

Cornelius Van Til. *Christianity and Barthianism.* Philadelphia 1962

Cornelius Van Til. *The Defence of the Faith.* 3rd ed. Philadelphia 1976

Cornelius Van Til. *Introduction to Systematic Theology.* Phillipsburg 1978

Cornelius Van Til. *Karl Barth and Evangelicalism.* Philadelphia 1965

C. R. Vaughan. *The Gifts of the Holy Spirit.* 1894 ed. Edinburgh 1975

Gene Edward Veith. *Guide to Contemporary Culture.* Leicester 1994

Richard Vines et al. *The Puritans on the Lord's Supper.* Morgan 1997

Geerhardus Vos. *Biblical Theology.* Grand Rapids 1948

Geerhardus Vos. *Redemptive History and Biblical Interpretation.* Ed. by R. B. Gaffin. Phillipsburg 1980

J. G. Vos. *The Scottish Covenanters.* Pittsburgh 1940

R. S. Wallace. *Calvin's Doctrine of the Word and Sacrament.* Edinburgh 1953

B. B. Warfield. *Studies in Theology.* New York 1932

Watchtower Bible and Tract Society. *You Can Live Forever in Paradise on Earth.* New York n.d.

Thomas Watson. *A Body of Divinity.* 1692 ed. Edinburgh 1965

Tom Wells. *A Vision for Missions.* Edinburgh 1985

John W. Wenham. *The Goodness of God.* London 1974

H. Westerink. *A Sign of Faithfulness.* Trans. J. Mark Beach. Neerlandia 1997

Lynn White. 'The Historical Roots of our Ecological Crisis'. *Science Magazine,* March 10 1967

J. B. Williams. *The Lives of Philip and Matthew Henry.* Edinburgh 1974

J. Rodman Williams. *Renewal Theology. Systematic Theology from a Charismatic Perspective.* 3 vols. Grand Rapids 1988-92

G. I. Williamson. *The Westminster Confession of Faith for Study Classes.* Philadelphia 1964

Ben Witherington III. *The Jesus Quest.* Downers Grove 1995

Herman Witsius. *The Economy of the Covenants Between God and Man.* 1677 ed. Trans. William Crookshank. Escondido 1990

Herman Witsius. *Sacred Dissertations on the Apostles' Creed.* Trans. Donald Fraser. 1823 ed. 2 vols. Escondido 1993

Johannes Wollebius. *Compendium of Christian Theology* (1626). In *Reformed Dogmatics.* Trans. and ed. by John W. Beardslee III. Grand Rapids 1977.

Al Wolters. '"Partners of the Deity": A Covenantal Reading of 2 Peter 1:4'. *Calvin Theological Journal,* vol. 25. no. 1. April 1990

N. T. Wright. *The Climax of the Covenant.* Edinburgh 1991

Raymond O. Zorn. *Christ Triumphant.* Edinburgh 1997

Persons Index

Elsdon, Ron 78
Erickson, Millard 249, 270
Eveson, Philip 154
Falwell Jerry 321
Ferguson, Marilyn 37
Finlayson, R.A. 246, 248, 250, 271, 299
Flavel, John 66, 192
Frame, John 230-1
Frase James 182, 183
Freeman, Anthony 61
Fudge, Edward William 300
Gaffin, Richard 131, 200-1, 289
Gandhi, Mahatma 113
Gillespie, George 209-10, 222, 304
Girardeau, John L. 156, 158, 160
Goodwin, Thomas 117, 124, 128, 133, 234
Grudem, Wayne 94, 214
Hanko, Herman 265
Harris, Murray 283
Harris, R.Laird 285
Hasker, William 61-2
Hawking, Stephen 32
Hendriksen, William 53, 180
Henry, Matthew 314
Hick, John 113
Hodge, Charles 49, 56, 65, 150, 178, 183, 200
Hodges, Zane 142, 144
Hoekema, A.A. 145, 277-8, 285, 287, 303, 322
Holwerda, David 302
Houston, Thomas 325-6
Hughes, Philip Edgecumbe 296, 300
Hull, Gretchen Gaebelein 228

Hurley, James 214
Hutcheson, George 211, 212, 268
Ironside, Harry A. 320
Jewett, Paul 262, 264
Johnston, Mark 159
Kaiser, Christopher 29-30
Kelly, William 320
Kingdon, David 262
Kistemaker, Simon 174, 291
Klooster, Fred 60
Knitter, Paul F. 113
Kroeger, Catherine Clark 214
Kuiper, R.B. 202, 207, 209, 214, 217, 229
Kuyper, Abraham 123, 125, 263, 306
Lee, Francis Nigel 232
Letham, Robert 100, 106, 254
Lillback, Peter 171
Lombard, Peter 246
MacLaine, Shirley 37
Macleod, Donald 16, 23, 186, 225, 257-8, 260-1, 287, 289, 291, 306
MacMillan, Douglas 124ff
McBrien, Richard P. 253
McCheyne, Robert Murray 286-7
McCrie, Thomas 209-10
McFague, Sally 61
McGrath, Alister 38, 46
McLeod, Alexander 316
Manton, Thomas 108
Marcel, Pierre 261
Martin, Hugh 105, 118
Mathison, Keith A. 287, 322
Melville, Andrew 212
Migliore, Daniel 139
Morey, Robert 282, 285, 298

Subject Index

providence 44, 96-97, 118, 229.
psalms 240-2.
punishment 21, 35, 50, 53, 81-82, 91, 104-108, 143, 159, 236, 285-6, 289, 297-302.
ransom 106.
reconciliation 106, 143, 209.
redemption 19-24, 50, 54, 57, 106-107, 112, 118, 121, 126, 127-134, 144, 156, 198, 202, 215, 233, 247, 260, 293, 302-5, 306.
regeneration 24, 51, 110, 132-134, 143, 144, 148, 157-158, 173, 179, 182, 198, 206, 207, 256, 261, 262, 263-4, 305.
regulative principle 230-2.
reign (of Christ): see kingship (of Christ).
repentance 24, 27, 29, 34, 60, 109, 138, 139, 142, 143-144, 161.
representation: see head (federal).
reprobation 60, 293, 294, 297.
responsibility (human) 13, 34, 51-52, 77, 236.
resurrection (of Christ) 45, 95, 108, 129, 131, 146, 169, 172, 178, 213, 233, 255, 277, 286, 288-92.
resurrection (of man) 129, 145, 160, 255, 282-4, 286, 288-92, 293, 303.
return (of Christ) 159, 279-80, 286-8, 302-5.
revelation 30, 31, 43-46, 52, 73, 76-78, 87, 100-101, 121, 127, 215, 219, 229, 306.
reward 23, 232, 296-7.
righteousness 22, 51, 71, 72, 85, 103, 104, 110, 137, 147-155, 167, 171, 188, 258, 266.
Roman Catholicism 153-154, 167,

210, 218-19, 220, 246, 253-4, 269-71.
rulers 111, 315-6.
Sabbath: see Lord's Day.
sacraments see also baptism, Lord's Supper, 111, 141, 221-2, 245-273.
sacrifice (of Christ) 23, 95, 97, 98, 101-108, 128, 268-273.
saint 201, 207, 208, 209, 215, 216.
salvation 19-27, 39, 40, 50, 53, 60, 63, 91-114, 117, 137-162, 180, 186, 201, 261, 278, 296, 302-4.
sanctification 26, 54, 71, 121, 144, 153, 159, 167-93, 198, 201, 203, 216-8, 222, 245, 266, 282, 302, 303, 306-7, 313.
Definitive sanctification 171
Progressive sanctification 174
Satan 80, 107, 127, 128, 159, 172, 280, 305.
satisfaction 95, 101-108.
Scholasticism 10.
seal 139, 160-161, 246, 249-50, 251, 257, 260, 268.
Second Coming: see return (of Christ).
security (eternal) 162.
seed 258, 260, 263-64.
servant 112.
sign 127-128, 246-54, 257, 260, 268.
sin 16, 17, 19, 21-27, 37, 43, 51, 62, 73, 77, 79, 80-86, 91-114, 127, 131, 132, 137-143, 145, 147-155, 159, 167-193, 208, 213, 219, 256, 260, 280, 281, 289, 292-302, 303, 313-4.
sinlessness (of Christ) 94, 96, 125.
sonship 125, 131.
soul 71, 72, 123, 146, 159, 160, 215, 279, 282-4.

David McKay is a graduate of the New University of Ulster (B.A.), the University of London (B.D.), the Reformed Presbyterian Theological Hall, Belfast, and Queen's University, Belfast (M.Th. and Ph.D.). He has been a minister of the Reformed Presbyterian Church of Ireland since 1984, and is presently minister of Cregagh Road congregation in Belfast. He is also Professor of Systematic Theology, Ethics and Apologetics at the Reformed Theological College, Belfast, and Editor of *The Covenanter Witness*. He is the author of *An Ecclesiastical Republic, Church Government in the Writings of George Gillespie* (Paternoster 1997) and has contributed to a number of theological journals. He is married to Valerie.